I0015232

Hands-On GPU-Accelerated Computer Vision with OpenCV and CUDA

Effective techniques for processing complex image data in real time using GPUs

Bhaumik Vaidya

BIRMINGHAM - MUMBAI

Hands-On GPU-Accelerated Computer Vision with OpenCV and CUDA

Acquisition Editor: Alok Dhuri
Content Development Editor: Pooja Parvatkar
Technical Editor: Divya Vadhyar
Copy Editor: Safis Editing
Project Coordinator: Ulhas Kambali
Proofreader: Safis Editing
Indexer: Mariammal Chettiyar
Graphics: Tom Scaria
Production Coordinator: Deepika Naik

First published: September 2018

Production reference: 1240918

Published by Packt Publishing Ltd.
Livery Place
35 Livery Street
Birmingham
B3 2PB, UK.

ISBN 978-1-78934-829-3

www.packtpub.com

`mapt.io`

Mapt is an online digital library that gives you full access to over 5,000 books and videos, as well as industry leading tools to help you plan your personal development and advance your career. For more information, please visit our website.

Why subscribe?

- Spend less time learning and more time coding with practical eBooks and Videos from over 4,000 industry professionals

- Improve your learning with Skill Plans built especially for you

- Get a free eBook or video every month

- Mapt is fully searchable

- Copy and paste, print, and bookmark content

Packt.com

Did you know that Packt offers eBook versions of every book published, with PDF and ePub files available? You can upgrade to the eBook version at `www.packt.com` and as a print book customer, you are entitled to a discount on the eBook copy. Get in touch with us at `customercare@packtpub.com` for more details.

At `www.packt.com`, you can also read a collection of free technical articles, sign up for a range of free newsletters, and receive exclusive discounts and offers on Packt books and eBooks.

Contributors

About the author

Bhaumik Vaidya is an experienced computer vision engineer and mentor. He has worked extensively on OpenCV Library in solving computer vision problems. He is a University gold medalist in masters and is now doing a PhD in the acceleration of computer vision algorithms built using OpenCV and deep learning libraries on GPUs. He has a background in teaching and has guided many projects in computer vision and VLSI(Very-large-scale integration). He has worked in the VLSI domain previously as an ASIC verification engineer, so he has very good knowledge of hardware architectures also. He has published many research papers in reputable journals to his credit. He, along with his PhD mentor, has also received an NVIDIA Jetson TX1 embedded development platform as a research grant from NVIDIA.

"I would like to thank my parents and family for their immense support. I would especially like to thank Parth Vaghasiya, who has stood like a pillar with me, for his continuous love and support. I really appreciate and thank Umang Shah and Ayush Vyas for their help in the development of content for this book. I would like to thank my friends Nihit, Arpit, Chirag, Vyom, Anupam, Bhavin, and Karan for their constant motivation and encouragement. I would like to thank Jay, Rangat, Manan, Rutvik, Smit, Ankit, Yash, Prayag, Jenish, Darshan, Parantap, Saif, Sarth, Shrenik, Sanjeet, and Jeevraj, who have been very special to me for their love, motivation, and support. I would like to thank Dr. Chirag Paunwala, Prof. Vandana Shah, Ms. Jagruti Desai and Prof. Mustafa Surti for their continuous guidance and support.

I gratefully acknowledge the support of NVIDIA Corporation and their donation of the Jetson TX1 GPU used for this book. I am incredibly grateful to Pooja Parvatkar, Alok Dhuri, and all the amazing people of Packt Publishing for taking their valuable time out to review this book in so much detail and for helping me during the development of the book.

To the memory of my grandmother, Urmilaben Vaidya, and to my family members, Vidyut Vaidya, Sandhya Vaidya, Bhartiben Joshi, Hardik Vaidya, and Parth Vaghasiya for their sacrifices, love, support, and inspiration."

About the reviewer

Vandana Shah gained her bachelor's degree in electronics in the year 2001. She has also gained an MBA in Human Resource management an a master's in Electronics Engineering specifically in the VLSI domain. She has also submitted her thesis for a PhD in electronics, specifically concerning the domain of image processing and deep learning for brain tumor detection, and is awaiting her award. Her area of interest is image processing with deep learning and embedded systems. She has more than 13 years of experience in research, as well as in teaching and guiding undergraduate and postgraduate students of electronics and communications. She has published many papers in renowned journals, such as IEEE, Springer, and Inderscience. She is also receiving a government grant for her upcoming research in the MRI image-processing domain. She has dedicated her life to mentoring students and researchers. She is also able to train students and faculty members in soft-skill development. Besides her prowess in technical fields, she also has a strong command of Kathak, an Indian dance.

"I thank my family members for their full support."

Packt is searching for authors like you

If you're interested in becoming an author for Packt, please visit `authors.packtpub.com` and apply today. We have worked with thousands of developers and tech professionals, just like you, to help them share their insight with the global tech community. You can make a general application, apply for a specific hot topic that we are recruiting an author for, or submit your own idea.

Table of Contents

Preface

Computer vision is revolutionizing a wide range of industries and OpenCV is the most widely chosen tool for computer vision with the ability to work in multiple programming languages. Nowadays, there is a need to process large images in real time in computer vision which is difficult to handle for OpenCV on its own. In this Graphics Processing Unit (GPU) and CUDA can help. So this book provides a detailed overview on integrating OpenCV with CUDA for practical applications. It starts with explaining the programming of GPU with CUDA which is essential for computer vision developers who have never worked with GPU. Then it explains OpenCV acceleration with GPU and CUDA by taking some practical examples. When computer vision applications are to be used in real life scenarios then it needs to deployed on embedded development boards. This book covers the deployment of OpenCV applications on NVIDIA Jetson Tx1 which is very popular for computer vision and deep learning applications. The last part of the book covers the concept of PyCUDA which can be used by Computer vision developers who are using OpenCV with Python. PyCUDA is a python library which leverages the power of CUDA and GPU for accelerations. This book provides a complete guide for developers using OpenCV in C++ or Python in accelerating their computer vision applications by taking a hands on approach.

Who this book is for

This book is a go-to guide for developers working with OpenCV who now want to learn how to process more complex image data by taking advantage of GPU processing. Most computer vision engineers or developers face problems when they try to process complex image data in real time. That is where the acceleration of computer vision algorithms using GPUs will help them in developing algorithms that can work on complex image data in real time. Most people think that hardware acceleration can only be done using FPGA and ASIC design, and for that, they need knowledge of hardware description languages such as Verilog or VHDL. However, that was only true before the invention of CUDA, which leverages the power of Nvidia GPUs and can be used to accelerate algorithms by using programming languages such as C++ and Python with CUDA. This book will help those developers in learning about these concepts by helping them to develop practical applications. This book will help developers to deploy computer vision applications on embedded platforms such as Nvidia Jetson TX1.

What this book covers

Chapter 1, *Introduction to CUDA and Getting Started with CUDA*, introduces the CUDA architecture and how it has redefined the parallel processing capabilities of GPUs. The application of the CUDA architecture in real-life scenarios is discussed. Readers are introduced to the development environment used for CUDA and how it can be installed on all operating systems.

Chapter 2, *Parallel Programming Using CUDA C*, teaches the reader to write programs using CUDA for GPUs. It starts with a simple Hello World program and then incrementally builds toward complex examples in CUDA C. It also covers how the kernel works and how to use device properties, and discusses terminologies associated with CUDA programming.

Chapter 3, *Threads, Synchronization, and Memory*, teaches the reader about how threads are called from CUDA programs and how multiple threads communicate with each other. It describes how multiple threads are synchronized when they work in parallel. It also describes constant memory and texture memory in detail.

Chapter 4, *Advanced Concepts in CUDA*, covers advanced concepts such as CUDA streams and CUDA events. It describes how sorting algorithms can be accelerated using CUDA, and looks at the acceleration of simple image-processing functions using CUDA.

Chapter 5, *Getting Started with OpenCV with CUDA Support,* describes the installation of the OpenCV library with CUDA support in all operating systems. It explains how to test this installation using a simple program. The chapter examines a performance comparison between image-processing programs that execute with and without CUDA support.

Chapter 6, *Basic Computer Vision Operations Using OpenCV and CUDA*, teaches the reader how to write basic computer vision operations such as pixel-level operations on images, filtering, and morphological operations using OpenCV.

Chapter 7, *Object Detection and Tracking Using OpenCV and CUDA*, looks at the steps for accelerating some real-life computer vision applications using OpenCV and CUDA. It describes the feature detection and description algorithms that are used for object detection. The chapter also covers the acceleration of face detection using Haar cascade and video analysis techniques, such as background subtraction for object tracking.

Chapter 8, *Introduction to Jetson Tx1 Development Board and Installing OpenCV on Jetson TX1*, introduces the Jetson TX1 embedded platform and how it can be used to accelerate and deploy computer vision applications. It describes the installation of OpenCV for Tegra on Jetson TX1 with Jetpack.

Chapter 9, *Deploying Computer Vision Applications on Jetson TX1*, covers deployment of computer vision applications on Jetson Tx1. It teaches the reader how to build different computer vision applications and how to interface the camera with Jetson Tx1 for video-processing applications.

Chapter 10, *Getting started with PyCUDA*, introduces PyCUDA, which is a Python library for GPU acceleration. It describes the installation procedure on all operating systems.

Chapter 11, *Working with PyCUDA*, teaches the reader how to write programs using PyCUDA. It describes the concepts of data transfer from host to device and kernel execution in detail. It covers how to work with arrays in PyCUDA and develop complex algorithms.

Chapter 12, *Basic Computer Vision Application Using PyCUDA*, looks at the development and acceleration of basic computer vision applications using PyCUDA. It describes color space conversion operations, histogram calculation, and different arithmetic operations as examples of computer vision applications.

To get the most out of this book

The examples covered in this book can be run with Windows, Linux, and macOS. All the installation instructions are covered in the book. A thorough understanding of computer vision concepts and programming languages such as C++ and Python is expected. It's preferable that the reader has Nvidia GPU hardware to execute examples covered in the book.

Download the example code files

You can download the example code files for this book from your account at www.packt.com. If you purchased this book elsewhere, you can visit www.packt.com/support and register to have the files emailed directly to you.

You can download the code files by following these steps:

1. Log in or register at www.packt.com.
2. Select the **SUPPORT** tab.
3. Click on **Code Downloads & Errata**.
4. Enter the name of the book in the **Search** box and follow the onscreen instructions.

Once the file is downloaded, please make sure that you unzip or extract the folder using the latest version of:

- WinRAR/7-Zip for Windows
- Zipeg/iZip/UnRarX for Mac
- 7-Zip/PeaZip for Linux

The code bundle for the book is also hosted on GitHub at `https://github.com/PacktPublishing/Hands-On-GPU-Accelerated-Computer-Vision-with-OpenCV-and-CUDA`. In case there's an update to the code, it will be updated on the existing GitHub repository.

We also have other code bundles from our rich catalog of books and videos available at `https://github.com/PacktPublishing/`. Check them out!

Download the color images

We also provide a PDF file that has color images of the screenshots/diagrams used in this book. You can download it here: `https://www.packtpub.com/sites/default/files/downloads/978-1-78934-829-3_ColorImages.pdf`.

Code in Action

Visit the following link to check out videos of the code being run: `http://bit.ly/2PZOYcH`

Conventions used

There are a number of text conventions used throughout this book.

`CodeInText`: Indicates code words in text, database table names, folder names, filenames, file extensions, pathnames, dummy URLs, user input, and Twitter handles. Here is an example: "Mount the downloaded `WebStorm-10*.dmg` disk image file as another disk in your system."

A block of code is set as follows:

```
html, body, #map {
  height: 100%;
  margin: 0;
  padding: 0
}
```

When we wish to draw your attention to a particular part of a code block, the relevant lines or items are set in bold:

```
[default]
exten => s,1,Dial(Zap/1|30)
exten => s,2,Voicemail(u100)
exten => s,102,Voicemail(b100)
exten => i,1,Voicemail(s0)
```

Any command-line input or output is written as follows:

```
$ mkdir css
$ cd css
```

Bold: Indicates a new term, an important word, or words that you see onscreen. For example, words in menus or dialog boxes appear in the text like this. Here is an example: "Select **System info** from the **Administration** panel."

Warnings or important notes appear like this.

Tips and tricks appear like this.

Get in touch

Feedback from our readers is always welcome.

General feedback: If you have questions about any aspect of this book, mention the book title in the subject of your message and email us at customercare@packtpub.com.

Errata: Although we have taken every care to ensure the accuracy of our content, mistakes do happen. If you have found a mistake in this book, we would be grateful if you would report this to us. Please visit www.packt.com/submit-errata, selecting your book, clicking on the Errata Submission Form link, and entering the details.

Piracy: If you come across any illegal copies of our works in any form on the Internet, we would be grateful if you would provide us with the location address or website name. Please contact us at copyright@packt.com with a link to the material.

If you are interested in becoming an author: If there is a topic that you have expertise in and you are interested in either writing or contributing to a book, please visit authors.packtpub.com.

Reviews

Please leave a review. Once you have read and used this book, why not leave a review on the site that you purchased it from? Potential readers can then see and use your unbiased opinion to make purchase decisions, we at Packt can understand what you think about our products, and our authors can see your feedback on their book. Thank you!

For more information about Packt, please visit packt.com.

Introducing CUDA and Getting Started with CUDA

1

This chapter gives you a brief introduction to CUDA architecture and how it has redefined the parallel processing capabilities of GPUs. The application of CUDA architecture in real-life scenarios will be demonstrated. This chapter will serve as a starting guide for software developers who want to accelerate their applications by using general-purpose GPUs and CUDA. The chapter describes development environments used for CUDA application development and how the CUDA toolkit can be installed on all operating systems. It covers how basic code can be developed using CUDA C and executed on Windows and Ubuntu operating systems.

The following topics will be covered in this chapter:

- Introducing CUDA
- Applications of CUDA
- CUDA development environments
- Installing CUDA toolkit on Windows, Linux, and macOS
- Developing simple code, using CUDA C

Technical requirements

This chapter requires familiarity with the basic C or C++ programming language. All the code used in this chapter can be downloaded from the following GitHub link: `https://github.com/bhaumik2450/Hands-On-GPU-Accelerated-Computer-Vision-with-OpenCV-and-CUDA /Chapter1`. The code can be executed on any operating system, though it is only tested on Windows 10 and Ubuntu 16.04.

Check out the following video to see the Code in Action:
`http://bit.ly/2PTQMUk`

Introducing CUDA

Compute Unified Device Architecture (**CUDA**) is a very popular parallel computing platform and programming model developed by NVIDIA. It is only supported on NVIDIA GPUs. OpenCL is used to write parallel code for other types of GPUs such as AMD and Intel, but it is more complex than CUDA. CUDA allows creating massively parallel applications running on **graphics processing units** (**GPUs**) with simple programming APIs. Software developers using C and C++ can accelerate their software application and leverage the power of GPUs by using CUDA C or C++. Programs written in CUDA are similar to programs written in simple C or C++ with the addition of keywords needed to exploit parallelism of GPUs. CUDA allows a programmer to specify which part of CUDA code will execute on the CPU and which part will execute on the GPU.

The next section describes the need for parallel computing and how CUDA architecture can leverage the power of the GPU, in detail.

Parallel processing

In recent years, consumers have been demanding more and more functionalities on a single hand held device. So, there is a need for packaging more and more transistors on a small area that can work quickly and consume minimal power. We need a fast processor that can carry out multiple tasks with a high clock speed, a small area, and minimum power consumption. Over many decades, transistor sizing has seen a gradual decrease resulting in the possibility of more and more transistors being packed on a single chip. This has resulted in a constant rise of the clock speed. However, this situation has changed in the last few years with the clock speed being more or less constant. So, what is the reason for this? Have transistors stopped getting smaller? The answer is no. The main reason behind clock speed being constant is high power dissipation with high clock rate. Small transistors packed in a small area and working at high speed will dissipate large power, and hence it is very difficult to keep the processor cool. As clock speed is getting saturated in terms of development, we need a new computing paradigm to increase the performance of the processors. Let's understand this concept by taking a small real-life example.

Suppose you are told to dig a very big hole in a small amount of time. You will have the following three options to complete this work in time:

- You can dig faster.
- You can buy a better shovel.
- You can hire more diggers, who can help you complete the work.

If we can draw a parallel between this example and a computing paradigm, then the first option is similar to having a faster clock. The second option is similar to having more transistors that can do more work per clock cycle. But, as we have discussed in the previous paragraph, power constraints have put limitations on these two steps. The third option is similar to having many smaller and simpler processors that can carry out tasks in parallel. A GPU follows this computing paradigm. Instead of having one big powerful processor that can perform complex tasks, it has many small and simple processors that can get work done in parallel. The details of GPU architecture are explained in the next section.

Introducing GPU architecture and CUDA

GeForce 256 was the first GPU developed by NVIDIA in 1999. Initially, GPUs were only used for rendering high-end graphics on monitors. They were only used for pixel computations. Later on, people realized that if GPUs can do pixel computations, then they would also be able to do other mathematical calculations. Nowadays, GPUs are used in many applications other than rendering graphics. These kinds of GPUs are called **General-Purpose GPUs** (**GPGPUs**).

The next question that may have come to your mind is the difference between the hardware architecture of a CPU and a GPU that allows it to carry out parallel computation. A CPU has a complex control hardware and less data computation hardware. Complex control hardware gives a CPU flexibility in performance and a simple programming interface, but it is expensive in terms of power. On the other hand, a GPU has simple control hardware and more hardware for data computation that gives it the ability for parallel computation. This structure makes it more power-efficient. The disadvantage is that it has a more restrictive programming model. In the early days of GPU computing, graphics APIs such as OpenGL and DirectX were the only way to interact with GPUs. This was a complex task for normal programmers, who were not familiar with OpenGL or DirectX. This led to the development of CUDA programming architecture, which provided an easy and efficient way of interacting with the GPUs. More details about CUDA architecture are given in the next section.

Normally, the performance of any hardware architecture is measured in terms of latency and throughput. *Latency* is the time taken to complete a given task, while *throughput* is the amount of the task completed in a given time. These are not contradictory concepts. More often than not, improving one improves the other. In a way, most hardware architectures are designed to improve either latency or throughput. For example, suppose you are standing in a queue at the post office. Your goal is to complete your work in a small amount of time, so you want to improve latency, while an employee sitting at a post office window wants to see more and more customers in a day. So, the employee's goal is to increase the throughput. Improving one will lead to an improvement in the other, in this case, but the way both sides look at this improvement is different.

In the same way, normal sequential CPUs are designed to optimize latency, while GPUs are designed to optimize throughput. CPUs are designed to execute all instructions in the minimum time, while GPUs are designed to execute more instructions in a given time. This design concept of GPUs makes them very useful in image processing and computer vision applications, which we are targeting in this book, because we don't mind a delay in the processing of a single pixel. What we want is that more pixels should be processed in a given time, which can be done on a GPU.

So, to summarize, parallel computing is what we need if we want to increase computational performance at the same clock speed and power requirement. GPUs provide this capability by having lots of simple computational units working in parallel. Now, to interact with the GPU and to take advantage of its parallel computing capabilities, we need a simple parallel programming architecture, which is provided by CUDA.

CUDA architecture

This section covers basic hardware modifications done in GPU architecture and the general structure of software programs developed using CUDA. We will not discuss the syntax of the CUDA program just yet, but we will cover the steps to develop the code. The section will also cover some basic terminology that will be followed throughout this book.

CUDA architecture includes several new components specifically designed for general-purpose computations in GPUs, which were not present in earlier architectures. It includes the unified shedder pipeline which allows all **arithmetic logical units** (**ALUs**) present on a GPU chip to be marshaled by a single CUDA program. The ALUs are also designed to comply with IEEE floating-point single and double-precision standards so that it can be used in general-purpose applications. The instruction set is also tailored to general purpose computation and not specific to pixel computations. It also allows arbitrary read and write access to memory. These features make CUDA GPU architecture very useful in general purpose applications.

All GPUs have many parallel processing units called *cores*. On the hardware side, these cores are divided into streaming processors and **streaming multiprocessors (SMs)**. The GPU has a grid of these streaming multiprocessors. On the software side, a CUDA program is executed as a series of multiple threads running in parallel. Each thread is executed on a different core. The GPU can be viewed as a combination of many blocks, and each block can execute many threads. Each block is bound to a different SM on the GPU. How mapping is done between a block and SM is not known to a CUDA programmer, but it is known and done by a scheduler. The threads from same block can communicate with one another. The GPU has a hierarchical memory structure that deals with communication between threads inside one block and multiple blocks. This will be dealt with in detail in the upcoming chapters.

As a programmer, you will be curious to know what will be the programming model in CUDA and how the code will understand whether it should be executed on the CPU or the GPU. For this book, we will assume that we have a computing platform comprising a CPU and a GPU. We will call a CPU and its memory the *host* and a GPU and its memory a *device*. A CUDA code contains the code for both the host and the device. The host code is compiled on CPU by a normal C or C++ compiler, and the device code is compiled on the GPU by a GPU compiler. The host code calls the device code by something called a *kernel* call. It will launch many threads in parallel on a device. The count of how many threads to be launched on a device will be provided by the programmer.

Now, you might ask how this device code is different from a normal C code. The answer is that it is similar to a normal sequential C code. It is just that this code is executed on a greater number of cores in parallel. However, for this code to work, it needs data on the device's memory. So, before launching threads, the host copies data from the host memory to the device memory. The thread works on data from the device's memory and stores the result on the device's memory. Finally, this data is copied back to the host memory for further processing. To summarize, the steps to develop a CUDA C program are as follows:

1. Allocate memory for data in the host and device memory.
2. Copy data from the host memory to the device memory.
3. Launch a kernel by specifying the degree of parallelism.
4. After all the threads are finished, copy the data back from the device memory to the host memory.
5. Free up all memory used on the host and the device.

CUDA applications

CUDA has seen an unprecedented growth in the last decade. It is being used in a wide variety of applications in various domains. It has transformed research in multiple fields. In this section, we will look at some of these domains and how CUDA is accelerating growth in each domain:

- **Computer vision applications**: Computer vision and image processing algorithms are computationally intensive. With more and more cameras capturing images at high definition, there is a need to process these large images in real time. With the CUDA acceleration of these algorithms, applications such as image segmentation, object detection, and classification can achieve a real-time frame rate performance of more than 30 frames per second. CUDA and the GPU allow the faster training of deep neural networks and other deep-learning algorithms; this has transformed research in computer vision. NVIDIA is developing several hardware platforms such as Jetson TX1, Jetson TX2, and Jetson TK1, which can accelerate computer vision applications. NVIDIA drive platform is also one of the platforms that is made for autonomous drive applications.

- **Medical imaging**: The medical imaging field is seeing widespread use of GPUs and CUDA in reconstruction and the processing of MRI images and **Computed tomography** (**CT**) images. It has drastically reduced the processing time for these images. Nowadays, there are several devices that are shipped with GPUs, and several libraries are available to process these images with CUDA acceleration.

- **Financial computing**: There is a need for better data analytics at a lower cost in all financial firms, and this will help in informed decision-making. It includes complex risk calculation and initial and lifetime margin calculation, which have to be done in real time. GPUs help financial firms to do these kinds of analytics in real time without adding too much overhead cost.

- **Life science, bioinformatics, and computational chemistry**: Simulating DNA genes, sequencing, and protein docking are computationally intensive tasks that need high computation resources. GPUs help in this kind of analysis and simulation. GPUs can run common molecular dynamics, quantum chemistry, and protein docking applications more than five times faster than normal CPUs.

- **Weather research and forecasting**: Several weather prediction applications, ocean modeling techniques, and tsunami prediction techniques utilize GPU and CUDA for faster computation and simulations, compared to CPUs.

- **Electronics Design Automation (EDA)**: Due to the increasing complexity in VLSI technology and the semiconductor fabrication process, the performance of EDA tools is lagging behind in this technological progress. It leads to incomplete simulations and missed functional bugs. Therefore, the EDA industry has been seeking faster simulation solutions. GPU and CUDA acceleration are helping this industry to speed up computationally intensive EDA simulations, including functional simulation, placement and routing, Signal integrity and electromagnetics, SPICE circuit simulation, and so on.
- **Government and defense**: GPU and CUDA acceleration is also widely used by governments and militaries. Aerospace, defense, and intelligence industries are taking advantage of CUDA acceleration in converting large amounts of data into actionable information.

CUDA development environment

To start developing an application using CUDA, you will need to set up the development environment for it. There are some prerequisites for setting up a development environment for CUDA. These include the following:

- A CUDA-supported GPU
- An NVIDIA graphics card driver
- A standard C compiler
- A CUDA development kit

How to check for these prerequisites and install them is discussed in the following sub section.

CUDA-supported GPU

As discussed earlier, CUDA architecture is only supported on NVIDIA GPUs. It is not supported on other GPUs such as AMD and Intel. Almost all GPUs developed by NVIDIA in the last decade support CUDA architecture and can be used to develop and execute CUDA applications. A detailed list of CUDA-supported GPUs can be found on the NVIDIA website: `https://developer.nvidia.com/cuda-gpus`. If you can find your GPU in this list, you will be able to run CUDA applications on your PC.

If you don't know which GPU is on your PC, then you can find it by following these steps:

- **On windows:**
    1. In the Start menu, type *device manager* and press *Enter*.
    2. In the device manager, expand the display adaptors. There, you will find the name of your NVIDIA GPU.

- **On Linux:**
    1. Open Terminal.
    2. Run `sudo lshw -C video`.

    This will list information regarding your graphics card, usually including its make and model.

- **On macOS:**
    1. Go to the Apple **Menu | About this Mac | More info**.
    2. Select **Graphics/Displays** under **Contents** list. There, you will find the name of your NVIDIA GPU.

If you have a CUDA-enabled GPU, then you are good to proceed to the next step.

NVIDIA graphics card driver

If you want to communicate with NVIDIA GPU hardware, then you will need a system software for it. NVIDIA provides a device driver to communicate with the GPU hardware. If the NVIDIA graphics card is properly installed, then these drivers are installed automatically with it on your PC. Still, it is good practice to check for driver updates periodically from the NVIDIA website: `http://www.nvidia.in/Download/index.aspx?lang=en-in`. You can select your graphics card and operating system for driver download from this link.

Standard C compiler

Whenever you are running a CUDA application, it will need two compilers: one for GPU code and one for CPU code. The compiler for the GPU code will come with an installation of CUDA toolkit, which will be discussed in the next section. You also need to install a standard C compiler for executing CPU code. There are different C compilers based on the operating systems:

- **On Windows**: For all Microsoft Windows editions, it is recommended to use Microsoft Visual Studio C compiler. It comes with Microsoft Visual Studio and can be downloaded from its official website: `https://www.visualstudio.com/downloads/`.

  The express edition for commercial applications needs to be purchased, but you can use community editions for free in non-commercial applications. For running the CUDA application, install Microsoft Visual Studio with a Microsoft Visual Studio C compiler selected. Different CUDA versions support different Visual Studio editions, so you can refer to the NVIDIA CUDA website for Visual Studio version support.

- **On Linux**: Mostly, all Linux distributions come with a standard **GNU C Complier** (**GCC**), and hence it can be used to compile CPU code for CUDA applications.
- **On Mac**: On the Mac operating system, you can install a GCC compiler by downloading and installing Xcode for macOS. It is freely available and can be downloaded from Apple's website:

  `https://developer.apple.com/xcode/`

CUDA development kit

CUDA needs a GPU compiler for compiling GPU code. This compiler comes with a CUDA development toolkit. If you have an NVIDIA GPU with the latest driver update and have installed a standard C compiler for your operating system, you are good to proceed to the final step of installing the CUDA development toolkit. A step-by-step guide for installing the CUDA toolkit is discussed in the next section.

Installing the CUDA toolkit on all operating systems

This section covers instructions on how to install CUDA on all supported platforms. It also describes steps to verify installation. While installing CUDA, you can choose between a network installer and an offline local installer. A network installer has a lower initial download size, but it needs an internet connection while installing. A local offline installer has a higher initial download size. The steps discussed in this book are for local installation. A CUDA toolkit can be downloaded for Windows, Linux, and macOS for both 32-bit and 64-bit architecture from the following link: https://developer.nvidia.com/cuda-downloads.

After downloading the installer, refer to the following steps for your particular operating system. CUDAx.x is used as notation in the steps, where x.x indicates the version of CUDA that you have downloaded.

Windows

This section covers the steps to install CUDA on Windows, which are as follows:

1. Double-click on the installer. It will ask you to select the folder where temporary installation files will be extracted. Select the folder of your choice. It is recommended to keep this as the default.
2. Then, the installer will check for system compatibility. If your system is compatible, you can follow the on screen prompt to install CUDA. You can choose between an express installation (default) and a custom installation. A custom installation allows you to choose which features of CUDA to install. It is recommended to select the express default installation.
3. The installer will also install CUDA sample programs and the CUDA Visual Studio integration.

 Please make sure you have Visual Studio installed before running this installer.

To confirm that the installation is successful, the following aspects should be ensured:

1. All the CUDA samples will be located at C:\ProgramData\NVIDIA Corporation\CUDA Samples\vx.x if you have chosen the default path for installation.
2. To check installation, you can run any project.
3. We are using the device query project located at C:\ProgramData\NVIDIA Corporation\CUDA Samples\vx.x\1_Utilities\deviceQuery.
4. Double-click on the *.sln file of your Visual Studio edition. It will open this project in Visual Studio.
5. Then you can click on the local **Windows debugger** in Visual Studio. If the build is successful and the following output is displayed, then the installation is complete:

```
C:\WINDOWS\system32\cmd.exe                                                              —    □    ×
Maximum Texture Dimension Size (x,y,z)          1D=(65536), 2D=(65536, 65536), 3D=(4096, 4096, 4096)
Maximum Layered 1D Texture Size, (num) layers   1D=(16384), 2048 layers
Maximum Layered 2D Texture Size, (num) layers   2D=(16384, 16384), 2048 layers
Total amount of constant memory:                65536 bytes
Total amount of shared memory per block:        49152 bytes
Total number of registers available per block:  65536
Warp size:                                      32
Maximum number of threads per multiprocessor:   2048
Maximum number of threads per block:            1024
Max dimension size of a thread block (x,y,z):   (1024, 1024, 64)
Max dimension size of a grid size    (x,y,z):   (2147483647, 65535, 65535)
Maximum memory pitch:                           2147483647 bytes
Texture alignment:                              512 bytes
Concurrent copy and kernel execution:           Yes with 1 copy engine(s)
Run time limit on kernels:                      Yes
Integrated GPU sharing Host Memory:             No
Support host page-locked memory mapping:        Yes
Alignment requirement for Surfaces:             Yes
Device has ECC support:                         Disabled
CUDA Device Driver Mode (TCC or WDDM):          WDDM (Windows Display Driver Model)
Device supports Unified Addressing (UVA):       Yes
Supports Cooperative Kernel Launch:             No
Supports MultiDevice Co-op Kernel Launch:       No
Device PCI Domain ID / Bus ID / location ID:    0 / 1 / 0
Compute Mode:
   < Default (multiple host threads can use ::cudaSetDevice() with device simultaneously) >

deviceQuery, CUDA Driver = CUDART, CUDA Driver Version = 9.0, CUDA Runtime Version = 9.0, NumDevs = 1
Result = PASS
Press any key to continue . . .
```

Linux

This section covers the steps to install CUDA on Linux distributions. In this section, the installation of CUDA in Ubuntu, which is a popular Linux distribution, is discussed using distribution-specific packages or using the `apt-get` command (which is specific to Ubuntu).

The steps to install CUDA using the `*.deb` installer downloaded from the CUDA website are as follows:

1. Open Terminal and run the `dpkg` command, which is used to install packages in Debian-based systems:

   ```
   sudo dpkg -i cuda-repo-<distro>_<version>_<architecture>.deb
   ```

2. Install the CUDA public GPG key using the following command:

   ```
   sudo apt-key add /var/cuda-repo-<version>/7fa2af80.pub
   ```

3. Then, update the `apt` repository cache using the following command:

   ```
   sudo apt-get update
   ```

4. Then you can install CUDA using the following command:

   ```
   sudo apt-get install cuda
   ```

5. Include the CUDA installation path in the PATH environment variable using the following command:

    If you have not installed CUDA at default locations, you need to change the path to point at your installation location.

   ```
   export PATH=/usr/local/cuda-x.x/bin${PATH:+:${PATH}}
   ```

6. Set the `LD_LIBRARY_PATH` environment variable:

   ```
   export LD_LIBRARY_PATH=/usr/local/cuda-x.x/lib64\
   ${LD_LIBRARY_PATH:+:${LD_LIBRARY_PATH}}
   ```

   You can also install the CUDA toolkit by using the `apt-get` package manager, available with Ubuntu OS. You can run the following command in Terminal:

   ```
   sudo apt-get install nvidia-cuda-toolkit
   ```

To check whether the CUDA GPU compiler has been installed, you can run the `nvcc -V` command from Terminal. It calls the GCC compiler for C code and the NVIDIA PTX compiler for the CUDA code.

You can install the NVIDIA Nsight Eclipse plugin, which will give the GUI Integrated Development Environment for executing CUDA programs, using the following command:

```
sudo apt install nvidia-nsight
```

After installation, you can run the `deviceQuery` project located at `~/NVIDIA_CUDA-x.x_Samples`. If the CUDA toolkit is installed and configured correctly, the output for `deviceQuery` should look similar to the following:

```
bhaumik@bhaumik-Lenovo-ideapad-520-15IKB: ~/NVIDIA_CUDA-9.0_Samples/1_Utilities/
Maximum number of threads per block:          1024
Max dimension size of a thread block (x,y,z): (1024, 1024, 64)
Max dimension size of a grid size    (x,y,z): (2147483647, 65535, 65535)
Maximum memory pitch:                         2147483647 bytes
Texture alignment:                            512 bytes
Concurrent copy and kernel execution:         Yes with 1 copy engine(s)
Run time limit on kernels:                    Yes
Integrated GPU sharing Host Memory:           No
Support host page-locked memory mapping:      Yes
Alignment requirement for Surfaces:           Yes
Device has ECC support:                       Disabled
Device supports Unified Addressing (UVA):     Yes
Supports Cooperative Kernel Launch:           No
Supports MultiDevice Co-op Kernel Launch:     .No
Device PCI Domain ID / Bus ID / location ID:  0 / 1 / 0
Compute Mode:
    < Default (multiple host threads can use ::cudaSetDevice() with device simu
ltaneously) >

deviceQuery, CUDA Driver = CUDART, CUDA Driver Version = 9.0, CUDA Runtime Versi
on = 9.0, NumDevs = 1
Result = PASS
bhaumik@bhaumik-Lenovo-ideapad-520-15IKB:~/NVIDIA_CUDA-9.0_Samples/1_Utilities/d
eviceQuery$ █
```

Mac

This section covers steps to install CUDA on macOS. It needs the `*.dmg` installer downloaded from the CUDA website. The steps to install after downloading the installer are as follows:

1. Launch the installer and follow the onscreen prompt to complete the installation. It will install all prerequisites, CUDA, toolkit, and CUDA samples.

2. Then, you need to set environment variables to point at CUDA installation using the following commands:

 If you have not installed CUDA at the default locations, you need to change the path to point at your installation location.

```
export PATH=/Developer/NVIDIA/CUDA-x.x/bin${PATH:+:${PATH}}
export DYLD_LIBRARY_PATH=/Developer/NVIDIA/CUDA-x.x/lib\
                    ${DYLD_LIBRARY_PATH:+:${DYLD_LIBRARY_PATH}}
```

3. Run the script: `cuda-install-samples-x.x.sh`. It will install CUDA samples with write permissions.
4. After it has completed, you can go to `bin/x86_64/darwin/release` and run the `deviceQuery` project. If the CUDA toolkit is installed and configured correctly, it will display your GPU's device properties.

A basic program in CUDA C

In this section, we will start learning CUDA programming by writing a very basic program using CUDA C. We will start by writing a `Hello, CUDA!` program in CUDA C and execute it. Before going into the details of code, one thing that you should recall is that host code is compiled by the standard C compiler and that the device code is executed by an NVIDIA GPU compiler. A NVIDIA tool feeds the host code to a standard C compiler such as Visual Studio for Windows and a GCC compiler for Ubuntu, and it uses macOS for execution. It is also important to note that the GPU compiler can run CUDA code without any device code. All CUDA code must be saved with a `*.cu` extension.

The following is the code for `Hello, CUDA!`:

```
#include <iostream>
 __global__ void myfirstkernel(void) {
 }
int main(void) {
  myfirstkernel << <1, 1 >> >();
  printf("Hello, CUDA!\n");
  return 0;
}
```

If you look closely at the code, it will look very similar to that of the simple Hello, CUDA! program written in C for the CPU execution. The function of this code is also similar. It just prints Hello, CUDA! on Terminal or the command line. So, two questions that should come to your mind is: how is this code different, and where is the role of CUDA C in this code? The answer to these questions can be given by closely looking at the code. It has two main differences, compared to code written in simple C:

- An empty function called myfirstkernel with __global__ prefix
- Call the myfirstkernel function with << <1,1> >>

__global__ is a qualifier added by CUDA C to standard C. It tells the compiler that the function definition that follows this qualifier should be complied to run on a device, rather than a host. So, in the previous code, myfirstkernel will run on a device instead of a host, though, in this code, it is empty.

Now where will the main function run? The NVCC compiler will feed this function to host the C compiler, as it is not decorated by the global keyword, and hence the main function will run on the host.

The second difference in the code is the call to the empty myfirstkernel function with some angular brackets and numeric values. This is a CUDA C trick to call device code from host code. It is called a *kernel* call. The details of a kernel call will be explained in later chapters. The values inside the angular brackets indicate arguments we want to pass from the host to the device at runtime. Basically, it indicates the number of blocks and the number of threads that will run in parallel on the device. So, in this code, << <1,1> >> indicates that myfirstkernel will run on one block and one thread or block on the device. Though this is not an optimal use of device resources, it is a good starting point to understand the difference between code executed on the host and code executed on a device.

Again, to revisit and revise the Hello, CUDA! code, the myfirstkernel function will run on a device with one block and one thread or block. It will be launched from the host code inside the main function by a method called **kernel launch**.

After writing code, how will you execute this code and see the output? The next section describes the steps to write and execute the Hello, CUDA! code on Windows and Ubuntu.

Steps for creating a CUDA C program on Windows

This section describes the steps to create and execute a basic CUDA C program on Windows using Visual Studio. The steps are as follows:

1. Open **Microsoft Visual Studio**.
2. Go to **File | New | Project**.
3. Select **NVIDIA | CUDA 9.0 | CUDA 9.0 Runtime**.
4. Give your desired name to the project and click on **OK**.
5. It will create a project with a sample `kernel.cu` file. Now open this file by double-clicking on it.
6. Delete existing code from the file and write the given code earlier.
7. Build the project from the **Build** tab and press *Ctrl + F5* to debug the code. If everything works correctly, you will see `Hello, CUDA!` displayed on the command line, as shown here:

Steps for creating a CUDA C program on Ubuntu

This section describes the steps to create and execute a basic CUDA C program on Ubuntu using the Nsight Eclipse plugin. The steps are as follows:

1. Open Nsight by opening Terminal and typing **nsight** into it.
2. Go to **File | New |CUDA C/C++ Projects**.
3. Give your desired name to the project and click on **OK**.
4. It will create a project with a sample file. Now open this file by double-clicking on it.

5. Delete the existing code from the file and write the given code earlier.
6. Run the code by pressing the play button. If everything works correctly, you will see `Hello, CUDA!` displayed on Terminal as shown here:

Summary

To summarize, in this chapter, you were introduced to CUDA and briefed upon the importance of parallel computing. Applications of CUDA and GPUs in various domains were discussed at length. The chapter described the hardware and software setup required to execute CUDA applications on your PCs. It gave a step-by-step procedure to install CUDA on local PCs.

The last section gave a starting guide for application development in CUDA C by developing a simple program and executing it on Windows and Ubuntu.

In the next chapter, we will build on this knowledge of programming in CUDA C. You will be introduced to parallel computing using CUDA C by way of several practical examples to show how it is faster compared to normal programming. You will also be introduced to the concepts of threads and blocks and how synchronization is performed between multiple threads and blocks.

Questions

1. Explain three methods to increase the performance of your computing hardware. Which method is used to develop GPUs?

2. True or false: Improving latency will improve throughput.

3. Fill in the blanks: CPUs are designed to improve ___ and GPUs are designed to improve ___ .

4. Take an example of traveling from one place to another that is 240 km away. You can take a car that can accommodate five people, with a speed of 60 kmph or a bus that can accommodate 40 people, with a speed of 40 kmph. Which option will provide better latency, and which option will provide better throughput?

5. Explain the reasons that make GPU and CUDA particularly useful in computer vision applications.

6. True or False: A CUDA compiler cannot compile code with no device code.

7. In the `Hello, CUDA!` example discussed in this chapter, will the `printf` statement be executed by the host or the device?

2
Parallel Programming using CUDA C

In the last chapter, we saw how easy it is to install CUDA and write a program using it. Though the example was not impressive, it was shown to convince you that it is very easy to get started with CUDA. In this chapter, we will build upon this concept. It teaches you to write advance programs using CUDA for GPUs in detail. It starts with a variable addition program and then incrementally builds towards complex vector manipulation examples in CUDA C. It also covers how the kernel works and how to use device properties in CUDA programs. The chapter discusses how vectors are operated upon in CUDA programs and how CUDA can accelerate vector operations compared to CPU processing. It also discusses terminologies associated with CUDA programming.

The following topics will be covered in this chapter:

- The concept of the kernel call
- Creating kernel functions and passing parameters to it in CUDA
- Configuring kernel parameters and memory allocation for CUDA programs
- Thread execution in CUDA programs
- Accessing GPU device properties from CUDA programs
- Working with vectors in CUDA programs
- Parallel communication patterns

Technical requirements

This chapter requires familiarity with the basic C or C++ programming language, particularly dynamic memory allocation functions. All the code used in this chapter can be downloaded from the following GitHub link: `https://github.com/PacktPublishing/` `Hands-On-GPU-Accelerated-Computer-Vision-with-OpenCV-and-CUDA`. The code can be executed on any operating system, though it is only tested on Windows 10 and Ubuntu 16.04.

Check out the following video to see the Code in Action:
`http://bit.ly/2PQmu4O`

CUDA program structure

We have seen a very simple `Hello, CUDA!` program earlier, that showcased some important concepts related to CUDA programs. A CUDA program is a combination of functions that are executed either on the host or on the GPU device. The functions that do not exhibit parallelism are executed on the CPU, and the functions that exhibit data parallelism are executed on the GPU. The GPU compiler segregates these functions during compilation. As seen in the previous chapter, functions meant for execution on the device are defined using the `__global__` keyword and compiled by the NVCC compiler, while normal C host code is compiled by the C compiler. A CUDA code is basically the same ANSI C code with the addition of some keywords needed for exploiting data parallelism.

So, in this section, a simple two-variable addition program is taken to explain important concepts related to CUDA programming, such as kernel calls, passing parameters to kernel functions from host to device, the configuration of kernel parameters, CUDA APIs needed to exploit data parallelism, and how memory allocation takes place on the host and the device.

Two-variable addition program in CUDA C

In the simple `Hello, CUDA!` code seen in Chapter 1, *Introducing Cuda and Getting Started with Cuda,* the device function was empty. It had nothing to do. This section explains a simple addition program that performs addition of two variables on the device. Though it is not exploiting any data parallelism of the device, it is very useful for demonstrating important programming concepts of CUDA C. First, we will see how to write a kernel function for adding two variables.

The code for the kernel function is shown here:

```
include <iostream>
#include <cuda.h>
#include <cuda_runtime.h>
//Definition of kernel function to add two variables
__global__ void gpuAdd(int d_a, int d_b, int *d_c)
{
    *d_c = d_a + d_b;
}
```

The gpuAdd function looks very similar to a normal add function implemented in ANSI C. It takes two integer variables d_a and d_b as inputs and stores the addition at the memory location indicated by the third integer pointer d_c. The return value for the device function is void because it is storing the answer in the memory location pointed to by the device pointer and not explicitly returning any value. Now we will see how to write the main function for this code. The code for the main function is shown here:

```
int main(void)
{
//Defining host variable to store answer
    int h_c;
//Defining device pointer
    int *d_c;
//Allocating memory for device pointer
    cudaMalloc((void**)&d_c, sizeof(int));
//Kernel call by passing 1 and 4 as inputs and storing answer in d_c
//<< <1,1> >> means 1 block is executed with 1 thread per block
    gpuAdd << <1, 1 >> > (1, 4, d_c);
//Copy result from device memory to host memory
    cudaMemcpy(&h_c, d_c, sizeof(int), cudaMemcpyDeviceToHost);
    printf("1 + 4 = %d\n", h_c);
//Free up memory
    cudaFree(d_c);
    return 0;
}
```

In the `main` function, the first two lines define variables for host and device. The third line allocates memory of the `d_c` variable on the device using the `cudaMalloc` function. The `cudaMalloc` function is similar to the `malloc` function in C. In the fourth line of the main function, `gpuAdd` is called with `1` and `4` as two input variables and `d_c`, which is a device memory pointer as an output pointer variable. The weird syntax of the `gpuAdd` function, which is also called a kernel call, is explained in the next section. If the answer of `gpuAdd` needs to be used on the host, then it must be copied from the device's memory to the host's memory, which is done by the `cudaMemcpy` function. Then, this answer is printed using the `printf` function. The penultimate line frees the memory used on the device by using the `cudafree` function. It is very important to free up all the memory used on the device explicitly from the program; otherwise, you might run out of memory at some point. The lines that start with `//` are comments for more code readability, and these lines are ignored by compilers.

The two-variable addition program has two functions, `main` and `gpuAdd`. As you can see, `gpuAdd` is defined by using the `__global__` keyword, and hence it is meant for execution on the device, while the main function will be executed on the host. The program adds two variables on the device and prints the output on the command line, as shown here:

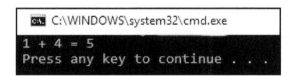

We will use a convention in this book that host variables will be prefixed with `h_` and device variables will be prefixed with `d_`. This is not compulsory; it is just done so that readers can understand the concepts easily without any confusion between host and device.

All CUDA APIs such as `cudaMalloc`, `cudaMemcpy`, and `cudaFree`, along with other important CUDA programming concepts such as kernel call, passing parameters to kernels, and memory allocation issues are discussed in upcoming sections.

A kernel call

The device code that is written using ANSI C keywords along with CUDA extension keywords is called a **kernel**. It is launched from the host code by a method called **kernel call**. Basically, the meaning of kernel call is that we are launching device code from the host code. A kernel call typically generates a large number of blocks and threads to exploit data parallelism on the GPU. Kernel code is very similar to normal C functions; it is just that this code is executed by several threads in parallel. It has a very weird syntax, which is as follows:

```
kernel << <number of blocks, number of threads per block, size of shared
memory > >> (parameters for kernel)
```

It starts with the name of the kernel that we want to launch. You should make sure that this kernel is defined using the __global__ keyword. Then, it has the << < > >> kernel launch operator that contains configuration parameters for kernel. It can include three parameters separated by a comma. The first parameter indicates the number of blocks you want to execute, and the second parameter indicates the number of threads each block will have. So, the total number of threads started by a kernel launch will be the product of these two numbers. The third parameter, which specifies the size of shared memory used by the kernel, is optional. In the program for variable addition, the kernel launch syntax is as follows:

```
gpuAdd << <1,1> >> (1 , 4, d_c)
```

Here, gpuAdd is the name of a kernel that we want to launch, and <<<1,1>>> indicates we want to start one block with one thread per block, which means that we are starting only one thread. Three arguments in round brackets are the parameters that are passed to the kernel. Here, we are passing two constants, 1 and 4. The third parameter is a pointer to device memory d_c. It points at the location on device memory where the kernel will store its answer after addition. One thing that the programmer has to keep in mind is that pointers passed as parameters to kernel should only point to device memory. If it is pointing to host memory, it can crash your program. After kernel execution is completed, the result pointed by the device pointer can be copied back to host memory for further use. Starting only one thread for execution on the device is not the optimal use of device resources. Suppose you want to start multiple threads in parallel; what is the modification that you have to make in the syntax of the kernel call? This is addressed in the next section and is termed "configuring kernel parameters".

Configuring kernel parameters

For starting multiple threads on the device in parallel, we have to configure parameters in the kernel call, which are written inside the kernel launch operator. They specify the number of blocks and the number of threads per block. We can launch many blocks in parallel with many threads in each block. Normally, there is a limit of 512 or 1,024 threads per block. Each block runs on the streaming multiprocessor, and threads in one block can communicate with one another via shared memory. The programmer can't choose which multiprocessor will execute a particular block and in which order blocks or threads will execute.

Suppose you want to start 500 threads in parallel; what is the modification that you can make to the kernel launch syntax that was shown previously? One option is to start one block of 500 threads via the following syntax:

```
gpuAdd<< <1,500> >> (1,4, d_c)
```

We can also start 500 blocks of one thread each or two blocks of 250 threads each. Accordingly, you have to modify values in the kernel launch operator. The programmer has to be careful that the number of threads per block does not go beyond the maximum supported limit of your GPU device. In this book, we are targeting computer vision applications where we need to work on two-and three-dimensional images. Here, it would be great if blocks and threads are not one-dimensional but more than that for better processing and visualization.

GPU supports a three-dimensional grids of blocks and three-dimensional blocks of threads. It has the following syntax:

```
mykernel<< <dim3(Nbx, Nby,Nbz), dim3(Ntx, Nty,Ntz) > >> ()
```

Here N_{bx}, N_{by}, and N_{bz} indicate the number of blocks in a grid in the direction of the x, y, and z axes, respectively. Similarly, N_{tx}, N_{ty}, and N_{tz} indicate the number of threads in a block in the direction of the x, y, and z axes. If the y and z dimensions are not specified, they are taken as 1 by default. So, for example, to process an image, you can start a 16 x 16 grid of blocks, all containing 16 x 16 threads. The syntax will be as follows:

```
mykernel << <dim3(16,16),dim3(16,16)> >> ()
```

To summarize, the configuration of the number of blocks and the number of threads is very important while launching the kernel. It should be chosen with proper care depending on the application that we are working on and the GPU resources. The next section will explain some important CUDA functions added over regular ANSI C functions.

CUDA API functions

In the variable addition program, we have encountered some functions or keywords that are not familiar to regular C or C++ programmers. These keywords and functions include `__global__` , `cudaMalloc`, `cudaMemcpy`, and `cudaFree`. So, in this section, these functions are explained in detail one by one:

- **__global__** : It is one of three qualifier keywords, along with `__device__` and `__host__` . This keyword indicates that a function is declared as a device function and will execute on the device when called from the host. It should be kept in mind that this function can only be called from the host. If you want your function to execute on the device and called from the device function, then you have to use the `__device__` keyword. The `__host__` keyword is used to define host functions that can only be called from other host functions. This is similar to normal C functions. By default, all functions in a program are host functions. Both `__host__` and `__device__` can be simultaneously used to define any function. It generates two copies of the same function. One will execute on the host, and the other will execute on the device.

- **cudaMalloc**: It is similar to the `Malloc` function used in C for dynamic memory allocation. This function is used to allocate a memory block of a specific size on the device. The syntax of `cudaMalloc` with an example is as follows:

```
cudaMalloc(void ** d_pointer, size_t size)
Example: cudaMalloc((void**)&d_c, sizeof(int));
```

As shown in the preceding example code, it allocates a memory block of size equal to the size of one integer variable and returns the pointer d_c, which points to this memory location.

- **cudaMemcpy**: This function is similar to the `Memcpy` function in C. It is used to copy one block of memory to other blocks on a host or a device. It has the following syntax:

```
cudaMemcpy ( void * dst_ptr, const void * src_ptr, size_t size,
enum cudaMemcpyKind kind )
Example: cudaMemcpy(&h_c, d_c, sizeof(int),
cudaMemcpyDeviceToHost);
```

This function has four arguments. The first and second arguments are the destination pointer and the source pointer, which point to the host or device memory location. The third argument indicates the size of the copy and the last argument indicates the direction of the copy. It can be from host to device, device to device, host to host, or device to host. But be careful, as you have to match this direction with the appropriate pointers as the first two arguments. As shown in the example, we are copying a block of one integer variable from the device to the host by specifying the device pointer d_c as the source, and the host pointer h_c as a destination.

- **cudaFree**: It is similar to the free function available in C. The syntax of cudaFree is as follows:

```
cudaFree ( void * d_ptr )
Example: cudaFree(d_c)
```

It frees the memory space pointed to by d_ptr. In the example code, it frees the memory location pointed to by d_c. Please make sure that d_c is allocated memory, using cudaMalloc to free it using cudaFree.

There are many other keywords and functions available in CUDA over and above existing ANSI C functions. We will be frequently using only these three functions, and hence they are discussed in this section. For more details, you can always visit the CUDA programming guide.

Passing parameters to CUDA functions

The gpuAdd kernel function of the variable addition program is very similar to the normal C function. So, like normal C functions, the kernel functions can also be passed parameters by value or by reference. Hence, in this section, we will see both the methods to pass parameters for CUDA kernels.

Passing parameters by value

If you recall, in the gpuAdd program, the syntax for calling the kernel was as follows:

```
gpuAdd << <1,1> >>(1,4,d_c)
```

On the other hand, the signature of the gpuAdd function in definition was as follows:

```
__global__  gpuAdd(int d_a, int d_b, int *d_c)
```

So, you can see that we are passing values of d_a and d_b while calling the kernel. First, parameter 1 will be copied to d_a and then parameter 4 will be copied to d_b while calling the kernal. The answer after addition will be stored at the address pointed by d_c on device memory. Instead of directly passing values 1 and 4 as inputs to the kernel, we can also write the following:

```
gpuAdd << <1,1> >>(a,b,d_c)
```

Here, a and b are integer variables that can contain any integer values. Passing parameters by values is not recommended, as it creates unnecessary confusion and complications in programs. It is better to pass parameters by reference.

Passing parameters by reference

Now we will see how to write the same program by passing parameters by reference. For that, we have to first modify the kernel function for addition of two variables. The modified kernel for passing parameters by reference is shown here:

```
#include <iostream>
#include <cuda.h>
#include <cuda_runtime.h>
//Kernel function to add two variables, parameters are passed by reference
__global__ void gpuAdd(int *d_a, int *d_b, int *d_c)
{
  *d_c = *d_a + *d_b;
}
```

Instead of using integer variables d_a and d_b as inputs to the kernel, the pointers to these variables on device *d_a and *d_b are taken as inputs. The answer which will be obtained after the addition is stored at the memory location pointed by third integer pointer d_c. The pointers passed as a reference to this device function should be allocated memory with the cudaMalloc function. The main function for this code is shown here:

```
int main(void)
{
  //Defining host and variables
  int h_a,h_b, h_c;
  int *d_a,*d_b,*d_c;
  //Initializing host variables
  h_a = 1;
  h_b = 4;
  //Allocating memory for Device Pointers
  cudaMalloc((void**)&d_a, sizeof(int));
  cudaMalloc((void**)&d_b, sizeof(int));
```

```
cudaMalloc((void**)&d_c, sizeof(int));
//Coping value of host variables in device memory
cudaMemcpy(d_a, &h_a, sizeof(int), cudaMemcpyHostToDevice);
cudaMemcpy(d_b, &h_b, sizeof(int), cudaMemcpyHostToDevice);
//Calling kernel with one thread and one block with parameters passed by
reference
gpuAdd << <1, 1 >> > (d_a, d_b, d_c);
//Coping result from device memory to host
cudaMemcpy(&h_c, d_c, sizeof(int), cudaMemcpyDeviceToHost);
printf("Passing Parameter by Reference Output: %d + %d = %d\n", h_a, h_b,
h_c);
//Free up memory
cudaFree(d_a);
cudaFree(d_b);
cudaFree(d_c);
return 0;
}
```

h_a, h_b, and h_c are variables in the host memory. They are defined like normal C code. On the other hand, d_a, d_b, and d_c are pointers residing on host memory, and they point to the device memory. They are allocated memory from the host by using the cudaMalloc function. The values of h_a and h_b are copied to the device memory pointed to by d_a and d_b by using the cudaMemcpy function, and the direction of data transfer is from the host to the device. Then, in kernel call, these three device pointers are passed to the kernel as parameters. The kernel computes addition and stores the result at the memory location pointed by d_c. The result is copied back to the host memory by using cudaMemcpy again, but this time with the direction of data transfer as the device to host. The output of the program is as follows:

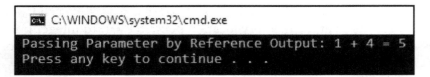

The memory used by three device pointers is freed by using the cudaFree at the end of the program. The sample memory map on the host and the device will look similar to the following:

Host Memory (CPU)		Device Memory (GPU)	
Address	Value	Address	Value
#01	h_a=1	#01	1
#02	h_b=4	#02	4
#03	h_c=5	#03	5

#04	d_a=#01	#04	
#05	d_b=#02	#05	
#06	d_c=#03	#06	

As you can see from the table, d_a, d_b, and d_c are residing on the host and pointing to values on the device memory. While passing parameters by reference to kernels, you should take care that all pointers are pointing to the device memory only. If it is not the case, then the program may crash.

While using device pointers and passing them to kernels, there are some restrictions that have to be followed by the programmer. The device pointers that are allocated memory using cudaMalloc can only be used to read or write from the device memory. They can be passed as parameters to the device function, and they should not be used to read and write memory from the host functions. To simplify, device pointers should be used to read and write device memory from the device function, and host pointers should be used to read and write host memory from host functions. So, in this book, you will always find the device pointer prefixed by d_ in kernel functions.

To summarize, in this section, concepts related to CUDA programming were explained in detail by taking two-variable additional programs as an example. After this section, you should be familiar with basic CUDA programming concepts and the terminology associated with CUDA programs. In the next section, you will learn how threads are executed on the device.

Executing threads on a device

We have seen that, while configuring kernel parameters, we can start multiple blocks and multiple threads in parallel. So, in which order do these blocks and threads start and finish their execution? It is important to know this if we want to use the output of one thread in other threads. To understand this, we have modified the kernel in the hello, CUDA! program we saw in the first chapter, by including a print statement in the kernel call, which prints the block number. The modified code is as follows:

```
#include <iostream>
#include <stdio.h>
__global__ void myfirstkernel(void)
{
  //blockIdx.x gives the block number of current kernel
    printf("Hello!!!I'm thread in block: %d\n", blockIdx.x);
}
int main(void)
```

```
{
    //A kernel call with 16 blocks and 1 thread per block
    myfirstkernel << <16,1>> >();

    //Function used for waiting for all kernels to finish
    cudaDeviceSynchronize();

    printf("All threads are finished!\n");
    return 0;
}
```

As can be seen from the code, we are launching a kernel with 16 blocks in parallel with each block having a single thread. In the kernel code, we are printing the block ID of the kernel execution. We can think that 16 copies of the same myfirstkernel start execution in parallel. Each of these copies will have a unique block ID, which can be accessed by the blockIdx.x CUDA directive, and a unique thread ID, which can be accessed by threadIdx.x. These IDs will tell us which block and thread are executing the kernel. When you run the program many times, you will find that, each time, blocks execute in a different order. One sample output can be shown as follows:

```
C:\WINDOWS\system32\cmd.exe
Hello!!!I'm thread in block: 2
Hello!!!I'm thread in block: 7
Hello!!!I'm thread in block: 6
Hello!!!I'm thread in block: 8
Hello!!!I'm thread in block: 1
Hello!!!I'm thread in block: 0
Hello!!!I'm thread in block: 5
Hello!!!I'm thread in block: 10
Hello!!!I'm thread in block: 9
Hello!!!I'm thread in block: 11
Hello!!!I'm thread in block: 4
Hello!!!I'm thread in block: 3
Hello!!!I'm thread in block: 14
Hello!!!I'm thread in block: 13
Hello!!!I'm thread in block: 12
Hello!!!I'm thread in block: 15
All threads are finished!
Press any key to continue . . .
```

One question you should ask is how many different output patterns will the previous program produce? The correct answer is 16! It will produce *n* factorial number of outputs, where *n* indicates the number of blocks started in parallel. So, whenever you are writing the program in CUDA, you should be careful that the blocks execute in random order.

This program also contains one more CUDA directive: `cudaDeviceSynchronize()`. Why is it used? It is used because a kernel launch is an asynchronous process, which means it returns control to the CPU thread immediately after starting up the GPU process before the kernel has finished executing. In the previous code, the next line in CPU thread is `print` and application exit will terminate console before the kernel has finished execution. So, if we do not include this directive, you will not see any print statements of the kernel execution. The output that is generated later by the kernel has nowhere to go, and you won't see it. To see the outputs generated by the kernel, we will include this directive, which ensures that the kernel finishes before the application is allowed to exit, and the output from the kernel will find a **waiting standard output queue**.

Accessing GPU device properties from CUDA programs

CUDA provides a simple interface to find the information such as determining which CUDA-enabled GPU devices (if any) are present and what capabilities each device supports. First, it is important to get a count of how many CUDA-enabled devices are present on the system, as a system may contain more than one GPU-enabled device. This count can be determined by the CUDA API `cudaGetDeviceCount()`. The program for getting a number of CUDA enabled devices on the system is shown here:

```
#include <memory>
#include <iostream>
#include <cuda_runtime.h>
// Main Program
int main(void)
{
  int device_Count = 0;
  cudaGetDeviceCount(&device_Count);
  // This function returns count of number of CUDA enable devices and 0 if
there are no CUDA capable devices.
  if (device_Count == 0)
  {
    printf("There are no available device(s) that support CUDA\n");
  }
  else
  {
```

```
    printf("Detected %d CUDA Capable device(s)\n", device_Count);
  }
}
```

The relevant information about each device can be found by querying the
cudaDeviceProp structure, which returns all the device properties. If you have more than
one CUDA-capable device, then you can start a for loop to iterate over all device properties.
The following section contains the list of device properties divided into different sets and
small code snippets used to access them from CUDA programs. These properties are
provided by the cudaDeviceProp structure in CUDA 9 runtime.

 For more details about properties in the different versions of CUDA, you
can check the programming guide for a particular version.

General device properties

cudaDeviceProp provides several properties that can be used to identify the device and
the versions being used. It provides the name property that returns the name of the device
as a string. We can also get a version of the driver and the runtime engine the device is
using by querying cudaDriverGetVersion and cudaRuntimeGetVersion properties.
Sometimes, if you have more than one device, you want to use the device that has more
multiprocessors. The multiProcessorCount property returns the count of the number of
multiprocessors on the device. The speed of the GPU in terms of clock rate can be fetched
by using the clockRate property. It returns clock rate in Khz. The following code snippet
shows how to use these properties from the CUDA program:

```
cudaDeviceProp device_Property;
cudaGetDeviceProperties(&device_Property, device);
printf("\nDevice %d: \"%s\"\n", device, device_Property.name);
cudaDriverGetVersion(&driver_Version);
cudaRuntimeGetVersion(&runtime_Version);
printf(" CUDA Driver Version / Runtime Version %d.%d / %d.%d\n",
driver_Version / 1000, (driver_Version % 100) / 10, runtime_Version / 1000,
(runtime_Version % 100) / 10);
printf( " Total amount of global memory: %.0f MBytes (%llu bytes)\n",
 (float)device_Property.totalGlobalMem / 1048576.0f, (unsigned long long)
device_Property.totalGlobalMem);
 printf(" (%2d) Multiprocessors", device_Property.multiProcessorCount );
printf("  GPU Max Clock rate: %.0f MHz (%0.2f GHz)\n",
device_Property.clockRate * 1e-3f, device_Property.clockRate * 1e-6f);
```

Memory-related properties

Memory on the GPU has a hierarchical architecture. It can be divided in terms of L1 cache, L2 cache, global memory, texture memory, and shared memory. The cudaDeviceProp provides many properties that help in identifying memory available with the device. memoryClockRate and memoryBusWidth provide clock rate and bus width of the memory respectively. The speed of the memory is very important. It affects the overall speed of your program. totalGlobalMem returns the size of global memory available with the device. totalConstMem returns the total constant memory available with the device. sharedMemPerBlock returns the total shared memory that can be used in tne device. The total number of registers available per block can be identified by using regsPerBlock. Size of L2 cache can be identified using the l2CacheSize property. The following code snippet shows how to use memory-related properties from the CUDA program:

```
printf( " Total amount of global memory: %.0f MBytes (%llu bytes)\n",
(float)device_Property.totalGlobalMem / 1048576.0f, (unsigned long long)
device_Property.totalGlobalMem);
printf(" Memory Clock rate: %.0f Mhz\n", device_Property.memoryClockRate *
1e-3f);
printf(" Memory Bus Width: %d-bit\n", device_Property.memoryBusWidth);
if (device_Property.l2CacheSize)
{
    printf(" L2 Cache Size: %d bytes\n", device_Property.l2CacheSize);
}
printf(" Total amount of constant memory: %lu bytes\n",
device_Property.totalConstMem);
printf(" Total amount of shared memory per block: %lu bytes\n",
device_Property.sharedMemPerBlock);
printf(" Total number of registers available per block: %d\n",
device_Property.regsPerBlock);
```

Thread-related properties

As seen in earlier sections, blocks and threads can be multidimensional. So, it would be nice to know how many threads and blocks can be launched in parallel in each dimension. There is also a limit on the number of threads per multiprocessor and the number of threads per block. This number can be found by using the maxThreadsPerMultiProcessor and the maxThreadsPerBlock. It is very important in the configuration of kernel parameters. If you launch more threads per block than the maximum threads possible per block, your program can crash. The maximum threads per block in each dimension can be identified by the maxThreadsDim. In the same way, the maximum blocks per grid in each dimension can be identified by using the maxGridSize. Both of them return an array with three values, which shows the maximum value in the x, y, and z dimensions respectively. The following code snippet shows how to use thread-related properties from the CUDA code:

```
printf(" Maximum number of threads per multiprocessor: %d\n",
device_Property.maxThreadsPerMultiProcessor);
printf(" Maximum number of threads per block: %d\n",
device_Property.maxThreadsPerBlock);
printf(" Max dimension size of a thread block (x,y,z): (%d, %d, %d)\n",
    device_Property.maxThreadsDim[0],
    device_Property.maxThreadsDim[1],
    device_Property.maxThreadsDim[2]);
printf(" Max dimension size of a grid size (x,y,z): (%d, %d, %d)\n",
    device_Property.maxGridSize[0],
    device_Property.maxGridSize[1],
    device_Property.maxGridSize[2]);
```

There are many other properties available in the cudaDeviceProp structure. You can check the CUDA programming guide for details of other properties. The output from all preceding code sections combined and executed on the NVIDIA Geforce 940MX GPU and CUDA 9.0 is as follows:

```
C:\WINDOWS\system32\cmd.exe
Detected 1 CUDA Capable device(s)

Device 0: "GeForce 940MX"
  CUDA Driver Version / Runtime Version          9.1 / 9.0
  CUDA Capability Major/Minor version number:    5.0
  Total amount of global memory:                 4096 MBytes (4294967296 bytes)
  ( 3) Multiprocessors  GPU Max Clock rate:                  1189 MHz (1.19 GHz)
  Memory Clock rate:                             2505 Mhz
  Memory Bus Width:                              64-bit
  L2 Cache Size:                                 1048576 bytes
  Maximum Texture Dimension Size (x,y,z)         1D=(65536), 2D=(65536, 65536), 3D=(4096, 4096, 4096)
  Maximum Layered 1D Texture Size, (num) layers  1D=(16384), 2048 layers
  Maximum Layered 2D Texture Size, (num) layers  2D=(16384, 16384), 2048 layers
  Total amount of constant memory:               65536 bytes
  Total amount of shared memory per block:       49152 bytes
  Total number of registers available per block: 65536
  Warp size:                                     32
  Maximum number of threads per multiprocessor:  2048
  Maximum number of threads per block:           1024
  Max dimension size of a thread block (x,y,z): (1024, 1024, 64)
  Max dimension size of a grid size    (x,y,z): (2147483647, 65535, 65535)
  Maximum memory pitch:                          2147483647 bytes
  Texture alignment:                             512 bytes
  Concurrent copy and kernel execution:          Yes with 1 copy engine(s)
  Run time limit on kernels:                     Yes
  Integrated GPU sharing Host Memory:            No
  Support host page-locked memory mapping:       Yes
  Alignment requirement for Surfaces:            Yes
  Device has ECC support:                        Disabled
  CUDA Device Driver Mode (TCC or WDDM):         WDDM (Windows Display Driver Model)
  Device supports Unified Addressing (UVA):      Yes
  Supports Cooperative Kernel Launch:            No
  Supports MultiDevice Co-op Kernel Launch:      No
  Device PCI Domain ID / Bus ID / location ID:   0 / 1 / 0
  Compute Mode:
     < Default (multiple host threads can use ::cudaSetDevice() with device simultaneously) >
Press any key to continue . . .
```

One question you might ask is why you should be interested in knowing the device properties. The answer is that this will help you in choosing a GPU device with more multiprocessors, if multiple GPU devices are present. If in your application the kernel needs close interaction with the CPU, then you might want your kernel to run on an integrated GPU that shares system memory with the CPU. These properties will also help you in finding the number of blocks and number of threads per block available on your device. This will help you with the configuration of kernel parameters. To show you one use of device properties, suppose you have an application that requires double precision for floating-point operation. Not all GPU devices support this operation. To know whether your device supports double precision floating-point operation and set that device for your application, the following code can be used:

```
#include <memory>
#include <iostream>
#include <cuda_runtime.h>
```

```
// Main Program
int main(void)
{
int device;
cudaDeviceProp device_property;
cudaGetDevice(&device);
printf("ID of device: %d\n", device);
memset(&device_property, 0, sizeof(cudaDeviceProp));
device_property.major = 1;
device_property.minor = 3;
cudaChooseDevice(&device, &device_property);
printf("ID of device which supports double precision is: %d\n", device);
cudaSetDevice(device);
}
```

This code uses two properties available in the `cudaDeviceprop` structure that help in identifying whether the device supports double precision operations. These two properties are major and minor. CUDA documentation says us that if major is greater than 1 and minor is greater than 3, then that device will support double precision operations. So, the program's `device_property` structure is filled with these two values. CUDA also provides the `cudaChooseDevice` API that helps in choosing a device with particular properties. This API is used on the current device to identify whether it contains these two properties. If it contains properties, then that device is selected for your application using the `cudaSetDevice` API. If more than one device is present in the system, this code should be written inside a for a loop to iterate over all devices.

Though trivial, this section is very important for you in finding out which applications can be supported by your GPU device and which cannot.

Vector operations in CUDA

Until now, the programs that we have seen were not leveraging any advantages of the parallel-processing capabilities of GPU devices. They were just written to get you familiar with the programming concepts in CUDA. From this section, we will start utilizing the parallel-processing capabilities of the GPU by performing vector or array operations on it.

Two-vector addition program

To understand vector operation on the GPU, we will start by writing a vector addition program on the CPU and then modify it to utilize the parallel structure of GPU. We will take two arrays of some numbers and store the answer of element-wise addition in the third array. The vector addition function on CPU is shown here:

```
#include "stdio.h"
#include<iostream>
 //Defining Number of elements in Array
#define N 5
 //Defining vector addition function for CPU
void cpuAdd(int *h_a, int *h_b, int *h_c)
{
    int tid = 0;
    while (tid < N)
    {
        h_c[tid] = h_a[tid] + h_b[tid];
        tid += 1;
    }
}
```

The `cpuAdd` should be very simple to understand. One thing you might find difficult to understand is the use of `tid`. It is included to make the program similar to the GPU program, in which `tid` indicated a particular thread ID. Here, also, if you have a multicore CPU, then you can initialize `tid` equal to 0 and 1 for each of them and then add 2 to it in the loop so that one CPU will perform a sum on even elements and one CPU will perform addition on odd elements. The main function for the code is shown here:

```
int main(void)
{
    int h_a[N], h_b[N], h_c[N];
    //Initializing two arrays for addition
    for (int i = 0; i < N; i++)
    {
      h_a[i] = 2 * i*i;
      h_b[i] = i;
      }
    //Calling CPU function for vector addition
    cpuAdd (h_a, h_b, h_c);
    //Printing Answer
    printf("Vector addition on CPU\n");
    for (int i = 0; i < N; i++)
    {
      printf("The sum of %d element is %d + %d = %d\n", i, h_a[i], h_b[i],
h_c[i]);
```

```
    }
    return 0;
}
```

There are two functions in the program: `main` and `cpuAdd`. In the main function, we start by defining two arrays to hold inputs and initialize it to some random numbers. Then, we pass these two arrays as input to the `cpuAdd` function. The `cpuAdd` function stores the answer in the third array. Then, we print this answer on the console, which is shown here:

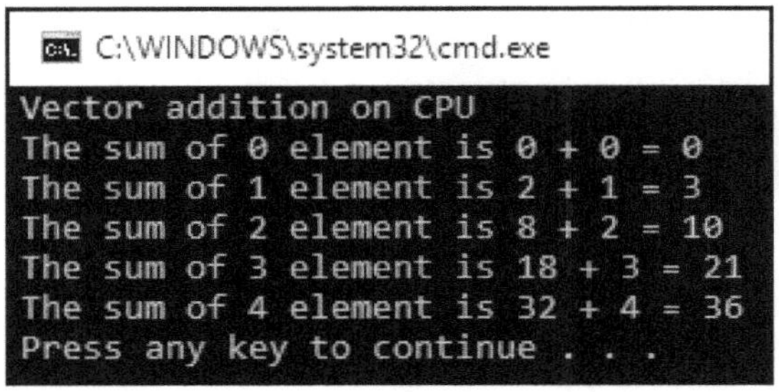

```
C:\WINDOWS\system32\cmd.exe
Vector addition on CPU
The sum of 0 element is 0 + 0 = 0
The sum of 1 element is 2 + 1 = 3
The sum of 2 element is 8 + 2 = 10
The sum of 3 element is 18 + 3 = 21
The sum of 4 element is 32 + 4 = 36
Press any key to continue . . .
```

This explanation of using the `tid in cpuadd` function may give you an idea of how to write the same function for the GPU execution, which can have many cores in parallel. If we initialize this add function with the ID of that core, then we can do the addition of all the elements in parallel. So, the modified kernel function for addition on the GPU is shown here:

```
#include "stdio.h"
#include<iostream>
#include <cuda.h>
#include <cuda_runtime.h>
 //Defining number of elements in Array
#define N 5
 //Defining Kernel function for vector addition
__global__ void gpuAdd(int *d_a, int *d_b, int *d_c)
{
 //Getting block index of current kernel
    int tid = blockIdx.x; // handle the data at this index
    if (tid < N)
    d_c[tid] = d_a[tid] + d_b[tid];
}
```

In the `gpuAdd` kernel function, `tid` is initialized with the block ID of the current block in which the kernel is executing. All kernels will add an array element indexed by this block ID. If the number of blocks are equal to the number of elements in an array, then all the addition operations will be done in parallel. How this kernel is called from the main function is explained next. The code for the main function is as follows:

```
int main(void)
{
 //Defining host arrays
 int h_a[N], h_b[N], h_c[N];
 //Defining device pointers
 int *d_a, *d_b, *d_c;
 // allocate the memory
 cudaMalloc((void**)&d_a, N * sizeof(int));
 cudaMalloc((void**)&d_b, N * sizeof(int));
 cudaMalloc((void**)&d_c, N * sizeof(int));
 //Initializing Arrays
 for (int i = 0; i < N; i++)
    {
    h_a[i] = 2*i*i;
    h_b[i] = i ;
    }

// Copy input arrays from host to device memory
 cudaMemcpy(d_a, h_a, N * sizeof(int), cudaMemcpyHostToDevice);
 cudaMemcpy(d_b, h_b, N * sizeof(int), cudaMemcpyHostToDevice);

//Calling kernels with N blocks and one thread per block, passing device
pointers as parameters
gpuAdd << <N, 1 >> >(d_a, d_b, d_c);
 //Copy result back to host memory from device memory
cudaMemcpy(h_c, d_c, N * sizeof(int), cudaMemcpyDeviceToHost);
printf("Vector addition on GPU \n");
 //Printing result on console
for (int i = 0; i < N; i++)
{
    printf("The sum of %d element is %d + %d = %d\n", i, h_a[i], h_b[i],
h_c[i]);
}
 //Free up memory
 cudaFree(d_a);
 cudaFree(d_b);
 cudaFree(d_c);
 return 0;
}
```

The GPU main function has the known structure as explained in the first section of this chapter:

- It starts with defining arrays and pointers for host and device. The device pointers are allocated memory using the cudaMalloc function.
- The arrays, which are to be passed to the kernel, are copied from the host memory to the device memory by using the cudaMemcpy function.
- The kernel is launched by passing the device pointers as parameters to it. If you see the values inside the kernel launch operator, they are *N* and *1*, which indicate we are launching *N* blocks with one thread per each block.
- The answer stored by the kernel on the device memory is copied back to the host memory by again using the cudaMemcpy, but this time with the direction of data transfer from the device to the host.
- And, finally, memory allocated to three device pointers is freed up by using the cudaFree function. The output of the program is as follows:

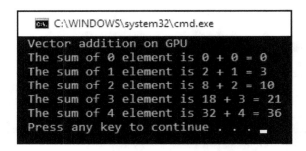

All CUDA programs follow the same pattern as shown before. We are launching N blocks in parallel. The meaning of this is that we are launching N copies of the same kernel simultaneously. You can understand this by taking a real-life example: Suppose you want to transfer five big boxes from one place to another. In the first method, you can perform this task by hiring one person who takes one block from one place to the other and repeat this five times. This option will take time, and it is similar to how vectors are added to the CPU. Now, suppose you hire five people and each of them carries one box. Each of them also knows the ID of the box they are carrying. This option will be much faster than the previous one. Each one of them just needs to be told that they have to carry one box with a particular ID from one place to the other.

This is exactly how kernels are defined and executed on the device. Each kernel copy knows the ID of it. This can be known by the `blockIdx.x` command. Each copy works on an array element indexed by its ID. All copies add all elements in parallel, which significantly reduces the processing time for the entire array. So, in a way, we are improving the throughput by doing operations in parallel over CPU sequential execution. The comparison of throughput between the CPU code and the GPU code is explained in the next section.

Comparing latency between the CPU and the GPU code

The programs for CPU and the GPU addition are written in a modular way so you can play around with the value of N. If N is small, then you will not notice any significant time difference between the CPU and the GPU code. But if you N is sufficiently large, then you will notice the significant difference in the CPU execution time and the GPU execution time for the same-vector addition. The time taken for the execution of a particular block can be measured by adding the following lines to the existing code:

```
clock_t start_d = clock();
printf("Doing GPU Vector add\n");
gpuAdd << <N, 1 >> >(d_a, d_b, d_c);
cudaThreadSynchronize();
clock_t end_d = clock();
double time_d = (double)(end_d - start_d) / CLOCKS_PER_SEC;
printf("No of Elements in Array:%d \n Device time %f seconds \n host time
%f Seconds\n", N, time_d, time_h);
```

Time is measured by calculating the total number of clock cycles taken to perform a particular operation. This can be done by taking the difference of starting and ending the clock tick count, measured using the clock() function. This is divided by the number of clock cycles per second, to get the execution time. When N is taken as 10,000,000 in the previous vector addition programs of the CPU and the GPU and executed simultaneously, the output is as follows:

```
No of Elements in Array:10000000
 Device time 0.001000 seconds
 host time 0.025000 Seconds
Press any key to continue . . .
```

As can be seen from the output, the execution time or throughput is improved from 25 milliseconds to almost 1 millisecond when the same function is implemented on GPU. This proves what we have seen in theory earlier that executing code in parallel on GPU helps in the improvement of throughput. CUDA provides an efficient and accurate method for measuring the performance of CUDA programs, using CUDA events, which will be explained in the later chapters.

Elementwise squaring of vectors in CUDA

Now, one question you can ask is, now that we are launching N blocks in parallel with one thread in each block, can we work in a reverse way? The answer is *yes*. We can launch only one block with N threads in parallel. To show that and make you more familiar with working around vectors in CUDA, we take the second example of the element-wise squaring of numbers in an array. We take one array of numbers and return an array that contains the square of these numbers. The kernel function to find the element-wise square is shown here:

```
#include "stdio.h"
#include<iostream>
#include <cuda.h>
#include <cuda_runtime.h>
 //Defining number of elements in Array
#define N 5
//Kernel function for squaring number
__global__ void gpuSquare(float *d_in, float *d_out)
{
    //Getting thread index for current kernel
    int tid = threadIdx.x; // handle the data at this index
    float temp = d_in[tid];
    d_out[tid] = temp*temp;
}
```

The gpuSquare kernel function has pointers to two arrays as arguments. The first pointer d_in points to the memory location where the input array is stored, while the second pointer d_out points to the memory location where output will be stored. In this program, instead of launching multiple blocks in parallel, we want to launch multiple threads in parallel, so tid is initialized with a particular thread ID using threadIdx.x. The main function for this program is as follows:

```
int main(void)
{
 //Defining Arrays for host
    float h_in[N], h_out[N];
    float *d_in, *d_out;
```

```
// allocate the memory on the cpu
    cudaMalloc((void**)&d_in, N * sizeof(float));
    cudaMalloc((void**)&d_out, N * sizeof(float));
//Initializing Array
    for (int i = 0; i < N; i++)
    {
        h_in[i] = i;
    }
//Copy Array from host to device
    cudaMemcpy(d_in, h_in, N * sizeof(float), cudaMemcpyHostToDevice);
//Calling square kernel with one block and N threads per block
    gpuSquare << <1, N >> >(d_in, d_out);
//Coping result back to host from device memory
    cudaMemcpy(h_out, d_out, N * sizeof(float), cudaMemcpyDeviceToHost);
//Printing result on console
    printf("Square of Number on GPU \n");
    for (int i = 0; i < N; i++)
    {
        printf("The square of %f is %f\n", h_in[i], h_out[i]);
    }
//Free up memory
    cudaFree(d_in);
    cudaFree(d_out);
    return 0;
}
```

This main function follows a similar structure to the vector addition program. One difference that you will see here from the vector addition program is that we are launching a single block with N threads in parallel. The output of the program is as follows:

Whenever you are using this way of launching N threads in parallel, you should take care that the maximum threads per block are limited to 512 or 1,024. So, the value of N should be less than this value. If N is 2,000 and the maximum number of threads per block for your device is 512, then you can't write << <1,2000 > >>. Instead, you should use something such as << <4,500> >>. The choice of a number of blocks and the number of threads per block should be made judiciously.

To summarize, we have learned how to work with vectors and how we can launch multiple blocks and multiple threads in parallel. We have also seen that by doing vector operations on GPU, it improves throughput, compared to the same operation on the CPU. In the last section of this chapter, we discuss the various parallel communication patterns that are followed by threads executing in parallel.

Parallel communication patterns

When several thread is executed in parallel, they follow a certain communication pattern that indicates where it is taking inputs and where it is writing its output in memory. We will discuss each communication pattern one by one. It will help you to identify communication patterns related to your application and how to write code for that.

Map

In this communication pattern, each thread or task takes a single input and produces a single output. Basically, it is a one-to-one operation. The vector addition program and element-wise squaring program, seen in the previous sections, are examples of the map pattern. The code of the map pattern will look as follows:

```
d_out[i] = d_in[i] * 2
```

Gather

In this pattern, each thread or task has multiple inputs, and it produces a single output to be written at a single location in memory. Suppose you want to write a program that finds a moving average of three numbers; this is an example of a gather operation. It takes three inputs from memory and writes single output to memory. So, there is data reuse on the input side. It is basically a many-to-one operation. The code for gather pattern will look as follows:

```
out[i] = (in [i-1] + in[i] + in[i+1])/3
```

Scatter

In a scatter pattern, a thread or a task takes a single input and computes where in the memory it should write the output. Array sorting is an example of a scatter operation. It can also be one-to-many operations. The code for scatter pattern will look as follows:

```
out[i-1] += 2 * in[i] and out[i+1] += 3*in[i]
```

Stencil

When threads or tasks read input from a fixed set of a neighborhood in an array, then this is called a **stencil communication pattern**. It is very useful in image-processing examples where we work on 3x3 or 5x5 neighborhood windows. It is a special form of a gather operation, so code syntax is similar to it.

Transpose

When the input is in the form of a row-major matrix, and we want the output to be in column-major form, we have to use this transpose communication pattern. It is particularly useful if you have a structure of arrays and you want to convert it in the form of an array of structures. It is also a one-to-one operation. The code for the transpose pattern will look as follows:

```
out[i+j*128] = in [j +i*128]
```

In this section, various communication patterns that CUDA programming follows is discussed. It is useful to find a communication pattern related to your application and use the code syntax of that pattern shown as an example.

Summary

To summarize, in this chapter, you were introduced to programming concepts in CUDA C and how parallel computing can be done using CUDA. It was shown that CUDA programs can run on any NVIDIA GPU hardware efficiently and in parallel. So, CUDA is both efficient and scalable. The CUDA API functions over and above existing ANSI C functions needed for parallel data computations were discussed in detail. How to call device code from the host code via a kernel call, configuring of kernel parameters, and a passing of parameters to the kernel were also discussed by taking a simple two-variable addition example. It was also shown that CUDA does not guarantee the order in which the blocks or thread will run and which block is assigned to which multi-processor in hardware. Moreover, vector operations, which take advantage of parallel-processing capabilities of GPU and CUDA, were discussed. It can be seen that, by performing vector operations on the GPU, it can improve the throughput drastically, compared to the CPU. In the last section, various common communication patterns followed in parallel programming were discussed in detail. Still, we have not discussed memory architecture and how threads can communicate with one another in CUDA. If one thread needs data of the other thread, then what can be done is also not discussed. So, in the next chapter, we will discuss memory architecture and thread synchronization in detail.

Questions

1. Write a CUDA program to subtract two numbers. Pass parameters by value in the kernel function.
2. Write a CUDA program to multiply two numbers. Pass parameters by reference in the kernel function.
3. Suppose you want to launch 5,000 threads in parallel. Configure kernel parameters in three different ways to accomplish this. Maximum 512 threads are possible per block.
4. True or false: The programmer can decide in which order blocks will execute on the device, and blocks will be assigned to which streaming multiprocessor?
5. Write a CUDA program to find out that your system contains a GPU device that has a major-minor version of 5.0 or greater.

6. Write a CUDA program to find a cube of a vector that contains numbers from 0 to 49.

7. For the following applications, which communication pattern is useful?
    1. Image processing
    2. Moving average
    3. Sorting array in ascending order
    4. Finding cube of numbers in array

Threads, Synchronization, and Memory

In the last chapter, we saw how to write CUDA programs that leverage the processing capabilities of a GPU by executing multiple threads and blocks in parallel. In all programs, until the last chapter, all threads were independent of each other and there was no communication between multiple threads. Most of the real-life applications need communication between intermediate threads. So, in this chapter, we will look in detail at how communication between different threads can be done, and explain the synchronization between multiple threads working on the same data. We will examine the hierarchical memory architecture of a CUDA and how different memories can be used to accelerate CUDA programs. The last part of this chapter explains a very useful application of a CUDA in the dot product of vectors and matrix multiplication, using all the concepts we have covered earlier.

The following topics will be covered in this chapter:

- Thread calls
- CUDA memory architecture
- Global, local, and cache memory
- Shared memory and thread synchronization
- Atomic operations
- Constant and texture memory
- Dot product and a matrix multiplication example

Technical requirements

This chapter requires familiarity with the basic C or C++ programming language and the codes that were explained in the previous chapters. All the code used in this chapter can be downloaded from the following GitHub link: `https://GitHub.com/PacktPublishing/Hands-On-GPU-Accelerated-Computer-Vision-with-OpenCV-and-CUDA`. The code can be executed on any operating system, though it has only been tested on Windows 10.

Check out the following video to see the code in action:
`http://bit.ly/2prnGAD`

Threads

The CUDA has a hierarchical architecture in terms of parallel execution. The kernel execution can be done in parallel with multiple blocks. Each block is further divided into multiple threads. In the last chapter, we saw that CUDA runtime can carry out parallel operations by launching the same copies of the kernel multiple times. We saw that it can be done in two ways: either by launching multiple blocks in parallel, with one thread per block, or by launching a single block, with many threads in parallel. So, two questions you might ask are, which method should I use in my code? And, is there any limitation on the number of blocks and threads that can be launched in parallel?

The answers to these questions are pivotal. As we will see later on in this chapter, threads in the same blocks can communicate with each other via shared memory. So, there is an advantage to launching one block with many threads in parallel so that they can communicate with each other. In the last chapter, we also saw the `maxThreadPerBlock` property that limits the number of threads that can be launched per block. Its value is 512 or 1,024 for the latest GPUs. Similarly, in the second method, the maximum number of blocks that can be launched in parallel is limited to 65,535.

Ideally, instead of launching multiple threads per single block or multiple blocks with a single thread, we launch multiple blocks with each having multiple threads (which can be equal to `maxThreadPerBlock`) in parallel. So, suppose you want to launch N = 50,000 threads in parallel in the vector add example, which we saw in the last chapter. The kernel call would be as follows:

```
gpuAdd<< <((N +511)/512),512 > >>(d_a,d_b,d_c)
```

The maximum threads per block are 512, and hence the total number of blocks is calculated by dividing the total number of threads (N) by 512. But if N is not an exact multiple of 512, then N divided by 512 may give a wrong number of blocks, which is one less than the actual count. So, to get the next highest integer value for the number of blocks, 511 is added to N and then it is divided by 512. It is basically the **ceil** operation on division.

Now, the question is, will this work for all values of N? The answer, sadly, is no. From the preceding discussion, the total number of blocks can't go beyond 65,535. So, in the afore as-mentioned kernel call, if `(N+511)/512` is above 65,535, then again the code will fail. To overcome this, a small constant number of blocks and threads are launched with some modification in the kernel code, which we will see further by rewriting the kernel for our vector addition program, as seen in `Chapter 2`, *Parallel Programming using Cuda C*:

```
#include "stdio.h"
#include<iostream>
#include <cuda.h>
#include <cuda_runtime.h>
//Defining number of elements in array
#define N 50000
__global__ void gpuAdd(int *d_a, int *d_b, int *d_c)
{
    //Getting index of current kernel
  int tid = threadIdx.x + blockIdx.x * blockDim.x;
  while (tid < N)
    {
        d_c[tid] = d_a[tid] + d_b[tid];
        tid += blockDim.x * gridDim.x;
    }
}
```

This kernel code is similar to what we wrote in the last chapter. It has two modifications. One modification is in the calculation of thread ID and the second is the inclusion of the `while` loop in the kernel function. The change in thread ID calculation is due to the launching of multiple threads and blocks in parallel. This calculation can be understood by considering blocks and threads as a two-dimensional matrix with the number of blocks equal to the number of rows, and the number of columns equal to the number of threads per block. We will take an example of three blocks and three threads/blocks, as shown in the following table:

Block 0	Thread 0	Thread 1	Thread 2
Block 1	Thread 0	Thread 1	Thread 2
Block 2	Thread 0	Thread 1	Thread 2

We can get the ID of each block by using `blockIdx.x` and the ID of each thread in the current block by the `threadIdx.x` command. So, for the thread shown in green, the block ID will be 2 and the thread ID will be 1. But what if we want a unique index for this thread among all the threads? This can be calculated by multiplying its block ID with the total number of threads per block, which is given by `blockDim.x`, and then summing it with its thread ID. This can be represented mathematically as follows:

```
tid = threadIdx.x + blockIdx.x * blockDim.x;
```

For example, in green, `threadIdx.x = 1`, `blockIdx.x = 2`, and `blockDim.x = 3` equals `tid = 7`. This calculation is very important to learn as it will be used widely in your code.

The `while` loop is included in the code because when N is very large, the total number of threads can't be equal to N because of the limitation described earlier. So, one thread has to do multiple operations separated by the total number of threads launched. This value can be calculated by multiplying `blockDim.x` by `gridDim.x`, which gives block and grid dimensions, respectively. Inside the `while` loop, the thread ID is incremented by this offset value. Now, this code will work for any value of N. To complete the program, we will write the main function for this code as follows:

```
int main(void)
{
    //Declare host and device arrays
    int h_a[N], h_b[N], h_c[N];
    int *d_a, *d_b, *d_c;

    //Allocate Memory on Device
    cudaMalloc((void**)&d_a, N * sizeof(int));
    cudaMalloc((void**)&d_b, N * sizeof(int));
    cudaMalloc((void**)&d_c, N * sizeof(int));
    //Initialize host array
    for (int i = 0; i < N; i++)
    {
        h_a[i] = 2 * i*i;
        h_b[i] = i;
    }

    cudaMemcpy(d_a, h_a, N * sizeof(int), cudaMemcpyHostToDevice);
    cudaMemcpy(d_b, h_b, N * sizeof(int), cudaMemcpyHostToDevice);
    //Kernel Call
    gpuAdd << <512, 512 >> >(d_a, d_b, d_c);

    cudaMemcpy(h_c, d_c, N * sizeof(int), cudaMemcpyDeviceToHost);
    //This ensures that kernel execution is finishes before going forward
    cudaDeviceSynchronize();
```

```
int Correct = 1;
printf("Vector addition on GPU \n");
for (int i = 0; i < N; i++)
{
  if ((h_a[i] + h_b[i] != h_c[i]))
    { Correct = 0; }
}
if (Correct == 1)
{
  printf("GPU has computed Sum Correctly\n");
}
else
{
  printf("There is an Error in GPU Computation\n");
}
  //Free up memory
cudaFree(d_a);
cudaFree(d_b);
 cudaFree(d_c);
  return 0;
}
```

Again, the main function is very similar to what we wrote last time. The only changes are in terms of how we launch the kernel function. The kernel is launched with 512 blocks, each having 512 threads in parallel. This will solve the problem for large values of N. Instead of printing the addition of a very long vector, only one print statement, which indicates whether the calculated answer is right or wrong, is printed. The output of the code will be seen as follows:

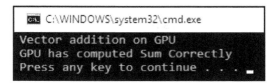

This section explained the hierarchical execution concept in a CUDA. The next section will take this concept further by explaining a hierarchical memory architecture.

Memory architecture

The execution of code on a GPU is divided among streaming multiprocessors, blocks, and threads. The GPU has several different memory spaces, with each having particular features and uses and different speeds and scopes. This memory space is hierarchically divided into different chunks, like global memory, shared memory, local memory, constant memory, and texture memory, and each of them can be accessed from different points in the program. This memory architecture is shown in preceding diagram:

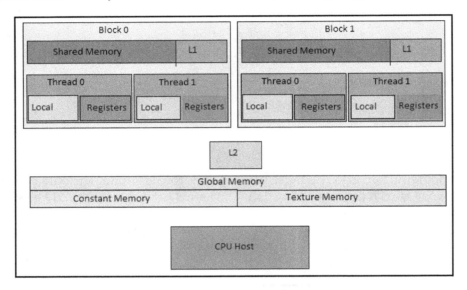

As shown in the diagram, each thread has its own local memory and a register file. Unlike processors, GPU cores have lots of registers to store local data. When the data of a thread does not fit in the register file, the local memory is used. Both of them are unique to each thread. The register file is the fastest memory. Threads in the same blocks have shared memory that can be accessed by all threads in that block. It is used for communication between threads. There is a global memory that can be accessed by all blocks and all threads. Global memory has a large memory access latency. There is a concept of caching to speed up this operation. L1 and L2 caches are available, as shown in the following table. There is a read-only constant memory that is used to store constants and kernel parameters. Finally, there is a texture memory that can take advantage of different two-dimensional or three-dimensional access patterns.

The features of all memories are summarized in the following table:

Memory	Access Pattern	Speed	Cached?	Scope	Lifetime
Global	Read and Write	Slow	Yes	Host and All Threads	Entire Program
Local	Read and Write	Slow	Yes	Each Thread	Thread
Registers	Read and Write	Fast	-	Each Thread	Thread
Shared	Read and Write	Fast	No	Each Block	Block
Constant	Read only	Slow	Yes	Host and All Threads	Entire Program
Texture	Read only	Slow	Yes	Host and All Threads	Entire Program

The preceding table describes important features of all memories. The scope defines the part of the program that can use this memory, and lifetime defines the time for which data in that memory will be visible to the program. Apart from this, L1 and L2 caches are also available for GPU programs for faster memory access.

To summarize, all threads have a register file, which is the fastest. Multiple threads in the same blocks have shared memory that is faster than global memory. All blocks can access global memory, which will be the slowest. Constant and texture memory are used for a special purpose, which will be discussed in the next section. Memory access is the biggest bottleneck in the fast execution of the program.

Global memory

All blocks have read and write access to global memory. This memory is slow but can be accessed from anywhere in your device code. The concept of caching is used to speed up access to a global memory. All memories allocated using cudaMalloc will be a global memory. The following simple example demonstrates how you can use a global memory from your program:

```
#include <stdio.h>
#define N 5

__global__ void gpu_global_memory(int *d_a)
{
  d_a[threadIdx.x] = threadIdx.x;
}

int main(int argc, char **argv)
{
  int h_a[N];
  int *d_a;
  cudaMalloc((void **)&d_a, sizeof(int) *N);
  cudaMemcpy((void *)d_a, (void *)h_a, sizeof(int) *N,
```

```
cudaMemcpyHostToDevice);
  gpu_global_memory << <1, N >> >(d_a);
  cudaMemcpy((void *)h_a, (void *)d_a, sizeof(int) *N,
cudaMemcpyDeviceToHost);
  printf("Array in Global Memory is: \n");
  for (int i = 0; i < N; i++)
  {
    printf("At Index: %d --> %d \n", i, h_a[i]);
  }
  return 0;
}
```

This code demonstrates how you can write in global memory from your device code. The memory is allocated using `cudaMalloc` from the host code and a pointer to this array is passed as a parameter to the kernel function. The kernel function populates this memory chunk with values of the thread ID. This is copied back to host memory for printing. The result is shown as follows:

As we are using global memory, this operation will be slow. There are advanced concepts to speed up this operation which will be explained later on. In the next section, we will explain local memory and registers that are unique to all threads.

Local memory and registers

Local memory and register files are unique to each thread. Register files are the fastest memory available for each thread. When variables of the kernel do not fit in register files, they use local memory. This is called **register spilling**. Basically, local memory is a part of global memory that is unique for each thread. Access to local memory will be slow compared to register files. Though local memory is cached in L1 and L2 caches, register spilling might not affect your program adversely.

A simple program to understand how to use local memory is shown as follows:

```
#include <stdio.h>
#define N 5

__global__ void gpu_local_memory(int d_in)
{
  int t_local;
  t_local = d_in * threadIdx.x;
  printf("Value of Local variable in current thread is: %d \n", t_local);
}
int main(int argc, char **argv)
{
  printf("Use of Local Memory on GPU:\n");
  gpu_local_memory << <1, N >> >(5);
  cudaDeviceSynchronize();
  return 0;
}
```

The `t_local` variable will be local to each thread and stored in a register file. When this variable is used for computation in the kernel function, the computation will be the fastest. The output of the preceding code is shown as follows:

```
C:\WINDOWS\system32\cmd.exe
Use of Local Memory on GPU:
Value of Local variable in current thread is: 0
Value of Local variable in current thread is: 5
Value of Local variable in current thread is: 10
Value of Local variable in current thread is: 15
Value of Local variable in current thread is: 20
Press any key to continue . . .
```

Cache memory

On the latest GPUs, there is an L1 cache per multiprocessor and an L2 cache, which is shared between all multiprocessors. Both global and local memories use these caches. As L1 is near to thread execution, it is very fast. As shown in the diagram for memory architecture earlier, the L1 cache and shared memory use the same 64 KB. Both can be configured for how many bytes they will use out of the 64 KB. All global memory access goes through an L2 cache. Texture memory and constant memory have their separate caches.

Thread synchronization

Up until now, whatever examples we have seen in this book had all threads independent of each other. But rarely, in real life, do you find examples where threads operate on data and terminate without passing results to any other threads. So there has to be some mechanism for threads to communicate with each other, and that is why the concept of shared memory is explained in this section. When many threads work in parallel and operate on the same data or read and write from the same memory location, there has to be synchronization between all threads. Thus, thread synchronization is also explained in this section. The last part of this section explains atomic operations, which are very useful in read-modified write conditions.

Shared memory

Shared memory is available on-chip, and hence it is much faster than global memory. Shared memory latency is roughly 100 times lower than uncached global memory latency. All the threads from the same block can access shared memory. This is very useful in many applications where threads need to share their results with other threads. However, it can also create chaos or false results if it is not synchronized. If one thread reads data from memory before the other thread has written to it, it can lead to false results. So, the memory access should be controlled or managed properly. This is done by the __syncthreads() directive, which ensures that all the write operations to memory are completed before moving ahead in the programs. This is also called a **barrier**. The meaning of barrier is that all threads will reach this line and wait for other threads to finish. After all threads have reached this barrier, they can move further. To demonstrate the use of shared memory and thread synchronization, an example of a moving average is taken. The kernel function for that is shown as follows:

```
#include <stdio.h>
__global__ void gpu_shared_memory(float *d_a)
{
  int i, index = threadIdx.x;
  float average, sum = 0.0f;
  //Defining shared memory
  __shared__ float sh_arr[10];
  sh_arr[index] = d_a[index];
 // This directive ensure all the writes to shared memory have completed

  __syncthreads();
  for (i = 0; i<= index; i++)
  {
    sum += sh_arr[i];
```

```
    }
    average = sum / (index + 1.0f);
    d_a[index] = average;
        //This statement is redundant and will have no effect on overall code
    execution
    sh_arr[index] = average;
    }
```

The moving average operation is nothing but finding an average of all elements in an array up to the current element. Many threads will need the same data of an array for their calculation. This is an ideal case of using shared memory, and it will provide faster data than global memory. This will reduce the number of global memory accesses per thread, which in turn will reduce the latency of the program. The shared memory location is defined using the __shared__ directive. In this example, the shared memory of ten float elements is defined. Normally, the size of shared memory should be equal to the number of threads per block. Here, we are working on an array of 10, and hence we have taken the shared memory of this size.

The next step is to copy data from global memory to this shared memory. All the threads copy the element indexed by its thread ID to the shared array. Now, this is a shared memory write operation and, in the next line, we will read from this shared array. So, before proceeding, we should ensure that all shared memory write operations are completed. Therefore, let's introduce the __synchronizethreads() barrier.

Next, the for loop calculates the average of all elements up to the current elements using the values in shared memory and stores the answer in global memory which is indexed by the current thread ID. The last line copies the calculated value in shared memory also. This line will have no effect on the overall execution of the code because shared memory has a lifetime up until the end of the current block execution, and this is the last line after which block execution is complete. It is just used to demonstrate this concept about shared memory. Now, we will try to write the main function for this code as follows:

```
int main(int argc, char **argv)
{
    float h_a[10];
    float *d_a;
        //Initialize host Array
    for (int i = 0; i < 10; i++)
    {
      h_a[i] = i;
    }
    // allocate global memory on the device
    cudaMalloc((void **)&d_a, sizeof(float) * 10);
    // copy data from host memory  to device memory
    cudaMemcpy((void *)d_a, (void *)h_a, sizeof(float) * 10,
```

```
cudaMemcpyHostToDevice);
    gpu_shared_memory << <1, 10 >> >(d_a);
    // copy the modified array back to the host
    cudaMemcpy((void *)h_a, (void *)d_a, sizeof(float) * 10,
cudaMemcpyDeviceToHost);
    printf("Use of Shared Memory on GPU: \n");
    for (int i = 0; i < 10; i++)
    {
      printf("The running average after %d element is %f \n", i, h_a[i]);
    }
    return 0;
}
```

In the `main` function, after allocating memory for host and device arrays, host array is populated with values from zero to nine. This is copied to device memory where the moving average is calculated and the result is stored. The result from device memory is copied back to host memory and then printed on the console. The output on the console is shown as follows:

```
C:\WINDOWS\system32\cmd.exe
Use of Shared Memory on GPU:
The running average after 0 element is 0.000000
The running average after 1 element is 0.500000
The running average after 2 element is 1.000000
The running average after 3 element is 1.500000
The running average after 4 element is 2.000000
The running average after 5 element is 2.500000
The running average after 6 element is 3.000000
The running average after 7 element is 3.500000
The running average after 8 element is 4.000000
The running average after 9 element is 4.500000
Press any key to continue . . .
```

This section demonstrated the use of shared memory when multiple threads use data from the same memory location. The next section demonstrates the use of the `atomic` operations, which are very important in read-modified write operations.

Atomic operations

Consider a situation in which a large number of threads try to modify a small portion of memory. This is a frequently occurring phenomenon. It creates more problems when we try to perform a read-modify-write operation. The example of this operation is d_out[i] ++, where the first d_out[i] is read from memory, then incremented and then written back to the memory. However, when multiple threads are doing this operation on the same memory location, it can give a wrong output.

Suppose one memory location has an initial value of six, and threads p and q are trying to increment this memory location, then the final answer should be eight. But at the time of execution, it may happen that both the p and q threads read this value simultaneously, then both will get the value six. They increment it to seven and both will store this seven in the memory. So instead of eight, our final answer is seven, which is wrong. How this can be dangerous is understood by taking an example of ATM cash withdrawal. Suppose you have a balance of Rs 5,000 in your account. You have two ATM cards of the same account. You and your friend go to two different ATMs simultaneously to withdraw Rs 4,000. Both of you swipe your card simultaneously; so, when the ATM checks for the balance, both will show a balance of Rs 5,000. When both of you withdraw Rs 4,000, then both machines will look at the initial balance, which was Rs 5,000. The amount to withdraw is less than the balance, and hence both machines will give Rs 4,000. Even though your balance was Rs 5,000, you got Rs 8,000, which is dangerous. To demonstrate this phenomenon, one example of large threads trying to access a small array is taken. The kernel function for this example is shown as follows:

```
include <stdio.h>

#define NUM_THREADS 10000
#define SIZE 10

#define BLOCK_WIDTH 100

__global__ void gpu_increment_without_atomic(int *d_a)
{
   int tid = blockIdx.x * blockDim.x + threadIdx.x;

   // Each thread increment elements which wraps at SIZE
   tid = tid % SIZE;
   d_a[tid] += 1;
}
```

The kernel function is just incrementing memory location in the `d_a[tid] +=1` line. The issue is how many times this memory location is incremented. The total number of threads is 10,000 and the array is only of size 10. We are indexing an array by taking the `modulo` operation between the thread ID and the size of the array. So, 1,000 threads will try to increment the same memory location. Ideally, every location in the array should be incremented 1,000 times. But as we will see in the output, this is not the case. Before seeing the output, we will try to write the `main` function:

```
int main(int argc, char **argv)
{
  printf("%d total threads in %d blocks writing into %d array elements\n",
  NUM_THREADS, NUM_THREADS / BLOCK_WIDTH, SIZE);
  // declare and allocate host memory
  int h_a[SIZE];
  const int ARRAY_BYTES = SIZE * sizeof(int);
  // declare and allocate GPU memory
  int * d_a;
  cudaMalloc((void **)&d_a, ARRAY_BYTES);
  // Initialize GPU memory with zero value.
  cudaMemset((void *)d_a, 0, ARRAY_BYTES);
  gpu_increment_without_atomic << <NUM_THREADS / BLOCK_WIDTH, BLOCK_WIDTH
>> >(d_a);
  // copy back the array of sums from GPU and print
  cudaMemcpy(h_a, d_a, ARRAY_BYTES, cudaMemcpyDeviceToHost);
  printf("Number of times a particular Array index has been incremented
without atomic add is: \n");
  for (int i = 0; i < SIZE; i++)
  {
    printf("index: %d --> %d times\n ", i, h_a[i]);
  }
  cudaFree(d_a);
  return 0;
}
```

In the `main` function, the device array is declared and initialized to zero. Here, a special `cudaMemSet` function is used to initialize memory on the device. This is passed as a parameter to the kernel, which increments these 10 memory locations. Here, a total of 10,000 threads are launched as 1,000 blocks and 100 threads per block. The answer stored on the device after the kernel's execution is copied back to the host, and the value of each memory location is displayed on the console.

The output is as follows:

```
C:\WINDOWS\system32\cmd.exe

10000 total threads in 100 blocks writing into 10 array elements
Number of times a particular Array index has been incremented without atomic add is:
index: 0 --> 16 times
 index: 1 --> 16 times
 index: 2 --> 16 times
 index: 3 --> 16 times
 index: 4 --> 16 times
 index: 5 --> 16 times
 index: 6 --> 17 times
 index: 7 --> 17 times
 index: 8 --> 17 times
 index: 9 --> 17 times
 Press any key to continue . . . _
```

As discussed previously, ideally, each memory location should have been incremented 1,000 times, but most of the memory locations have values of 16 and 17. This is because many threads read the same locations simultaneously and hence increment the same value and store it in memory. As the timing of the thread's execution is beyond the control of the programmer, how many times simultaneous memory access will happen is not known. If you run your program a second time, then will your output be same as the first time? Your output might look like the following:

```
C:\WINDOWS\system32\cmd.exe

10000 total threads in 100 blocks writing into 10 array elements
Number of times a particular Array index has been incremented without atomic add is:
index: 0 --> 19 times
 index: 1 --> 19 times
 index: 2 --> 19 times
 index: 3 --> 19 times
 index: 4 --> 19 times
 index: 5 --> 19 times
 index: 6 --> 19 times
 index: 7 --> 19 times
 index: 8 --> 19 times
 index: 9 --> 19 times
 Press any key to continue . . .
```

As you might have guessed, every time you run your program, the memory locations may have different values. This happens because of the random execution of all threads on the device.

To solve this problem, CUDA provides an API called `atomicAdd` operations. It is a `blocking` operation, which means that when multiple threads are trying to access the same memory location, only one thread can access the memory location at a time. Other threads have to wait for this thread to finish and `write` its answer on memory. The kernel function to use the `atomicAdd` operation is shown as follows:

```
#include <stdio.h>
#define NUM_THREADS 10000
#define SIZE 10
#define BLOCK_WIDTH 100

__global__ void gpu_increment_atomic(int *d_a)
{
    // Calculate thread index
    int tid = blockIdx.x * blockDim.x + threadIdx.x;

    // Each thread increments elements which wraps at SIZE
    tid = tid % SIZE;
    atomicAdd(&d_a[tid], 1);
}
```

The `kernel` function is quite similar to what we saw earlier. Instead of incrementing memory location using the += operator, the `atomicAdd` function is used. It takes two arguments. The first is the memory location we want to increment, and the second is the value by which this location has to be incremented. In this code, 1,000 threads will again try to access the same location; so when one thread is using this location, the other 999 threads have to wait. This will increase the cost in terms of execution time. The `main` function of increment using `atomic` operations is shown as follows:

```
int main(int argc, char **argv)
{
    printf("%d total threads in %d blocks writing into %d array
elements\n",NUM_THREADS, NUM_THREADS / BLOCK_WIDTH, SIZE);

    // declare and allocate host memory
    int h_a[SIZE];
    const int ARRAY_BYTES = SIZE * sizeof(int);

    // declare and allocate GPU memory
    int * d_a;
    cudaMalloc((void **)&d_a, ARRAY_BYTES);
    // Initialize GPU memory withzero value
    cudaMemset((void *)d_a, 0, ARRAY_BYTES);
    gpu_increment_atomic << <NUM_THREADS / BLOCK_WIDTH, BLOCK_WIDTH >>
>(d_a);
    // copy back the array from GPU and print
```

```
cudaMemcpy(h_a, d_a, ARRAY_BYTES, cudaMemcpyDeviceToHost);
printf("Number of times a particular Array index has been incremented is:
\n");
for (int i = 0; i < SIZE; i++)
{
    printf("index: %d --> %d times\n ", i, h_a[i]);
}
cudaFree(d_a);
return 0;
}
```

In the `main` function, the array with 10 elements is initialized with a zero value and passed to the kernel. But now, the kernel will do the `atomic add` operation. So, the output of this program should be accurate. Each element in the array should be incremented 1,000 times. The following will be the output:

If you measure the execution time of the program with atomic operations, it may take a longer time than that taken by simple programs using global memory. This is because many threads are waiting for memory access in the atomic operation. Use of shared memory can help to speed up operations. Also, if the same number of threads are accessing more memory locations, then the atomic operation will incur less time overhead as a smaller number of threads having to wait for memory access.

In this section, we have seen that atomic operations help in avoiding race conditions in memory operations and make the code simpler to write and understand. In the next section, we will explain two special types of memories, constant and texture, which help in accelerating certain types of code.

Constant memory

The CUDA language makes another type of memory available to the programmer, which is known as **constant** memory. NVIDIA hardware provides 64 KB of this constant memory, which is used to store data that remains constant throughout the execution of the kernel. This constant memory is cached on-chip so that the use of constant memory instead of global memory can speed up execution. The use of constant memory will also reduce memory bandwidth to the device's global memory. In this section, we will see how to use constant memory in CUDA programs. A simple program that performs a simple math operation, a*x + b, where a and b are constants, is taken as an example. The kernel function code for this program is shown as follows:

```
#include "stdio.h"
#include<iostream>
#include <cuda.h>
#include <cuda_runtime.h>

//Defining two constants
__constant__ int constant_f;
__constant__ int constant_g;
#define N 5

//Kernel function for using constant memory
__global__ void gpu_constant_memory(float *d_in, float *d_out)
{
  //Getting thread index for current kernel
  int tid = threadIdx.x;
  d_out[tid] = constant_f*d_in[tid] + constant_g;
}
```

Constant memory variables are defined using the __constant__ keyword. In the preceding code, two float variables, constant_f and constant_g, are defined as constants that will not change throughout the kernel's execution. The second thing to note is that once variables are defined as constants, they should not be defined again in the kernel function. The kernel function computes a simple mathematical operation using these two constants. There is a special way in which constant variables are copied to memory from the main function. This is shown in the following code:

```
int main(void)
{
  //Defining Arrays for host
  float h_in[N], h_out[N];
  //Defining Pointers for device
  float *d_in, *d_out;
  int h_f = 2;
```

```
    int h_g = 20;
    // allocate the memory on the cpu
    cudaMalloc((void**)&d_in, N * sizeof(float));
    cudaMalloc((void**)&d_out, N * sizeof(float));
    //Initializing Array
    for (int i = 0; i < N; i++)
    {
      h_in[i] = i;
    }
    //Copy Array from host to device
    cudaMemcpy(d_in, h_in, N * sizeof(float), cudaMemcpyHostToDevice);
    //Copy constants to constant memory
    cudaMemcpyToSymbol(constant_f, &h_f,
sizeof(int),0,cudaMemcpyHostToDevice);
    cudaMemcpyToSymbol(constant_g, &h_g, sizeof(int));

    //Calling kernel with one block and N threads per block
    gpu_constant_memory << <1, N >> >(d_in, d_out);
    //Coping result back to host from device memory
    cudaMemcpy(h_out, d_out, N * sizeof(float), cudaMemcpyDeviceToHost);
    //Printing result on console
    printf("Use of Constant memory on GPU \n");
    for (int i = 0; i < N; i++)
    {
      printf("The expression for index %f is %f\n", h_in[i], h_out[i]);
    }
    cudaFree(d_in);
    cudaFree(d_out);
    return 0;
}
```

In the main function, the h_f and h_g constants are defined and initialized on the host, which will be copied to constant memory. The cudaMemcpyToSymbol instruction is used to copy these constants onto constant memory for kernel execution. It has five arguments. First is the destination, which is defined using the __constant__ keyword. Second is the host address, third is the size of the transfer, fourth is memory offset, which is taken as zero, and fifth is the direction of data transfer, which is taken as the host to the device. The last two arguments are optional, and hence they are omitted in the second call to the cudaMemcpyToSymbol instruction.

The output of the code is shown as follows:

```
C:\WINDOWS\system32\cmd.exe
Use of Constant memory on GPU
The expression for input 0.000000 is 20.000000
The expression for input 1.000000 is 22.000000
The expression for input 2.000000 is 24.000000
The expression for input 3.000000 is 26.000000
The expression for input 4.000000 is 28.000000
Press any key to continue . . .
```

One thing to note is that constant memory is a `Read-only` memory. This example is used just to explain the use of the constant memory from the CUDA program. It is not the optimal use of constant memory. As discussed earlier, constant memory helps in conserving memory bandwidth to global memory. To understand this, you have to understand the concept of warp. One warp is a collection of 32 threads woven together and executed in lockstep. A single read from constant memory can be broadcast to half warp, which can reduce up to 15 memory transactions. Also, constant memory is cached so that memory access to a nearby location will not incur an additional memory transaction. When each half warp, which contains 16 threads, operates on the same memory locations, the use of constant memory saves a lot of execution time. It should also be noted that if half-warp threads use completely different memory locations, then the use of constant memory may increase the execution time. So, the constant memory should be used with proper care.

Texture memory

Texture memory is another read-only memory that can accelerate the program and reduce memory bandwidth when data is read in a certain pattern. Like constant memory, it is also cached on a chip. This memory was originally designed for rendering graphics, but it can also be used for general purpose computing applications. It is very effective when applications have memory access that exhibits a great deal of spatial locality. The meaning of spatial locality is that each thread is likely to read from the nearby location what other nearby threads read. This is great in image processing applications where we work on 4-point connectivity and 8-point connectivity. A two-dimensional spatial locality for accessing memory location by threads may look something like this:

Thread 0	Thread 2
Thread 1	Thread 3

General global memory cache will not be able to capture this spatial locality and will result in lots of memory traffic to global memory. Texture memory is designed for this kind of access pattern so that it will only read from memory once, and then it will be cached so that execution will be much faster. Texture memory supports one and two-dimensional fetch operations. Using texture memory in your CUDA program is not trivial, especially for those who are not programming experts. In this section, a simple example of how to copy array values using texture memory is explained. The kernel function for using texture memory is explained as follows:

```
#include "stdio.h"
#include<iostream>
#include <cuda.h>
#include <cuda_runtime.h>

#define NUM_THREADS 10
#define N 10

//Define texture reference for 1-d access
texture <float, 1, cudaReadModeElementType> textureRef;

__global__ void gpu_texture_memory(int n, float *d_out)
{
    int idx = blockIdx.x*blockDim.x + threadIdx.x;
    if (idx < n) {
      float temp = tex1D(textureRef, float(idx));
      d_out[idx] = temp;
    }
}
```

The part of texture memory that should be fetched is defined by texture reference. In code, it is defined using the texture API. It has three arguments. The first argument indicates the data type of texture elements. In this example, it is a float. The second argument indicates the type of texture reference, which can be one-dimensional, two-dimensional, and so on. Here, it is a one-dimensional reference. The third argument specifies the read mode and it is an optional argument. Please make sure that this texture reference is declared as a static global variable, and it should not be passed as parameters to any function. In the kernel function, data stored at the thread ID is read from this texture reference and copied to the d_out global memory pointer. Here, we are not using any spatial locality as this example is only taken to show you how to use texture memory from CUDA programs. The spatial locality will be explained in the next chapter when we see some image processing applications with CUDA. The main function for this example is shown as follows:

```
int main()
{
    //Calculate number of blocks to launch
```

```
    int num_blocks = N / NUM_THREADS + ((N % NUM_THREADS) ? 1 : 0);
    float *d_out;
    // allocate space on the device for the results
    cudaMalloc((void**)&d_out, sizeof(float) * N);
    // allocate space on the host for the results
    float *h_out = (float*)malloc(sizeof(float)*N);
    float h_in[N];
    for (int i = 0; i < N; i++)
    {
      h_in[i] = float(i);
    }
    //Define CUDA Array
    cudaArray *cu_Array;
    cudaMallocArray(&cu_Array, &textureRef.channelDesc, N, 1);
    cudaMemcpyToArray(cu_Array, 0, 0, h_in, sizeof(float)*N,
  cudaMemcpyHostToDevice);
    // bind a texture to the CUDA array
    cudaBindTextureToArray(textureRef, cu_Array);
    gpu_texture_memory << <num_blocks, NUM_THREADS >> >(N, d_out);
    // copy result to host
    cudaMemcpy(h_out, d_out, sizeof(float)*N, cudaMemcpyDeviceToHost);
    printf("Use of Texture memory on GPU: \n");
    // Print the result
    for (int i = 0; i < N; i++)
    {
      printf("Average between two nearest element is : %f\n", h_out[i]);
    }
    free(h_out);
    cudaFree(d_out);
    cudaFreeArray(cu_Array);
    cudaUnbindTexture(textureRef);
}
```

In the `main` function, after declaring and allocating memory for host and device arrays, the host array is initialized with values from zero to nine. In this example, you will see the first use of CUDA arrays. They are similar to normal arrays, but they are dedicated to textures. They are read-only to kernel functions and can be written to device memory from the host by using the `cudaMemcpyToArray` function, as shown in the preceding code. The second and third arguments in that function are width and height offset that are taken as 0, 0, meaning that we are starting from the top left corner. They are opaque memory layouts optimized for texture memory fetches.

The `cudaBindTextureToArray` functions bind texture reference to this CUDA array. This means, it copies this array to a texture reference starting from the top left corner. After binding the texture reference, the kernel is called, which uses this texture reference and computes the array to be stored on device memory. After the kernel finishes, the output array is copied back to the host for displaying on the console. When using texture memory, we have to unbind the texture from our code. This is done by using the `cudaUnbindTexture` function. The `cudaFreeArray` function is used to free up memory used by the CUDA array. The output of the program displayed on the console is shown as follows:

```
C:\WINDOWS\system32\cmd.exe

Use of Texture memory on GPU:
Texture element at 0 is : 0.000000
Texture element at 1 is : 1.000000
Texture element at 2 is : 2.000000
Texture element at 3 is : 3.000000
Texture element at 4 is : 4.000000
Texture element at 5 is : 5.000000
Texture element at 6 is : 6.000000
Texture element at 7 is : 7.000000
Texture element at 8 is : 8.000000
Texture element at 9 is : 9.000000
Press any key to continue . . .
```

This section finishes our discussion on memory architecture in CUDA. When the memories available in CUDA are used judiciously according to your application, it improves the performance of the program drastically. You need to look carefully at the memory access pattern of all threads in your application and then select which memory you should use for your application. The last section of this chapter briefly describes the complex CUDA program, which uses all the concepts we have used up until this point.

Dot product and matrix multiplication example

Up to this point, we have learned almost all the important concepts related to basic parallel programming using CUDA. In this section, we will show you how to write CUDA programs for important mathematical operations like dot product and matrix multiplication, which are used in almost all applications. This will make use of all the concepts we saw earlier and help you in writing code for your applications.

Dot product

The dot product between two vectors is an important mathematical operation. It will also explain one important concept in CUDA programming that is called **reduction** operation. The dot product between two vectors can be defined as follows:

```
(x1,x1,x3) . (y1,y2,y3) = x1y1 + x2y2 +x3y3
```

Now, if you see this operation, it is very similar to an element-wise addition operation on vectors. Instead of addition, you have to perform element-wise multiplication. All threads also have to keep running the sum of multiplication they have performed because all individual multiplications need to be summed up to get a final answer of the dot product. The answer of the dot product will be a single number. This operation where the final answer is the reduced version of the original two arrays is called a **reduce** operation in CUDA. It is useful in many applications. To perform this operation in CUDA, we will start by writing a kernel function for it, as follows:

```
#include <stdio.h>
#include<iostream>
#include <cuda.h>
#include <cuda_runtime.h>
#define N 1024
#define threadsPerBlock 512


__global__ void gpu_dot(float *d_a, float *d_b, float *d_c)
{
  //Define Shared Memory
  __shared__ float partial_sum[threadsPerBlock];
  int tid = threadIdx.x + blockIdx.x * blockDim.x;
  int index = threadIdx.x;

  float sum = 0;
  while (tid < N)
  {
    sum += d_a[tid] * d_b[tid];
    tid += blockDim.x * gridDim.x;
  }

  // set the partial sum in shared memory
  partial_sum[index] = sum;

  // synchronize threads in this block
  __syncthreads();

  //Calculate Patial sum for a current block using data in shared memory
```

```
    int i = blockDim.x / 2;
    while (i != 0) {
      if (index < i)
        {partial_sum[index] += partial_sum[index + i];}
      __syncthreads();
      i /= 2;
    }
    //Store result of partial sum for a block in global memory
    if (index == 0)
      d_c[blockIdx.x] = partial_sum[0];
  }
```

The `kernel` function takes two input arrays as input and stores the final partial sum in the third array. Shared memory is defined to store intermediate answers of the partial answer. The size of the shared memory is equal to the number of threads per block, as all separate blocks will have the separate copy of this shared memory. After that, two indexes are calculated; the first one, which calculates the unique thread ID, is similar to what we have done in the vector addition example. The second index is used to store the partial product answer on shared memory. Again, every block has a separate copy of shared memory, so only the thread ID used to index the shared memory is of a given block.

The `while` loop will perform element-wise multiplication of elements indexed by the thread ID. It will also do multiplication of elements that is offset by the total threads to the current thread ID. The partial sum of this element is stored in the shared memory. We are going to use these results from the shared memory to calculate the partial sum for a single block. So, before reading this shared memory block, we must ensure that all threads have finished writing to this shared memory. This is ensured by using the `__syncthreads()` directive.

Now, one method to get an answer for the dot product is that one thread iterates over all these partial sums to get a final answer. One thread can perform the reduce operation. This will take N operations to complete, where N is the number of partial sums to be added (equal to the number of threads per block) to get a final answer.

The question is, can we do this reduce operation in parallel? The answer is yes. The idea is that every thread will add two elements of the partial sum and store the answer in the location of the first element. Since each thread combines two entries in one, the operation can be completed in half entries. Now, we will repeat this operation for the remaining half until we get the final answer that calculates the partial sum for this entire block. The complexity of this operation is $\log_2(N)$, which is far better than the complexity of N when one thread performs the reduce operation.

The operation explained is calculated by the block starting with `while (i != 0)`. The block sums the partial answer of the current thread and the thread offset by `blockdim/2`. It continues this addition until we get a final single answer, which is a sum of all partial products in a given block. The final answer is stored in the global memory. Each block will have a separate answer to be stored in the global memory so that it is indexed by the block ID, which is unique for each block. Still, we have not got the final answer. This can be performed in the `device` function or the `main` function.

Normally, the last few additions in the reduce operation need very little resources. Much of the GPU resource remains idle, and that is not the optimal use of the GPU. So, the final addition operation of all partial sums for an individual block is done in the `main` function. The `main` function is as follows:

```
int main(void)
{
  float *h_a, *h_b, h_c, *partial_sum;
  float *d_a, *d_b, *d_partial_sum;

  //Calculate number of blocks and number of threads
  int block_calc = (N + threadsPerBlock - 1) / threadsPerBlock;
  int blocksPerGrid = (32 < block_calc ? 32 : block_calc);
  // allocate memory on the cpu side
  h_a = (float*)malloc(N * sizeof(float));
  h_b = (float*)malloc(N * sizeof(float));
  partial_sum = (float*)malloc(blocksPerGrid * sizeof(float));

  // allocate the memory on the gpu
  cudaMalloc((void**)&d_a, N * sizeof(float));
  cudaMalloc((void**)&d_b, N * sizeof(float));
  cudaMalloc((void**)&d_partial_sum, blocksPerGrid * sizeof(float));

  // fill in the host mempory with data
  for (int i = 0; i<N; i++) {
    h_a[i] = i;
    h_b[i] = 2;
  }


  // copy the arrays to the device
  cudaMemcpy(d_a, h_a, N * sizeof(float), cudaMemcpyHostToDevice);
  cudaMemcpy(d_b, h_b, N * sizeof(float), cudaMemcpyHostToDevice);

  gpu_dot << <blocksPerGrid, threadsPerBlock >> >(d_a, d_b, d_partial_sum);

  // copy the array back to the host
  cudaMemcpy(partial_sum, d_partial_sum, blocksPerGrid * sizeof(float),
```

```
cudaMemcpyDeviceToHost);

  // Calculate final dot prodcut
  h_c = 0;
  for (int i = 0; i<blocksPerGrid; i++)
  {
    h_c += partial_sum[i];
  }
}
```

Three arrays are defined and memory is allocated for both host and device to store inputs and output. The two host arrays are initialized inside a `for` loop. One array is initialized with 0 to N and the second is initialized with a constant value 2. The calculation of the number of blocks in a grid and number of threads in a block is also done. It is similar to what we did at the start of this chapter. Bear in mind, you can also keep these value as constants, like we did in the first program of this chapter, to avoid complexity.

These arrays are copied to device memory and passed as parameters to the `kernel` function. The `kernel` function will return an array, which has answers of the partial products of individual blocks indexed by their block ID. This array is copied back to the host in the `partial_sum` array. The final answer of the dot product is calculated by iterating over this `partial_sum` array, using the `for` loop starting from zero to the number of blocks per grid. The final dot product is stored in `h_c`. To check whether the calculated dot product is correct or not, the following code can be added to the `main` function:

```
printf("The computed dot product is: %f\n", h_c);
#define cpu_sum(x) (x*(x+1))
  if (h_c == cpu_sum((float)(N - 1)))
  {
    printf("The dot product computed by GPU is correct\n");
  }
  else
  {
    printf("Error in dot product computation");
  }
  // free memory on the gpu side
  cudaFree(d_a);
  cudaFree(d_b);
  cudaFree(d_partial_sum);
  // free memory on the cpu side
  free(h_a);
  free(h_b);
  free(partial_sum);
```

The answer is verified with the answer calculated mathematically. In two input arrays, if one array has values from 0 to N−1 and the second array has a constant value of 2, then the dot product will be N*(N+1). We print the answer of the dot product calculated mathematically, along with whether it has been calculated correctly or not. The host and device memory is freed up in the end. The output of the program is as follows:

```
C:\WINDOWS\system32\cmd.exe
The computed dot product is: 1047552.000000
The dot product computed by GPU is correct
Press any key to continue . . .
```

Matrix multiplication

The second most important mathematical operation performed on a GPU using CUDA is matrix multiplication. It is a very complicated mathematical operation when the sizes of the matrices are very large. It should be kept in mind that for matrix multiplication, the number of columns in the first matrix should be equal to the number of rows in the second matrix. Matrix multiplication is not a cumulative operation. To avoid complexity, in this example, we are taking a square matrix of the same size. If you are familiar with the mathematics of matrix multiplication, then you may recall that a row in the first matrix will be multiplied with all the columns in the second matrix. This is repeated for all rows in the first matrix. It is shown as follows:

$$
\begin{bmatrix} 0 & 0 & 0 & 0 \\ 1 & 1 & 1 & 1 \\ 2 & 2 & 2 & 2 \\ 3 & 3 & 3 & 3 \end{bmatrix} * \begin{bmatrix} 0 & 1 & 2 & 3 \\ 0 & 1 & 2 & 3 \\ 0 & 1 & 2 & 3 \\ 0 & 1 & 2 & 3 \end{bmatrix} = \begin{bmatrix} 0*0+0*0+0*0+0*0 & 0 & 0 & 0 \\ 1*0+1*0+1*0+1*0 & 4 & 8 & 12 \\ 2*0+2*0+2*0+2*0 & 8 & 16 & 24 \\ 3*0+3*0+3*0+3*0 & 12 & 24 & 36 \end{bmatrix}
$$

Same data is reused many times, so this is an ideal case of using shared memory. In this section, we will make two separate kernel functions, with and without using shared memory. You can compare the execution of two kernels to get an idea of how shared memory improves the performance of the program. We will first start by writing a kernel function without using shared memory:

```
#include <stdio.h>
#include<iostream>
#include <cuda.h>
#include <cuda_runtime.h>
#include <math.h>
```

```
//This defines size of a small square box or thread dimensions in one block
#define TILE_SIZE 2

//Matrix multiplication using non shared kernel
__global__ void gpu_Matrix_Mul_nonshared(float *d_a, float *d_b, float
*d_c, const int size)
{
  int row, col;
  col = TILE_SIZE * blockIdx.x + threadIdx.x;
  row = TILE_SIZE * blockIdx.y + threadIdx.y;

  for (int k = 0; k< size; k++)
  {
    d_c[row*size + col] += d_a[row * size + k] * d_b[k * size + col];
  }
}
```

Matrix multiplication is performed using two-dimensional threads. If we launch two-dimensional threads with each thread performing a single element of the output matrix, then up to 16 x 16 matrices can be multiplied. If the size is greater than this, then it will need more than 512 threads for computation, which is not possible on most GPUs. So, we need to launch multiple blocks with each containing less than 512 threads. To accomplish this, the output matrix is divided into small square blocks having dimensions of TILE_SIZE in both directions. Each thread in a block will calculate elements of this square block. The total number of blocks for matrix multiplication will be calculated by dividing the size of the matrix by the size of this small square defined by TILE_SIZE.

If you understand this, then calculating the row and column index for the output will be very easy. It is similar to what we have done up till now, with blockdim.x being equal to TILE_SIZE. Now, every element in the output will be the dot product of one row in the first matrix and one column in the second matrix. Both the matrices have the same size so the dot product has to be performed for a number of elements equal to the size variable. So the for loop in the kernel function is running from 0 to size.

To calculate the individual index of both matrices, consider that this matrix is stored as a linear array in system memory in row-major fashion. Its meaning is that all elements in the first row are placed in a consecutive memory location and then rows are placed one after the other, as follows:

$$\begin{bmatrix} M_{00} & M_{01} \\ M_{10} & M_{11} \end{bmatrix} \rightarrow \begin{bmatrix} M_{00} & M_{01} & M_{10} & M_{11} \end{bmatrix}$$

The index of a linear array can be calculated by its row ID multiplied by the size of the matrix plus its column ID. So, the index for $M_{1,0}$ will be 2 as its row ID is 1, the matrix size is 2 and the column ID is zero. This method is used to calculate the element index in both the matrices.

To calculate the element at `[row, col]` in the resultant matrix, the index in the first matrix will be equal to `row*size + k` , and for the second matrix, it will be `k*size + col`. This is a very simple `kernel` function. There is a large amount of data reuse in matrix multiplication. This function is not utilizing the advantage of shared memory. So, we will try to modify the kernel function that makes use of shared memory. The modified `kernel` function is shown as follows:

```
// shared
__global__ void gpu_Matrix_Mul_shared(float *d_a, float *d_b, float *d_c,
const int size)
{
  int row, col;

  __shared__ float shared_a[TILE_SIZE][TILE_SIZE];

  __shared__ float shared_b[TILE_SIZE][TILE_SIZE];

  // calculate thread id
  col = TILE_SIZE * blockIdx.x + threadIdx.x;
  row = TILE_SIZE * blockIdx.y + threadIdx.y;

  for (int i = 0; i< size / TILE_SIZE; i++)
  {
    shared_a[threadIdx.y][threadIdx.x] = d_a[row* size + (i*TILE_SIZE +
threadIdx.x)];
    shared_b[threadIdx.y][threadIdx.x] = d_b[(i*TILE_SIZE + threadIdx.y) *
size + col];
  }
    __syncthreads();

    for (int j = 0; j<TILE_SIZE; j++)
      d_c[row*size + col] += shared_a[threadIdx.x][j] *
shared_b[j][threadIdx.y];
    __syncthreads(); // for synchronizing the threads

  }
}
```

A two-shared memory with size equal to the size of a small square block, which is TILE_SIZE, is defined for storing data for reuse. Row and column indexes are calculated in the same way as seen earlier. First, this shared memory is filled up in the first for loop. After that, __syncthreads() is included so that memory read from shared memory only happens when all threads have finished writing to it. The last for loop again calculates the dot product. As this is done by only using shared memory, this considerably reduces memory traffic to a global memory, which in turn improves the performance of the program for larger matrix dimensions. The main function of this program is shown as follows:

```
int main()
{
   //Define size of the matrix
   const int size = 4;
   //Define host and device arrays
   float h_a[size][size], h_b[size][size],h_result[size][size];
   float *d_a, *d_b, *d_result; // device array
   //input in host array
   for (int i = 0; i<size; i++)
   {
      for (int j = 0; j<size; j++)
      {
         h_a[i][j] = i;
         h_b[i][j] = j;
      }
   }


   cudaMalloc((void **)&d_a, size*size*sizeof(int));
   cudaMalloc((void **)&d_b, size*size * sizeof(int));
   cudaMalloc((void **)&d_result, size*size* sizeof(int));
   //copy host array to device array
   cudaMemcpy(d_a, h_a, size*size* sizeof(int), cudaMemcpyHostToDevice);
   cudaMemcpy(d_b, h_b, size*size* sizeof(int), cudaMemcpyHostToDevice);
   //calling kernel
   dim3 dimGrid(size / TILE_SIZE, size / TILE_SIZE, 1);
   dim3 dimBlock(TILE_SIZE, TILE_SIZE, 1);

   gpu_Matrix_Mul_nonshared << <dimGrid, dimBlock >> > (d_a, d_b, d_result,
size);
   //gpu_Matrix_Mul_shared << <dimGrid, dimBlock >> > (d_a, d_b, d_result,
size);

   cudaMemcpy(h_result, d_result, size*size * sizeof(int),
cudaMemcpyDeviceToHost);
   return 0;
```

```
}
```

After defining and allocating memory for host and device arrays, the host array is filled with some random values. These arrays are copied to device memory so that it can be passed to the `kernel` functions. The number of grid blocks and the number of block threads is defined using the `dim3` structure, with the dimensions equal to that calculated earlier. You can call any of the kernels. The calculated answer is copied back to the host memory. To display the output on the console, the following code is added to the `main` function:

```
printf("The result of Matrix multiplication is: \n");
  for (int i = 0; i< size; i++)
  {
    for (int j = 0; j < size; j++)
    {
      printf("%f ", h_result[i][j]);
    }
    printf("\n");
  }
cudaFree(d_a)
cudaFree(d_b)
cudaFree(d_result)
```

The memory used to store matrices on device memory is also freed up. The output on the console is as follows:

```
C:\WINDOWS\system32\cmd.exe
The result of Matrix multiplication is:
0.000000    0.000000    0.000000    0.000000    0.000000    0.000000
0.000000    6.000000    12.000000   18.000000   24.000000   30.000000
0.000000    12.000000   24.000000   36.000000   48.000000   60.000000
0.000000    18.000000   36.000000   54.000000   72.000000   90.000000
0.000000    24.000000   48.000000   72.000000   96.000000   120.000000
0.000000    30.000000   60.000000   90.000000   120.000000  150.000000
Press any key to continue . . .
```

This section demonstrated CUDA programs for two important mathematical operations used in a wide range of applications. It also explained the use of shared memory and multidimensional threads.

Summary

This chapter explained the launch of multiple blocks, with each having multiple threads from the kernel function. It showed the method for choosing the two parameters for a large value of threads. It also explained the hierarchical memory architecture that can be used by CUDA programs. The memory nearest to the thread being executed is fast, and as we move away from it, memories get slower. When multiple threads want to communicate with each other, then CUDA provides the flexibility of using shared memory, by which threads from the same blocks can communicate with each other. When multiple threads use the same memory location, then there should be synchronization between the memory access; otherwise, the final result will not be as expected. We also saw the use of an atomic operation to accomplish this synchronization. If some parameters remain constant throughout the kernel's execution, then it can be stored in constant memory for speed up. When CUDA programs exhibit a certain communication pattern like spatial locality, then texture memory should be used to improve the performance of the program. To summarize, to improve the performance of CUDA programs, we should reduce memory traffic to slow memories. If this is done efficiently, drastic improvement in the performance of the program can be achieved.

In the next chapter, the concept of CUDA streams will be discussed, which is similar to multitasking in CPU programs. How we can measure the performance of CUDA programs will also be discussed. It will also show the use of CUDA in simple image processing applications.

Questions

1. Suppose you want to launch 100,000 threads in parallel. What is the best choice of the number of blocks in a grid and number of threads in a block and why?
2. Write a CUDA program to find out the cube of every element in an array when the number of elements in the array is 100,000.
3. State whether the following statement is true or false and give a reason: An assignment operator between local variables will be faster than an assignment operator between global variables.
4. What is register spilling? How it can harm the performance of your CUDA program?
5. State whether the following line of code will give the required output or not: `d_out[i] = d_out[i-1]`.

6. State whether the following statement is true or false and give a reason: Atomic operations increase the execution time for CUDA programs.

7. Which kinds of communication patterns are ideal for using texture memory in your CUDA programs?

8. What will be the effect of using the __syncthreads directive inside an if statement?

Advanced Concepts in CUDA

4

In the last chapter, we looked at memory architecture in CUDA and saw how it can be used efficiently to accelerate applications. Up until now, we have not seen a method to measure the performance of CUDA programs. In this chapter, we will discuss how we can do that using CUDA events. The Nvidia Visual Profiler will also be discussed, as well as how to resolve errors in CUDA programs from within the CUDA code and using debugging tools. How we can improve the performance of CUDA programs will also be discussed. This chapter will describe how CUDA streams can be used for multitasking and how we can use them to accelerate applications. You will also learn how array-sorting algorithms can be accelerated using CUDA. Image processing is an application where we need to process a large amount of data in a very small amount of time, so CUDA can be an ideal choice for this kind of application to manipulate pixel values in an image. This chapter describes the acceleration of a simple and widely used image-processing function a histogram calculation, using CUDA.

The following topics will be covered in this chapter:

- Performance measurement in CUDA
- Error handling in CUDA
- Performance improvement of CUDA programs
- CUDA streams and how they can be used to accelerate applications
- Acceleration of sorting algorithms using CUDA
- Introduction to image processing applications with CUDA

Technical requirements

This chapter requires familiarity with the basic C or C++ programming language and all the code examples explained in the previous chapters. All the code used in this chapter can be downloaded from the following GitHub link: `https://github.com/PacktPublishing/` `Hands-On-GPU-Accelerated-Computer-Vision-with-OpenCV-and-CUDA`. The code can be executed on any operating system, although it has only been tested on Windows 10 and Ubuntu. Check out the following video to see the Code in Action: `http://bit.ly/2Nt4DEy`

Performance measurement of CUDA programs

Up until now, we have not determined the performance of the CUDA programs explicitly. In this section, we will see how to measure the performance of CUDA programs using CUDA Events and also visualize the performance using the Nvidia Visual Profiler. This is a very important concept in CUDA because it will allow you to choose the best-performing algorithms for a particular application from many options. First, we will measure performance using CUDA Events.

CUDA Events

We can use a CPU timer for measuring the performance of CUDA programs, but it will not give accurate results. It will include thread latency overhead and scheduling in the OS, among many other factors. The time measured using the CPU will also depend on the availability of a high precision CPU timer. Many times, the host is performing asynchronous computation while the GPU kernel is running, hence CPU timers may not give the correct time for kernel executions. So, to measure the GPU kernel computation time, CUDA provides an event API.

A CUDA event is a GPU timestamp that's recorded at a specified point from your CUDA program. In this API, the GPU records the timestamp, which eliminates the issues that were present when using CPU timers for measuring performance. There are two steps to measure time using CUDA Events: creating an event and recording an event. We will record two events, one at the start of our code and one at the end. Then, we will try to calculate the difference in time between these two events, and that will give the overall performance of our code.

In your CUDA code, you can include the following lines to measure performance using the CUDA event API:

```
cudaEvent_t e_start, e_stop;
cudaEventCreate(&e_start);
cudaEventCreate(&e_stop);
cudaEventRecord(e_start, 0);
//All GPU code for which performance needs to be measured allocate the
memory
cudaMalloc((void**)&d_a, N * sizeof(int));
cudaMalloc((void**)&d_b, N * sizeof(int));
cudaMalloc((void**)&d_c, N * sizeof(int));
   //Copy input arrays from host to device memory
cudaMemcpy(d_a, h_a, N * sizeof(int), cudaMemcpyHostToDevice);
cudaMemcpy(d_b, h_b, N * sizeof(int), cudaMemcpyHostToDevice);
gpuAdd << <512, 512 >> >(d_a, d_b, d_c);
//Copy result back to host memory from device memory
cudaMemcpy(h_c, d_c, N * sizeof(int), cudaMemcpyDeviceToHost);
cudaDeviceSynchronize();
cudaEventRecord(e_stop, 0);
cudaEventSynchronize(e_stop);
float elapsedTime;
cudaEventElapsedTime(&elapsedTime, e_start, e_stop);
printf("Time to add %d numbers: %3.1f ms\n",N, elapsedTime);
```

We will create two events, `e_start` and `e_stop`, for starting and ending the code. `cudaEvent_t` is used to define event objects. To create an event, we will use the `cudaEventCreate` API. We can pass in event objects as arguments to this API. At the beginning of the code, we will record the GPU timestamp in the `e_start` event; this will be done using the `cudaEventRecord` API. The second argument to this function is zero, which indicates the CUDA stream number, which we will discuss later in this chapter.

After recording the timestamp in the beginning, you can start writing your GPU code. After the code ends, we will again record the time in the `e_stop` event. This will be done with the `cudaEventRecord(e_stop, 0)` line. Once we have recorded both the start and end times, the difference between them should give us the actual performance of the code. But there's still one issue with directly calculating the difference in time between these two events.

As we have discussed in previous chapters, execution in CUDA C can be asynchronous. When the GPU is executing the kernel, the CPU might be executing the next lines of our code until the GPU finishes its execution. So, measuring time directly without synchronizing the GPU and CPU may give incorrect results. `CudaEventRecord()` will record a timestamp when all GPU instructions prior to its call finish. We should not read the `e_stop` event until this point, when prior work on the GPU is finished. So, to synchronize CPU operations with the GPU, we will use `cudaEventSynchronize(e_stop)`. It ensures that the correct timestamp is recorded in the `e_stop` event.

Now, to calculate the difference between these two timestamps, CUDA provides an API called `cudaEventElapsedTime`. It has three arguments. The first is the variable in which we want to store the difference, the second is the start event, and the third is the end event. After calculating this time, we will print it on the console in the next line. We added this performance measurement code to the vector addition code seen in the previous chapter, using multiple threads and blocks. The output after adding these lines is as follows:

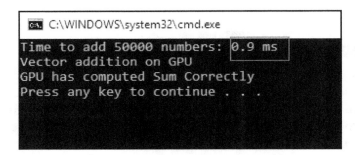

The time taken to add 50,000 elements on the GPU is around **0.9 ms**. This output will depend on your system configurations, hence you might get a different output in the red box. So, you can include this performance measurement code in all the code examples we have seen in this book to measure their performance. You can also quantify performance gains using constant and texture memories by using this event API.

It should be kept in mind that CUDA Events can only be used to measure the timing of device code blocks. This only includes memory allocation, memory copies, and kernel execution. It should not be used to measure the timings of the host code. As the GPU is recording time in the event API, using it to measure the performance of the host code may give incorrect results.

The Nvidia Visual Profiler

We now know that CUDA provides an efficient way to improve the performance of parallel computing applications. However, sometimes, it may happen that even after incorporating CUDA in your application, the performance of the code does not improve. In this kind of scenario, it is very useful to visualize which part of the code is taking the most time to complete. This is called **profiling of kernel execution code**. Nvidia provides a tool for this and it comes with the standard CUDA installation. This tool is called the **Nvidia Visual Profiler**. In the standard CUDA 9.0 installation on Windows 10, it can be found on the following path: C:\Program Files\NVIDIA GPU Computing Toolkit\CUDA\v9.0\libnvvp. You can run the nvvp application available on this path, which will open the Nvidia Visual Profile tool as follows:

This tool will execute your code and, based on the performance of your GPU, give you a detailed report on the execution time of each kernel, detailed timestamps for each operation in your code, the memory used in your code, and the memory bandwidth, among others. To visualize and get detailed reports for any applications you have developed, you can go to **File -> New Session**. Select the .exe file of the application. We have selected the vector addition example seen in the previous chapter. The result will be as follows:

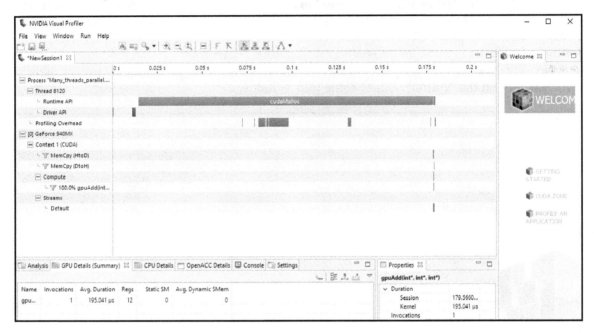

The result displays the timing of all operations in the program. It can be seen that the cudaMalloc operation takes the most time to complete. It also displays the order in which each operation is performed in your code. It shows that the kernel is called only once and it needs an average of 192.041 microseconds to execute. The details of memory copy operations can also be visualized. The properties of memory copy operations from the host to the device are shown as follows:

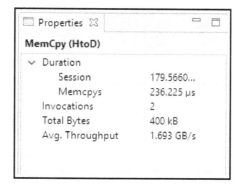

It can be seen that, as we are copying two arrays from the host to the device, the memory copy operation is invoked twice. The total number of bytes copied are 400 KB with a throughput of 1.693 GB/s. This tool is very important in the analysis of kernel execution. It can also be used to compare the performance of two kernels. It will show you the exact operation that is slowing down the performance of your code.

To summarize, in this section, we have seen two methods to measure and analyze CUDA code. CUDA Events is an efficient API for measuring the timing of device code. The Nvidia Visual Profiler gives a detailed analysis and profiling of CUDA code, which can be used to analyze performance. In the next section, we will see how to handle errors in CUDA code.

Error handling in CUDA

We have not checked the availability of GPU devices or memory for our CUDA programs. It may happen that, when you run your CUDA program, the GPU device is not available or is out of memory. In that case, you may find it difficult to understand the reason for the termination of your program. Therefore, it is a good practice to add error handling code in CUDA programs. In this section, we will try to understand how we can add this error handling code to CUDA functions. When the code is not giving the intended output, it is useful to check the functionality of the code line-by-line or by adding a breakpoint in the program. This is called **debugging**. CUDA provides debugging tools that can help. So, in the following section, we will see some debugging tools that are provided by Nvidia with CUDA.

Error handling from within the code

When we discussed CUDA API functions in Chapter 2, *Parallel Programming using CUDA C*, we saw that they also return the flag that indicates whether the operation has finished successfully or not. This can be used to handle errors from within CUDA programs. Of course, this will not help in resolving errors, but it will indicate which CUDA operation is causing errors. It is a very good practice to wrap CUDA functions with this error handling code. The sample error handling code for a cudaMalloc function is as follows:

```
cudaError_t cudaStatus;
cudaStatus = cudaMalloc((void**)&d_a, sizeof(int));
if (cudaStatus != cudaSuccess) {
        fprintf(stderr, "cudaMalloc failed!");
        goto Error;
}
```

The cudaError_t API is used to create an error object that will store the return value of all CUDA operations. So the output of a cudaMalloc function is assigned to this error object. If the error object is not equal to cudaSuccess, then there was some error in assigning memory on the device. This is handled by an if statement. It will print the error on the console and jump to the end of the program. The wrapper code for error handling during a memory copy operation is shown as follows:

```
cudaStatus = cudaMemcpy(d_a,&h_a, sizeof(int), cudaMemcpyHostToDevice);
if (cudaStatus != cudaSuccess) {
  fprintf(stderr, "cudaMemcpy failed!");
  goto Error;
  }
```

Again, it has a similar structure to the error handling code for cudaMalloc. The wrapper code for the kernel call is shown as follows:

```
gpuAdd<<<1, 1>>>(d_a, d_b, d_c);
// Check for any errors launching the kernel
cudaStatus = cudaGetLastError();
if (cudaStatus != cudaSuccess) {
  fprintf(stderr, "addKernel launch failed: %s\n",
cudaGetErrorString(cudaStatus));
  goto Error;
}
```

The kernel call does not return a flag that indicates success or failure, so it is not directly assigned to an error object. Instead, if there is any error during the kernel's launch, then we can fetch it with the `cudaGetLastError()` API, which is used to handle an error during kernel calls. It is assigned to the `cudaStatus` error object and, if it is not equal to `cudaSuccess`, it prints the error on the console and jumps to the end of the program. All the error handling code jumps to the code section defined by the `Error` label. It can be defined as follows:

```
Error:
    cudaFree(d_a);
```

Whenever any error is encountered in a program, we jump to this section. We free up memory allocated on the device and then exit the `main` function. This is a very efficient way of writing CUDA programs. We suggest that you use this method for writing your CUDA code. It was not explained earlier to avoid unnecessary complexity in the code examples. The addition of error handling code in CUDA programs will make them longer, but it will be able to pinpoint which CUDA operation is causing problems in the code.

Debugging tools

There are always two types of errors that we may encounter in programming: **syntax** errors and **semantic** errors. Syntax errors can be handled by compilers, but semantic errors are difficult to find and debug. Semantic errors cause the program to work unexpectedly. When your CUDA program is not working as intended, then there is a need to execute your code line-by-line to visualize the output after each line. This is called **debugging**. It is a very important operation for any kind of programming. CUDA provides debugging tools that help resolve this kind of error.

For Linux-based systems, Nvidia provides a very helpful debugger known as **CUDA-GDB**. It has a similar interface to the normal GDB debugger used for C code. It helps you in debugging your kernel directly on the GPU with features such as setting breakpoints, inspecting the GPU memory, and inspecting blocks and threads. It also provides a memory checker to check illegal memory accesses.

For Windows-based systems, Nvidia provides the Nsight debugger integrated with Microsoft Visual Studio. Again, it has features for adding breakpoints in the program and inspecting blocks or thread execution. The device's global memory can be viewed from a Visual Studio memory interface.

To summarize, in this section, we have seen two methods for handling errors in CUDA. One method helps in solving GPU hardware-related errors, such as the device or memory not being available, from CUDA programs. The second method of using debugging helps when the program is not working as per expectations. In the next section, we will see some advanced concepts that can help improve the performance of CUDA programs.

Performance improvement of CUDA programs

In this section, we will see some basic guidelines that we can follow to improve the performance of CUDA programs. These are explained one by one.

Using an optimum number of blocks and threads

We have seen two parameters that need to be specified during a kernel call: the number of blocks and the number of threads per block. GPU resources should not be idle during a kernel call; only then it will give the optimum performance. If resources remain idle, then it may degrade the performance of the program. The number of blocks and threads per block help in keeping GPU resources busy. It has been researched that if the number of blocks are double the number of multiprocessors on the GPU, it will give the best performance. The total number of multiprocessors on the GPU can be found out by using device properties, as seen in `Chapter 2`, *Parallel Programming Using CUDA C*. In the same way, the maximum number of threads per block should be equal to the `maxThreadperblock` device property. These values are just for guidance. You can play around with these two parameters to get optimum performance in your application.

Maximizing arithmetic efficiency

Arithmetic efficiency is defined as the ratio of the number of mathematical computations to the number of memory access operations. The value of arithmetic efficiency should be as high as possible for good performance. It can be increased by maximizing computations per thread and minimizing the time spent on the memory per thread. Sometimes, the opportunity to maximize computations per thread is limited, but certainly, you can reduce the time spent on the memory. You can minimize it by storing frequently accessed data in fast memory.

We saw in the last chapter that the local memory and register files are the fastest memory types available on the GPU. So, they can be used to store data that needs frequent access. We also saw the use of shared memory, constant memory, and texture memory for performance improvement. Caching also helps in reducing memory access time. Ultimately, if we reduce the bandwidth of global memory, we can reduce the time spent on the memory. Efficient memory usage is very important in improving the performance of CUDA programs, as memory bandwidth is the biggest bottleneck in fast execution.

Using coalesced or strided memory access

Coalesced memory access means that every thread reads or writes into contiguous memory locations. GPU is most efficient when this memory access method is used. If threads use memory locations that are offset by a constant value, then this is called **strided memory access**. It still gives better performance than random memory access. So, if you try to use coalesced memory access in the program, it can drastically improve performance. Here are examples of these memory access patterns:

```
Coalesce Memory Access: d_a[i] = a
Strided Memory Access: d_a[i*2] = a
```

Avoiding thread divergence

Thread divergence happens when all threads in a kernel call follow different paths of execution. It can happen in the following kernel code scenarios:

```
Thread divergence by way of branching
tid = ThreadId
if (tid%2 == 0)
{
  Some Branch code;
}
else
{
  Some other code;
}

Thread divergence by way of looping
Pre-loop code
for (i=0; i<tid;i++)
{
  Some loop code;
}
Post loop code;
```

In the first code snippet, there is separate code for odd and even number threads because of the condition in the `if` statement. This makes odd and even number threads follow different paths for execution. After the `if` statement, these threads will again merge. This will incur time overhead because fast threads will have to wait for slow threads.

In the second example, using the `for` loop, each thread runs the `for` loop for a different number of iterations, hence all threads will take different amounts of time to finish. `Post loop code` has to wait for all these threads to finish. It will incur time overhead. So, as much as possible, avoid this kind of thread divergence in your code.

Using page-locked host memory

In every example until this point, we have used the `malloc` function to allocate memory on the host, which allocates standard pageable memory on the host. CUDA provides another API called `cudaHostAlloc()`, which allocates page-locked host memory or what is sometimes referred to as pinned memory. It guarantees that the operating system will never page this memory out of this disk and that it will remain in physical memory. So, any application can access the physical address of the buffer. This property helps the GPU copy data to and from the host via **Direct Memory Access (DMA)** without CPU intervention. This helps improve the performance of memory transfer operations. But page-locked memory should be used with proper care because this memory is not swapped out of disk; your system may run out of memory. It may effect the performance of other applications running on the system. You can use this API to allocate memory that is used to transfer data to a device, using the `Memcpy` operation. The syntax of using this API is shown as follows:

```
Allocate Memory: cudaHostAlloc ( (void **) &h_a, sizeof(*h_a),
cudaHostAllocDefault);
Free Memory: cudaFreeHost(h_a);
```

The syntax of `cudaHostAlloc` is similar to a simple `malloc` function. The last argument, `cudaHostAllocDefault`, which is a flag used to modify the behavior of pinned memory, is added. `cudaFreeHost` is used to free memory allocated using a `cudaHostAlloc` function.

CUDA streams

We have seen that the GPU provides a great performance improvement in data parallelism when a single instruction operates on multiple data items. We have not seen task parallelism where more than one kernel function, which are independent of each other, operate in parallel. For example, one function may be computing pixel values while another function is downloading something from the internet. We know that the CPU provides a very flexible method for this kind of task parallelism. The GPU also provides this capability, but it is not as flexible as the CPU. This task parallelism is achieved by using CUDA streams, which we will see in detail in this section.

A CUDA stream is nothing but a queue of GPU operations that execute in a specific order. These functions include kernel functions, memory copy operations, and CUDA event operations. The order in which they are added to the queue will determine the order of their execution. Each CUDA stream can be considered a single task, so we can start multiple streams to do multiple tasks in parallel. We will look at how multiple streams work in CUDA in the next section.

Using multiple CUDA streams

We will understand the working of CUDA streams by using multiple CUDA streams in the vector addition program that we developed in the previous chapter. The kernel function for this is as follows:

```
#include "stdio.h"
#include<iostream>
#include <cuda.h>
#include <cuda_runtime.h>
//Defining number of elements in Array
#define N 50000

//Defining Kernel function for vector addition
__global__ void gpuAdd(int *d_a, int *d_b, int *d_c) {
  //Getting block index of current kernel

  int tid = threadIdx.x + blockIdx.x * blockDim.x;
  while (tid < N)
  {
    d_c[tid] = d_a[tid] + d_b[tid];
    tid += blockDim.x * gridDim.x;
  }
}
```

The `kernel` function is similar to what we developed earlier. It is just that multiple streams will execute this kernel in parallel. It should be noted that not all GPU devices support CUDA streams. GPU devices that support the `deviceOverlap` property can perform memory transfer operations and kernel executions simultaneously. This property will be used in CUDA streams for task parallelism. Before proceeding further in this code, please ensure that your GPU device supports this property. You can use code from Chapter 2, *Parallel Programming Using CUDA C*, to verify this property. We will use two parallel streams, which will execute this kernel in parallel and operate on half of the input data each. We will start by creating these two streams in the main function, as follows:

```
int main(void) {
  //Defining host arrays
  int *h_a, *h_b, *h_c;
  //Defining device pointers for stream 0
  int *d_a0, *d_b0, *d_c0;
  //Defining device pointers for stream 1
  int *d_a1, *d_b1, *d_c1;
  cudaStream_t stream0, stream1;
  cudaStreamCreate(&stream0);
  cudaStreamCreate(&stream1);

  cudaEvent_t e_start, e_stop;
  cudaEventCreate(&e_start);
  cudaEventCreate(&e_stop);
  cudaEventRecord(e_start, 0);
```

Two stream objects, `stream 0` and `stream 1`, are defined using the `cudaStream_t` and `cudaStreamCreate` APIs. We have also defined host pointers and two sets of device pointers, which will be used for each stream separately. We defined and created two events for performance measurement of this program. Now, we need to allocate memory for these pointers. The code is as follows:

```
  //Allocate memory for host pointers
  cudaHostAlloc((void**)&h_a, 2*N* sizeof(int),cudaHostAllocDefault);
  cudaHostAlloc((void**)&h_b, 2*N* sizeof(int), cudaHostAllocDefault);
  cudaHostAlloc((void**)&h_c, 2*N* sizeof(int), cudaHostAllocDefault);
  //Allocate memory for device pointers
  cudaMalloc((void**)&d_a0, N * sizeof(int));
  cudaMalloc((void**)&d_b0, N * sizeof(int));
  cudaMalloc((void**)&d_c0, N * sizeof(int));
  cudaMalloc((void**)&d_a1, N * sizeof(int));
  cudaMalloc((void**)&d_b1, N * sizeof(int));
  cudaMalloc((void**)&d_c1, N * sizeof(int));
  for (int i = 0; i < N*2; i++) {
    h_a[i] = 2 * i*i;
    h_b[i] = i;
```

```
}
```

CUDA streams need an access to page-locked memory for its memory copy operation, hence we are defining host memory using a cudaHostAlloc function instead of simple malloc. We have seen the advantage of page-locked memory in the last section. Two sets of device pointers are allocated memory using cudaMalloc. It should be noted that host pointers hold the entire data so their size is 2*N*sizeof(int), whereas each device pointer operates on half the data elements so their size is only N*sizeof(int). We have also initialized host arrays with some random values for addition. Now, we will try to enqueue memory copy operations and kernel execution operations in both of the streams. The code for this is as follows:

```
//Asynchrnous Memory Copy Operation for both streams
cudaMemcpyAsync(d_a0, h_a , N * sizeof(int), cudaMemcpyHostToDevice,
stream0);
cudaMemcpyAsync(d_a1, h_a+ N, N * sizeof(int), cudaMemcpyHostToDevice,
stream1);
cudaMemcpyAsync(d_b0, h_b , N * sizeof(int), cudaMemcpyHostToDevice,
stream0);
cudaMemcpyAsync(d_b1, h_b + N, N * sizeof(int), cudaMemcpyHostToDevice,
stream1);
//Kernel Call
gpuAdd << <512, 512, 0, stream0 >> > (d_a0, d_b0, d_c0);
gpuAdd << <512, 512, 0, stream1 >> > (d_a1, d_b1, d_c1);
//Copy result back to host memory from device memory
cudaMemcpyAsync(h_c , d_c0, N * sizeof(int), cudaMemcpyDeviceToHost,
stream0);
cudaMemcpyAsync(h_c + N, d_c1, N * sizeof(int), cudaMemcpyDeviceToHost,
stream0);
```

Instead of using a simple cudaMemcpy API, we are using a cudaMemcpyAsync API, which is used for asynchronous memory transfer. It enqueues a request of a memory copy operation in a given stream specified as the last argument to the function. When this function returns, the memory copy operation may not have even started, hence it is called an asynchronous operation. It just puts a request of the memory copy in a queue. As we can see in the memory copy operations, stream0 operates on data between 0 to N and stream 1 operates on data from N+1 to 2N.

The order of operation is important in stream operations as we want to overlap memory copy operations with kernel execution operations. So, instead of enqueuing all the stream0 operations and then enqueuing the stream 1 operations, we are first enqueuing memory copy operations in both streams and then enqueuing both kernel computation operations. This will ensure that memory copy and kernel computation overlaps with each other. If both operations take the same amount of time, we can achieve two times the speedup. We can get a better idea about the order of operations by looking at the following diagram:

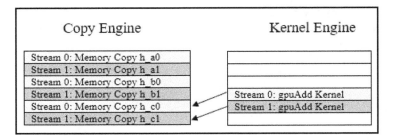

The time increases from top to bottom. We can see that two memory copy operations and kernel execute operations are performed in the same time period, which will accelerate your program. We have also seen that the memory copy operations, defined by cudaMemcpyAsync, are asynchronous; so, when one stream returns, the memory copy operation may not have started. If we want to use the result of the last memory copy operation, then we have to wait for both streams to finish their queue operations. This can be ensured by using the following code:

```
cudaDeviceSynchronize();
cudaStreamSynchronize(stream0);
cudaStreamSynchronize(stream1);
```

cudaStreamSynchronize ensures that all operations in the stream are finished before proceeding to the next line. To measure the performance of the code, the following code is inserted:

```
cudaEventRecord(e_stop, 0);
cudaEventSynchronize(e_stop);
float elapsedTime;
cudaEventElapsedTime(&elapsedTime, e_start, e_stop);
printf("Time to add %d numbers: %3.1f ms\n",2* N, elapsedTime);
```

It will record the stop time and, based on the difference between the start and stop time, it will calculate the overall execution time for this program and print the output on the console. To check whether the program has calculated the correct output, we will insert the following code for verification:

```
int Correct = 1;
printf("Vector addition on GPU \n");
//Printing result on console
for (int i = 0; i < 2*N; i++)
{
    if ((h_a[i] + h_b[i] != h_c[i]))
    {
        Correct = 0;
    }
}
if (Correct == 1)
{
    printf("GPU has computed Sum Correctly\n");
}
else
{
    printf("There is an Error in GPU Computation\n");
}
//Free up memory
cudaFree(d_a0);
cudaFree(d_b0);
cudaFree(d_c0);
cudaFree(d_a0);
cudaFree(d_b0);
cudaFree(d_c0);
cudaFreeHost(h_a);
cudaFreeHost(h_b);
cudaFreeHost(h_c);
return 0;
}
```

The verification code is similar to what we have seen earlier. Memory allocated on the device is freed up using `cudaFree` and memory allocated on the host using `cudaHostAlloc` is freed up using the `cudaFreeHost` function. This is mandatory, otherwise your system may run out of memory very quickly. The output of the program is shown as follows:

```
C:\WINDOWS\system32\cmd.exe
Time to add 100000 numbers: 0.9 ms
Vector addition on GPU
GPU has computed Sum Correctly
Press any key to continue . . . _
```

As can be seen in the preceding screenshot, **0.9 ms** is needed to add 100,000 elements, which is a double increment over code without streams, which needed **0.9 ms** to add 50,000 numbers, as seen in the first section of this chapter.

To summarize, we have seen CUDA streams in this section, which helps achieve task parallelism on the GPU. The order in which operations are queued in streams is very important to achieve speedup using CUDA streams.

Acceleration of sorting algorithms using CUDA

Sorting algorithms are widely used in many computing applications. There are many sorting algorithms, such as enumeration or rank sort, bubble sort, and merge sort. All algorithms have different levels of complexity, so it takes a different amount of time to sort a given array. For a large array, all algorithms take a long time to complete. If this can be accelerated using CUDA, then it can be of great help in any computing application.

To show an example of how CUDA can accelerate different sorting algorithms, we will implement a rank sort algorithm in CUDA.

Enumeration or rank sort algorithms

In this algorithm, we count every element in an array to find out how many elements in an array are less than the current element. From that, we can get the position of the current element in a sorted array. Then, we put this element in that position. We repeat this process for all elements in an array to get a sorted array. This is implemented as the `kernel` function, which is shown as follows:

```
#include "device_launch_parameters.h"
#include <stdio.h>

#define arraySize 5
#define threadPerBlock 5
//Kernel Function for Rank sort
__global__ void addKernel(int *d_a, int *d_b)
{
  int count = 0;
  int tid = threadIdx.x;
  int ttid = blockIdx.x * threadPerBlock + tid;
  int val = d_a[ttid];
  __shared__ int cache[threadPerBlock];
  for (int i = tid; i < arraySize; i += threadPerBlock) {
    cache[tid] = d_a[i];
    __syncthreads();
    for (int j = 0; j < threadPerBlock; ++j)
      if (val > cache[j])
        count++;
        __syncthreads();
  }
  d_b[count] = val;
}
```

The `Kernel` function takes two arrays as parameters. `d_a` is an input array and `d_b` is the output array. The `count` variable is taken, which stores the position of the current element in the sorted array. The current thread index in the block is stored in `tid` and the unique thread index among all blocks is stored in `ttid`. Shared memory is used to reduce the time in accessing data from global memory. The size of shared memory is equal to the number of threads in a block, as discussed earlier. The `value` variable holds the current element. Shared memory is filled up with the values of global memory. These values are compared with the `value` variable and the count of the number of values that are less is stored in the `count` variable. This continues until all elements in an array are compared with the `value` variable. After the loop finishes, the `count` variable has the position of the element in a sorted array, and the current element is stored at that position in `d_b`, which is an output array.

The `main` function for this code is as follows:

```
int main()
{
    //Define Host and Device Array
    int h_a[arraySize] = { 5, 9, 3, 4, 8 };
    int h_b[arraySize];
    int *d_a, *d_b;
    //Allocate Memory on the device
    cudaMalloc((void**)&d_b, arraySize * sizeof(int));
    cudaMalloc((void**)&d_a, arraySize * sizeof(int));
    // Copy input vector from host memory to device memory.
    cudaMemcpy(d_a, h_a, arraySize * sizeof(int), cudaMemcpyHostToDevice);
    // Launch a kernel on the GPU with one thread for each element.
    addKernel<<<arraySize/threadPerBlock, threadPerBlock>>>(d_a, d_b);

    //Wait for device to finish operations
    cudaDeviceSynchronize();
    // Copy output vector from GPU buffer to host memory.
    cudaMemcpy(h_b, d_b, arraySize * sizeof(int), cudaMemcpyDeviceToHost);
    printf("The Enumeration sorted Array is: \n");
    for (int i = 0; i < arraySize; i++)
    {
      printf("%d\n", h_b[i]);
    }
    //Free up device memory
    cudaFree(d_a);
    cudaFree(d_b);
    return 0;
}
```

The `main` function should be very familiar to you by now. We are defining host and device arrays and allocating memory on the device for device arrays. The host array is initialized with some random values and copied to the device's memory. The kernel is launched by passing device pointers as parameters. The kernel computes the sorted array by the rank sort algorithm and returns it to the host. This sorted array is printed on the console as follows:

This is a very trivial case and you might not see any performance improvement between the CPU and GPU. But if you go on increasing the value of `arraySize`, then the GPU will drastically improve the performance of this algorithm. It can be a hundredfold improvement for an array size equal to 15,000.

Rank sort is the simplest sorting algorithm available. This discussion will help you in developing code for other sorting algorithms, such as bubble sort and merge sort.

Image processing using CUDA

Today, we live in an age of high definition camera sensors that capture high-resolution images. An image can have a size of up to 1920 x 1920 pixels. So, processing of these pixels on computers in real time involves billions of floating point operations to be performed per second. This is difficult for even the fastest of CPUs. A GPU can help in this kind of situation. It provides high computation power, which can be leveraged using CUDA in your code.

Images are stored as multidimensional arrays in a computer with two dimensions for a grayscale image and three dimensions for a color image. CUDA also supports multidimensional grid blocks and threads. So, we can process an image by launching multidimensional blocks and threads, as seen previously. The number of blocks and threads can vary depending on the size of an image. It will also depend on your GPU specifications. If it supports 1,024 threads per block, then 32 x 32 threads per block can be launched. The number of blocks can be determined by dividing the image size by the number of these threads. As discussed many times previously, the choice of parameters affects the performance of your code. So, they should be chosen properly.

It is very easy to convert a simple image processing code developed in C or C++ to a CUDA code. It can be done by an inexperienced programmer also by following a set pattern. Image processing code has a set pattern, as in the following code:

```
for (int i=0; i < image_height; i++)
{
    for (int j=0; j < image_width; j++)
    {
        //Pixel Processing code for pixel located at (i,j)
    }
}
```

Images are nothing but multidimensional matrices stored on a computer, so getting a single pixel value from an image involves using nested `for` loops to iterate over all pixels. To convert this code to CUDA, we want to launch a number of threads equal to the number of pixels in an image. The pixel value in a thread can be obtained by the following code in the `kernel` function:

```
int i = blockIdx.y * blockDim.y + threadIdx.y;
int j = blockIdx.x * blockDim.x + threadIdx.x;
```

The `i` and `j` values can be used as an index to an image array to find the pixel values. So, as can be seen in the previous code, with a simple conversion process of converting `for` loops into a thread index, we can write device code for a CUDA program. We are going to develop many image processing applications using the `OpenCV` library from the next section onward. We will not cover actual image manipulation in this chapter, but we will end this chapter by developing a CUDA program for the very important statistical operation of calculating a histogram. Histogram calculation is very important for image processing applications as well.

Histogram calculation on the GPU using CUDA

A histogram is a very important statistical concept used in a variety of applications such as machine learning, computer vision, data science, and image processing. It represents a count of the frequency of each element in a given dataset. It shows which data items occur the most frequently and which occur the least frequently. You can also get an idea about the distribution of data by just looking at the values of the histogram. In this section, we will develop an algorithm that calculates the histogram of a given data distribution.

We will start by calculating a histogram on the CPU so that you can get an idea of how to calculate a histogram. Let's assume that we have data with 1,000 elements, and each element has a value between 0 to 15. We want to calculate the histogram of this distribution. The sample code for this calculation on the CPU is as follows:

```
int h_a[1000] = Random values between 0 and 15

int histogram[16];
for (int i = 0; i<16; i++)
{
    histogram[i] = 0;
}
for (i=0; i < 1000; i++)
{
    histogram[h_a[i]] +=1;
}
```

We have 1,000 data elements and they are stored in h_a. The h_a array contains values between 0 and 15; it has 16 distinct values. So the number of bins, which indicates the number of distinct values for which histogram needs to be calculated, is 16. So we have defined a histogram array that will store the final histogram with a size equal to the number of bins. This array needs to be initialized to zero as it will be incremented with each occurrence. This is done in the first for loop that runs from 0 to the number of bins.

For the calculation of the histogram, we need to iterate through all of the elements in h_a. Whichever value is found in h_a, the particular index in that histogram array needs to be incremented. That is done by the second for loop, which calculates the final histogram by running from 0 to the size of the array and incrementing the histogram array indexed by the value found in h_a. The histogram array will contain the frequency of each element between 0 to 15 after the for loop finishes.

Now, we will develop this same code for the GPU. We will try to develop this code using three different methods. The kernel code for the first two methods is as follows:

```
#include <stdio.h>
#include <cuda_runtime.h>

#define SIZE 1000
#define NUM_BIN 16

__global__ void histogram_without_atomic(int *d_b, int *d_a)
{
  int tid = threadIdx.x + blockDim.x * blockIdx.x;
  int item = d_a[tid];
  if (tid < SIZE)
  {
    d_b[item]++;
  }
}


__global__ void histogram_atomic(int *d_b, int *d_a)
{
  int tid = threadIdx.x + blockDim.x * blockIdx.x;
  int item = d_a[tid];
  if (tid < SIZE)
  {
    atomicAdd(&(d_b[item]), 1);
  }
}
```

The first function is the simplest kernel function for histogram computation. Each thread is operating on one data element. The value of the data element is fetched using the thread ID as an index to the input array. This value is used as an index into the d_b output array, which is incremented. The d_b array should contain the frequency of each value between 0 to 15 in the input data. But if you recall from Chapter 3, *Threads, Synchronization, and Memory,* this may not give you a correct answer, as many threads are trying to modify the same memory location simultaneously. In this example, 1,000 threads are trying to modify 16 memory locations simultaneously. We need to use the atomic add operation for this kind of scenario.

The second device function is developed using the atomic add operation. This kernel function will give you the correct answer but it will take more time to complete, as the atomic operation is a blocking operation. All other threads have to wait when one thread is using a particular memory location. So, this second kernel function will add overhead time, which makes it even slower than the CPU version. To complete the code, we will try to write the main function for it as follows:

```
int main()
{
  int h_a[SIZE];
  for (int i = 0; i < SIZE; i++) {
  h_a[i] = i % NUM_BIN;
  }
  int h_b[NUM_BIN];
  for (int i = 0; i < NUM_BIN; i++) {
    h_b[i] = 0;
  }

  // declare GPU memory pointers
  int * d_a;
  int * d_b;

  // allocate GPU memory
  cudaMalloc((void **)&d_a, SIZE * sizeof(int));
  cudaMalloc((void **)&d_b, NUM_BIN * sizeof(int));

  // transfer the arrays to the GPU
  cudaMemcpy(d_a, h_a, SIZE * sizeof(int), cudaMemcpyHostToDevice);
  cudaMemcpy(d_b, h_b, NUM_BIN * sizeof(int), cudaMemcpyHostToDevice);

  // launch the kernel
  //histogram_without_atomic << <((SIZE+NUM_BIN-1) / NUM_BIN), NUM_BIN >>
>(d_b, d_a);
  histogram_atomic << <((SIZE+NUM_BIN-1) / NUM_BIN), NUM_BIN >> >(d_b,
  d_a);
```

```
// copy back the sum from GPU
cudaMemcpy(h_b, d_b, NUM_BIN * sizeof(int), cudaMemcpyDeviceToHost);
printf("Histogram using 16 bin without shared Memory is: \n");
for (int i = 0; i < NUM_BIN; i++) {
  printf("bin %d: count %d\n", i, h_b[i]);
}

// free GPU memory allocation
cudaFree(d_a);
cudaFree(d_b);
return 0;
}
```

We have started the main function by defining the host and device arrays and allocating memory for it. The h_a input data array is initialized with values from 0 to 15 in the first for loop. We are using the modulo operation, hence 1,000 elements will be evenly divided between values of 0 to 15. The second array, which will store the histogram, is initialized to zero. These two arrays are copied to the device memory. The kernel will compute the histogram and return it to the host. We will print this histogram on the console. The output is shown here:

When we try to measure the performance of this code using the atomic operation and compare it with CPU performance, it is slower than the CPU for large-sized arrays. That begs the question: should we use CUDA for histogram computation, or is it possible to make this computation faster?

The answer to this question is: *yes*. If we use shared memory for computing a histogram for a given block and then add this block histogram to the overall histogram on global memory, then it can speed up the operation. This is possible because addition is a cumulative operation. The kernel code of using shared memory for histogram computation is shown as follows:

```
#include <stdio.h>
#include <cuda_runtime.h>
#define SIZE 1000
#define NUM_BIN 256
__global__ void histogram_shared_memory(int *d_b, int *d_a)
{
  int tid = threadIdx.x + blockDim.x * blockIdx.x;
  int offset = blockDim.x * gridDim.x;
  __shared__ int cache[256];
  cache[threadIdx.x] = 0;
  __syncthreads();
  while (tid < SIZE)
  {
    atomicAdd(&(cache[d_a[tid]]), 1);
    tid += offset;
  }
  __syncthreads();
  atomicAdd(&(d_b[threadIdx.x]), cache[threadIdx.x]);
}
```

In this code, the number of bins are 256 instead of 16, for more capacity. We are defining shared memory of a size equal to the number of threads in a block, which is equal to 256 bins. We will calculate a histogram for the current block, so shared memory is initialized to zero and a histogram is computed for this block in the same way as discussed earlier. But, this time, the result is stored in shared memory and not in global memory. In this case, only 256 threads are trying to access 256 memory elements in shared memory, instead of 1,000 elements, as in the previous code. This will help reduce the time overhead in the atomic operation. The final atomic add operation in the last line will add a histogram of one block to the overall histogram values. As addition is a cumulative operation, we do not have to worry about the order in which each block is executed. The main function for this is similar to the previous function.

The output for this `kernel` function is as follows:

```
C:\WINDOWS\system32\cmd.exe                                                    —    □    ×
bin 227: count 4
bin 228: count 4
bin 229: count 4
bin 230: count 4
bin 231: count 4
bin 232: count 3
bin 233: count 3
bin 234: count 3
bin 235: count 3
bin 236: count 3
bin 237: count 3
bin 238: count 3
bin 239: count 3
bin 240: count 3
bin 241: count 3
bin 242: count 3
bin 243: count 3
bin 244: count 3
bin 245: count 3
bin 246: count 3
bin 247: count 3
bin 248: count 3
bin 249: count 3
bin 250: count 3
bin 251: count 3
bin 252: count 3
bin 253: count 3
bin 254: count 3
bin 255: count 3
Press any key to continue . . . _
```

If you measure the performance of the preceding program, it will beat both GPU versions without shared memory and the CPU implementation for large array sizes. You can check whether the histogram computed by the GPU is correct or not by comparing results with the CPU computation.

This section demonstrated the implementation of the histogram on the GPU. It also re-emphasized the use of shared memory and atomic operations in CUDA programs. It also demonstrated how CUDA is helpful in image processing applications and how easy it is to convert existing CPU code into CUDA code.

Summary

In this chapter, we saw some advanced concepts in CUDA that can help us to develop a complex application using CUDA. We saw the method for measuring the performance of the device code and how to see a detailed profile of the kernel function using the Nvidia Visual Profiler tool. It helps us in identifying the operation that slows down the performance of our program. We saw the methods to handle errors in hardware operation from the CUDA code itself, and we saw methods of debugging the code using certain tools. The CPU provides efficient task parallelism where two completely different functions execute in parallel. We saw that the GPU also provides this functionality using CUDA streams and achieves a twofold speedup on the same vector addition program using CUDA streams.

Then, we saw an acceleration of sorting algorithms using CUDA, which is an important concept to understand in order to build complex computing applications. Image processing is a computationally intensive task, which needs to be performed in real time. Almost all image processing algorithms can utilize parallelism of the GPU and CUDA. So, in the last section, we saw the use of CUDA in the acceleration of image processing application and how we can convert existing C++ code to CUDA code. We have also developed CUDA code for histogram calculation, which is an important image processing application.

This chapter also marks an end to concepts related to CUDA programming. From the next chapter onward, we will start with the exciting part of developing computer vision applications using the OpenCV library, which utilizes the CUDA acceleration concepts that we have seen up until this point. We will start dealing with real images and not matrices from the next chapter.

Questions

1. Why aren't CPU timers used to measure the performance of kernel functions?
2. Try to visualize the performance of the matrix multiplication code implemented in the previous chapter using the Nvidia Visual Profiler tool.
3. Give different examples of semantic errors encountered in programs.
4. What is the drawback of thread divergence in kernel functions? Explain with an example.
5. What is the drawback of using the `cudahostAlloc` function to allocate memory on the host?
6. Justify the following statement: the order of operations in CUDA streams is very important to improve the performance of a program.
7. How many blocks and threads should be launched for a 1024 x 1024 image for good performance using CUDA?

Getting Started with OpenCV with CUDA Support

5

So far, we have seen all the concepts related to parallel programming using CUDA and how it can leverage the GPU for acceleration. From this chapter on, we will try to use the concept of parallel programming in CUDA for computer vision applications. Though we have worked on matrices, we have not worked on actual images. Basically, working on images is similar to manipulation of two-dimensional matrices. We will not develop the entire code from scratch for computer vision applications in CUDA, but we will use the popular computer vision library that is called OpenCV. Though this book assumes that the reader has some familiarity with working with OpenCV, this chapter revises the concepts of using OpenCV in C++. This chapter describes the installation of the OpenCV library with CUDA support on Windows and Ubuntu. Then it describes how to test this installation and run a simple program. This chapter describes the use of OpenCV in working with images and videos by developing simple codes for it. This chapter also compares the performance of a program with CUDA support to one without it.

The following topics will be covered in this chapter:

- Introduction to image processing and computer vision
- Introduction to OpenCV with CUDA support
- Installation of OpenCV with CUDA support on Windows and Ubuntu
- Working with images using OpenCV
- Working with videos using OpenCV
- Arithmetic and logical operations on images
- Color-space conversions and image thresholding
- Performance comparison between CPU and GPU OpenCV programs

Technical requirements

This chapter requires a basic understanding of image processing and computer vision. It needs familiarity with the basic C or C++ programming language and all the code samples explained in previous chapters. All of the code used in this chapter can be downloaded from the following GitHub link: `https://github.com/PacktPublishing/Hands-On-GPU-Accelerated-Computer-Vision-with-OpenCV-and-CUDA`. The code can be executed on any operating system, though it has only been tested on Ubuntu 16.04.

Check out the following video to see the Code in Action:
`http://bit.ly/2xF5cQV`

Introduction to image processing and computer vision

The volume of image and video data available in the world is increasing day by day. The increasing use of mobile devices to capture images and use of the internet to post them has allowed production of enormous amounts of video and image data every day. Image processing and computer vision are used in many applications across various domains. Doctors use MRI and X-ray images for medical diagnoses. Space scientists and chemical engineers use images for space exploration and analysis of various genes at the molecular level. Images can be used to develop autonomous vehicles and video surveillance applications. They can also be used in agricultural applications and to identify faulty products during manufacturing. All these applications need to process images on a computer at a high speed. We are not going to look at how images are captured by a camera sensor and converted into digital images for computer storage. In this book, we will only cover the processing of an image on a computer, where we assume it is already stored.

Many people use the terms **image processing** and **computer vision** interchangeably. However, there is a difference between these two fields. Image processing is concerned with improving the visual quality of images by modifying pixel values, whereas computer vision is concerned with extracting important information from the images. So in image processing, both input and output are images, while in computer vision, input is an image but output is the information extracted from that image. Both have a wide variety of applications, but image processing is mainly used at the pre-processing stage of computer vision applications.

An image is stored as a multidimensional matrix. So processing an image on a computer is nothing more than manipulating this matrix. We saw how to work with matrices in CUDA in previous chapters. The code for reading, manipulating, and displaying images in CUDA might get very long, tedious, and hard to debug. So we will use a library that contains APIs for all of these functions and which can leverage the advantage of CUDA-GPU acceleration for processing images. This library is called OpenCV, which is an acronym for Open Computer Vision. In the next section, this library is explained in detail.

Introduction to OpenCV

OpenCV is a computer vision library developed with computational efficiency in mind and keeping the focus on real-time performance. It is written in C/C++ and it contains more than a hundred functions that help in computer vision applications. The main advantage of OpenCV is that it is open source and released under a Berkley software distribution (BSD) license which allows free use of OpenCV in research and commercial applications. This library has an interface in C, C++, Java, and Python languages and it can be used in all operating systems, such as Windows, Linux, macOS, and Android, without modifying a single line of code.

This library can also take advantage of multi-core processing and OpenGL and CUDA for parallel processing. As OpenCV is lightweight, it can be used on embedded platforms such as Raspberry Pi as well. This makes it ideal for deploying computer vision applications on embedded systems in real-life scenarios. We are going to explore this in the next few chapters. These features have made OpenCV a default choice for computer vision developers. It has a wide developer base and user community that helps constantly in improving the library. The downloads for OpenCV are in the millions and increasing day by day. The other popular computer vision and image processing tool is MATLAB, so you might wonder what are the advantages of using OpenCV over MATLAB. The following table shows a comparison between these two tools:

Parameter	OpenCV	MATLAB
Program speed	Higher because it is developed using C/C++	Lower than OpenCV
Resources needed	OpenCV is a lightweight library so it consumes very little memory both in terms of hard disk and RAM. A normal OpenCV program will require less than 100MB RAM.	MATLAB is very bulky. The latest MATLAB version installation can consume more than 15 GB space on the hard disk and a large chunk of RAM (more than 1 GB) when it is in use.
Portability	OpenCV can run on all operating systems that can run C language.	MATLAB can only run on Windows, Linux, and MAC.

Cost	The use of OpenCV in commercial or academic applications is completely free.	MATLAB is a licensed software so you have to pay a large amount to use it in your academic or commercial applications.
Ease of use	OpenCV is comparatively difficult to use as it has less documentation and difficult to remember syntax. It also does not have its own development environment.	MATLAB has its own integrated development environment with built-in help resources, which makes it easy for a new programmer to use.

MATLAB and OpenCV both have their pros and cons. But when we want to use computer vision in embedded applications and take advantage of parallel processing, OpenCV is the ideal choice. So, in this book, OpenCV is described for accelerating computer vision applications using GPU and CUDA. OpenCV has APIs in C, C++, Python, and Java. It is written in C/C++ so API in those languages will be the fastest. Moreover, CUDA acceleration is more supported in C/C++ API, so, in this book, we will use OpenCV with C/C++ API. In the next section, we will see how to install OpenCV on various operating systems.

Installation of OpenCV with CUDA support

Installation of OpenCV with CUDA is not as trivial as you might think. It involves many steps. In this section, all the steps for installing OpenCV in Windows and Ubuntu are explained with screenshots, so you can set your environment up easily.

Installation of OpenCV on Windows

This section explains the steps needed to install OpenCV with CUDA on a Windows operating system. The steps are performed on the Windows 10 operating system, but it will work on any Windows operating system.

Using pre-built binaries

There are pre-built binaries available for OpenCV that can be downloaded and used directly in your program. It doesn't take full advantage of CUDA so it is not recommended for this book. The following steps describe the procedure for installing OpenCV without CUDA support on Windows:

1. Make sure that Microsoft Visual Studio is installed for a compilation of C Programs.

2. Download the latest version of OpenCV from `https://sourceforge.net/projects/opencvlibrary/files/opencv-win/`.

3. Double click on the downloaded `.exe` file and extract it to your folder of choice. Here we are extracting it to the `C://opencv` folder.

4. Set up the environment variable `OPENCV_DIR` by right-clicking on **My Computer** | **Advance Setting** | **Environment Variables** | **New**. Set its value as `C:\opencv\build\x64\vc14`, as shown in the following screenshot. Here `vc14` will depend on the version of Microsoft Visual Studio:

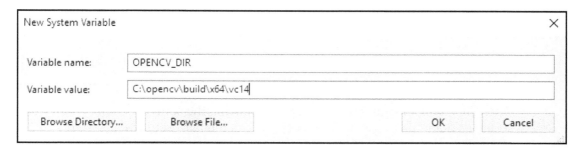

Now you can use this installation for OpenCV applications using C/C++.

Building libraries from source

If you want to compile OpenCV with CUDA support, follow these steps for installation:

1. OpenCV with CUDA will require a C compiler and GPU compiler. It will require Microsoft Visual Studio and the latest CUDA installation. The procedure to install them is covered in `Chapter 1`, *Introducing CUDA and Getting Started with CUDA*. So before moving ahead, please check that they are installed properly.

2. Download the source for the latest version of OpenCV by visiting the link: `https://github.com/opencv/opencv/`.

3. There are some extra modules that are not included in OpenCV, but they are available in the extra module call `opencv_contrib`, which can be installed along with OpenCV. The functions available in this module are not stable; once they get stable they are moved to an actual OpenCV source. If you want to install this module, download it from `https://github.com/opencv/opencv_contrib`.

4. Install `cmake` from the following link: `https://cmake.org/download/`. It is needed for compilation of OpenCV library.

5. Extract ZIP files of `opencv` and `opencv_contrib` in any folder. Here they are extracted to the `C://opencv` and `C://opencv_contrib` folders.

6. Open CMake to compile OpenCV. In that, you need to select the path for the OpenCV source and select the folder in which this source will be built. It is shown in the following screenshot:

7. Then click on **Configure**. It will start configuring the source. CMake will try to locate as many packages as possible based on the path settings in system variables. The configuration process is shown in the following screenshot:

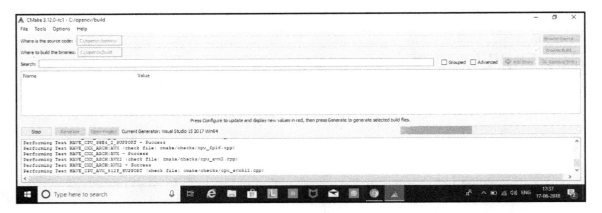

8. If some of the packages are not located then you can locate them manually. To configure OpenCV for installation with CUDA support, you have to check the `WITH_CUDA` variable, as shown in the following screenshot, and then click on **Configure** again:

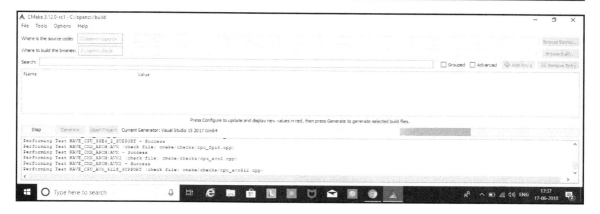

9. After configuration is finished, click on **Generate**. This will create the Visual Studio project file based on the version of Visual Studio you select. When generating is finished, the window should be something like the following:

10. Go to the build directory of the `opencv` folder and find the Visual Studio project with the name `OpenCV.sln`, as shown in the following screenshot:

11. This will open the project in Microsoft Visual Studio. In **Solution Explorer**, find the project with the name `ALL_BUILD`. Right-click on it and build it. Build this project for both debug and release options in Visual Studio. This is shown in the following screenshot:

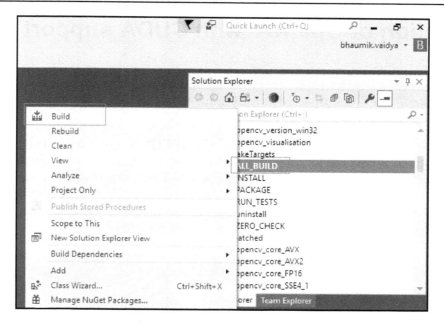

12. It will take a long time to build this entire project, though it will vary depending on your processor and Visual Studio version. After successful completion of the build operation, you are ready to use the OpenCV library in your C/C++ projects.

13. Set up the environment variable OPENCV_DIR by right-clicking on **My Computer** | **Advance System Settings** | **Environment Variables** | **New**. Set its value as C:\opencv\build\x64\vc14. Here, vc14 will depend on your version of Microsoft Visual Studio:

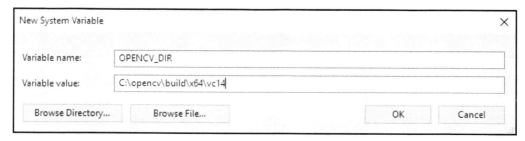

You can check the installation by going to the C://opencv/build/bin/Debug directory and running any .exe application.

Installation of OpenCV with CUDA support on Linux

This section covers the installation steps for OpenCV with CUDA support on a Linux operating system. The steps are tested on Ubuntu 16.04, but they should work on any Unix distribution:

1. OpenCV with CUDA will require the latest CUDA installation. The procedure to install it is covered in Chapter 1, *Introducing CUDA and Getting Started with CUDA*. So before moving ahead, please check that it is installed properly. You can check the installation of the CUDA toolkit and supporting Nvidia device driver by executing the nvidia-smi command. You should see output similar to the following if your installation is working correctly:

```
bhaumik@bhaumik-Lenovo-ideapad-520-15IKB: ~/Desktop/opencv/opencv/samples/gpu
bhaumik@bhaumik-Lenovo-ideapad-520-15IKB:~$ nvidia-smi
Sat Jun 16 14:13:59 2018
+-----------------------------------------------------------------------------+
| NVIDIA-SMI 396.26                 Driver Version: 396.26                     |
|-------------------------------+----------------------+----------------------+
| GPU  Name        Persistence-M| Bus-Id        Disp.A | Volatile Uncorr. ECC |
| Fan  Temp  Perf  Pwr:Usage/Cap|         Memory-Usage | GPU-Util  Compute M. |
|===============================+======================+======================|
|   0  GeForce 940MX       Off  | 00000000:01:00.0 Off |                  N/A |
| N/A   53C    P0    N/A /  N/A |     91MiB /  4046MiB |      2%      Default |
+-------------------------------+----------------------+----------------------+

+-----------------------------------------------------------------------------+
| Processes:                                                       GPU Memory |
|  GPU       PID   Type   Process name                             Usage      |
|=============================================================================|
|    0      1192      G   /usr/lib/xorg/Xorg                            69MiB |
|    0      2117      G   compiz                                        21MiB |
+-----------------------------------------------------------------------------+
```

2. Download the source for the latest version of OpenCV by visiting the link: `https://github.com/opencv/opencv/` . Extract it to the `opencv` folder.

3. There are some extra modules that are not included in OpenCV, but they are available in the extra module called `opencv_contrib`, which can be installed along with OpenCV. The functions available in this module are not stable; once they get stable, they are moved to an actual OpenCV source. If you want to install this module, download it from: `https://github.com/opencv/opencv_contrib`. Extract it to the `opencv_contrib` folder in the same directory as the `opencv` folder.

4. Open the `opencv` folder and create a build directory. Then go inside this newly created `build` directory. These steps can be done by executing the following commands from the Command Prompt:

```
$ cd opencv
$ mkdir build
$ cd build
```

5. The `cmake` command is used to compile `opencv` with CUDA support. Make sure the `WITH_CUDA` flag is set to ON in this command, along with a proper path for extra modules downloaded and saved in the `opencv_contrib` directory. The entire `cmake` command is shown as follows:

```
cmake -D CMAKE_BUILD_TYPE=RELEASE CMAKE_INSTALL_PREFIX=/usr/local
WITH_CUDA=ON  ENABLE_FAST_MATH=1 CUDA_FAST_MATH=1 -D WITH_CUBLAS=1
OPENCV_EXTRA_MODULES_PATH=../../opencv_contrib/modules
BUILD_EXAMPLES=ON ..
```

It will start the configuration and creation of `makefile`. It will locate all the extra modules based on the values in the system path. The output of the `cmake` command with selected CUDA installation is shown in the following screenshot:

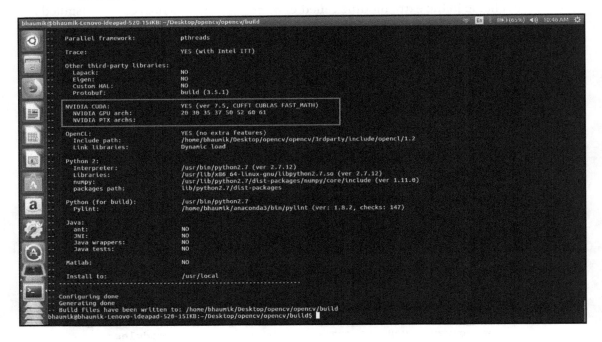

6. CMake will create a makefile in the build directory after successful configuration. To compile OpenCV using this makefile, execute the command `make -j8` from the command window, as shown:

7. After successful compilation, to install OpenCV, you have to execute the command `sudo make install` from the command line. The following will be the output of that command:

8. Run the `sudo ldconfig` command to finish the installation. It creates the necessary links and cache to the `opencv` libraries.

9. You can check the installation by running any example from the `opencv/samples/gpu` folder.

For using OpenCV in the program, you have to include the `opencv2/opencv.hpp` header file. This header file will include all other header files necessary for the program. So all the OpenCV programs have to include this header file on the top.

Working with images in OpenCV

Now that OpenCV is installed on the system, we can start using it to work with images. In this section, we will learn how images are represented inside OpenCV, develop programs to read an image, display an image, and save an image to disk. We will also see the method for creating synthetic images in OpenCV. We will also use OpenCV to draw different shapes on an image. Along with this, important syntax and features of OpenCV will be explained.

Image representation inside OpenCV

As described earlier, images are nothing but two-dimensional arrays, so they should be stored as an array inside a computer for processing. OpenCV provides a Mat class, which is nothing but an image container used to store an image. The Mat object can be created and assigned to an image in two separate lines as follows:

```
Mat img;
img= imread("cameraman.tif");
```

The data type of an image and size of the two-dimensional array can also be defined while creating an object. The data type of an image is very important as it signifies the number of channels and number of bits used to specify a single pixel value. Grayscale images have a single channel, while color images are a combination of three separate channels: Red, Green, and Blue.

The number of bits used for a single pixel specifies the number of discrete gray level values. An 8-bit image can have gray levels between 0 and 255, while 16-bit images can have gray levels between 0 to 65,535. OpenCV supports many data types with CV_8U as default, which indicates an 8-bit unsigned image with a single channel. It is equivalent to CV_8UC1. The color images can be specified as CV_8UC3, which indicates an 8-bit unsigned image with three channels. OpenCV supports up to 512 channels. Five or more channels have to be defined in round brackets, for example, CV_8UC(5) which indicates an 8-bit image with five channels. OpenCV also supports signed numbers so the data type can also be CV_16SC3, which specifies a 16-bit signed image with three channels.

A `Mat` object can be used to define the size of an image. This is also called the resolution of an image. It indicates the number of pixels in horizontal and vertical directions. Normally, the resolution of an image is defined in terms of width x height. While the size of an array in a `Mat` object should be defined in terms of the number of rows x number of columns. Some examples of using Mat to define image containers are shown as follows:

```
Mat img1(6,6,CV_8UC1);
//This defines img1 object with size of 6x6, unsigned 8-bit integers and
single channel.

Mat img2(256,256, CV_32FC1)
//This defines img2 object with size of 256x256, 32 bit floating point
numbers and single channel.

Mat img3(1960,1024, CV_64FC3)
//This defines img3 object with size of 1960x1024, 64 bit floating point
numbers and three channels.
```

The resolution and size of the image will determine the space needed to save an image on disk. Suppose the size of a color image with three channels is 1024 x 1024, then it will take 3 x 1024 x 1024 bytes = 3 MB to store the image on disk. In the next section, we will see how to use this Mat object and OpenCV to read and display an image.

Reading and displaying an image

In this section, we will try to develop the code for reading and displaying an image using C++ and OpenCV. The entire code for this is as follows it is then explained line by line:

```cpp
#include <opencv2/opencv.hpp>
#include <iostream>

using namespace cv;
using namespace std;

int main(int argc, char** argv)
{
  // Read the image
  Mat img = imread("images/cameraman.tif",0);

  // Check for failure in reading an Image
  if (img.empty())
  {
    cout << "Could not open an image" << endl;
    return -1;
  }
```

```
//Name of the window
String win_name = "My First Opencv Program";

// Create a window
namedWindow(win_name);

// Show our image inside the created window.
imshow(win_name, img);

// Wait for any keystroke in the window
waitKey(0);

//destroy the created window
destroyWindow(win_name);

return 0;
}
```

The program starts with including header files for standard input-output and image processing.

The functions from the std namespace, such as cout and endl, are used in the program, so the std namespace is added. All of the OpenCV classes and functions are defined using the cv namespace. So, to use functions defined in the cv namespace, we are specifying the using namespace cv line. If that line is omitted, then every function in the cv namespace has to be used in the following way:

```
Mat img = cv::imread("cameraman.tif")
```

The main function contains the code for reading and displaying an image. The imread command is used to read an image in OpenCV. It returns a Mat object. The imread command has two arguments. The first argument is the name of an image along with its path. The path can be specified in two ways. You can specify a fully qualified path of an image in your PC or you can specify a relative path of an image from your code file. In the preceding example, the relative path is used, where an image is located in the images folder that is in the same directory as the code file.

The second argument is optional and specifies whether the image is to be read as a grayscale or color image. If the image is to be read as a color image, then specify IMREAD_COLOR or 1. If the image is to be read as a grayscale image, then specify IMREAD_GRAYSCALE or 0. If the image is to be read in its saved form, then specify IMREAD_UNCHANGED or −1 as a second argument. If an image is read as a color image, the imread command will return three channels starting with **blue, green,** and **red (BGR** format). If the second argument is not provided, then the default value is IMREAD_COLOR which reads an image as a color image.

If, somehow, the image can't be read or it is not available on the disk, then the `imread` command will return a `Null Mat` object. If this happens, there is no need to continue with further image processing code and we can exit at this point by notifying the user about the error. This is handled by the code inside the `if` loop.

A window in which an image will be displayed should be created. OpenCV provides a function called `namedWindow` for that. It requires two arguments. The first argument is the name of the window. It has to be a string. The second argument specifies the size of the window that is to be created. It can take two values: `WINDOW_AUTOSIZE` or `WINDOW_NORMAL`. If `WINDOW_AUTOSIZE` is specified, then the user will not be able to resize the window and the image will be displayed in its original size. If `WINDOW_NORMAL` is specified, the user will be able to resize the window. This argument is optional and its default value is `WINDOW_AUTOSIZE` if it is not specified.

To display an image in the created window, the `imshow` command is used. This command requires two arguments. The first argument is the name of the window created using the `namedWindow` command and the second argument is the image variable that has to be displayed. This variable has to be a `Mat` object. For displaying multiple images, separate windows with unique names have to be created. The name of the window will appear as a title on the image window.

The `imshow` function should be provided for enough time to display an image in the created window. This is done by using the `waitKey` function. So the `imshow` function should be followed by the `waitkey` function in all OpenCV programs, otherwise the image will not be displayed. `waitKey` is a keyboard binding function and it accepts one argument, which is a time in milliseconds. It will wait, for a specified time, for a keystroke, then it will move to the next line of code. If no argument is specified or 0 is specified, it will wait for an indefinite time period for a keystroke. It will move to the next line only when any key is pressed on the keyboard. We can also detect whether a specific key is pressed and, depending on the key pressed, we can make certain decisions. We will use this feature later on in this chapter.

All the windows created for displaying the windows need to be closed before the termination of the program. This can be done using the `distroyAllWindows` function. It will close all the windows created using the `namedWindow` function during the program for displaying an image. There is a function called `distroyWindow`, which closes specific windows. The name of the window should be provided as an argument to the `distroyWindow` function.

For the execution of a program, just copy the code and paste it in Visual Studio if using it on Windows, or make a cpp file of it in Ubuntu. The build method is similar to a normal cpp application in Visual Studio, so it is not repeated here. For execution on Ubuntu, execute the following commands on the command prompt from the folder of a saved cpp file:

```
For compilation:
$ g++ -std = c++11 image_read.cpp 'pkg_config --libs --cflags opencv' -o
image_read

For execution:
$ ./image_read
```

The output of the preceding program after execution is as follows:

Reading and displaying a color image

In the preceding program, the second argument for imread is specified as 0, which means that it will read an image as a grayscale image. Suppose you want to read any color image. To do this, you can change the imread command in the following way:

```
Mat img = imread("images/autumn.tif",1);
```

The second argument is specified as 1, which means that it will read an image in BGR form. It is important to note that OpenCV's imread and imshow use BGR format for color images, which is different from the RGB format used by MATLAB and other image processing tools. The output after changing imread is as follows:

The same image can be read as a grayscale image even though it is a color image by providing 0 as a second argument. This will convert an image into grayscale implicitly and then read. The image will look as follows:

It is very important to remember how you are reading the image using the imread function because it will affect your program's other image processing code.

To summarize, in this section, we saw how to read an image and display it using OpenCV. In the process, we also learned about some important functions available in OpenCV. In the next section, we will see how to create a synthetic image using OpenCV.

Creating images using OpenCV

Sometimes, we may encounter the need to create our own image or draw some shapes on top of existing images. Or we may want to draw bounding boxes around a detected object or display labels on an image. So in this section, we will see how to create blank grayscale and color images. We will also see the functions for drawing lines, rectangles, ellipses, circles, and text on images.

To create an empty black image of the size 256 x 256, the following code can be used:

```cpp
#include <opencv2/opencv.hpp>
#include <iostream>

using namespace cv;
using namespace std;

int main(int argc, char** argv)
{
  //Create blank black grayscale Image with size 256x256
  Mat img(256, 256, CV_8UC1, Scalar(0));
  String win_name = "Blank Image";
  namedWindow(win_name);
  imshow(win_name, img);
  waitKey(0);
  destroyWindow(win_name);
  return 0;
}
```

The code is more or less similar to the code developed for reading an image, but instead of using the imread command here, the image is created using the constructor of the Mat class only. As discussed earlier, we can provide the size and data type while creating a Mat object. So while creating an img object, we have provided four arguments. The first two arguments specify the size of an image, which first defines the number of rows (height) and second defines the number of columns (width). The third argument defines the data type of an image. We have used CV_8UC1, which means an 8-bit unsigned integer image with a single channel. The last argument specifies the initialization value for all pixels in an array.

Here we have used 0, which is the value for black. When this program is executed, it will create a black image of size 256 x 256, as follows:

Similar code can be used for creating blank images of any color, as follows:

```
#include <opencv2/opencv.hpp>
#include <iostream>

using namespace cv;
using namespace std;

int main(int argc, char** argv)
{
  //Create blank blue color Image with size 256x256
  Mat img(256, 256, CV_8UC3, Scalar(255,0,0));
  String win_name = "Blank Blue Color Image";
  namedWindow(win_name);
  imshow(win_name, img);
  waitKey(0);
  destroyWindow(win_name);
  return 0;
}
```

While creating a `Mat` object, instead of using the `CV_8UC1` data type, `CV_8UC3` is used, which specifies an 8-bit image with three channels. So there are 24 bits for a single pixel. The fourth argument specifies the starting pixel values. It is specified using the scalar keyword and a tuple of three values specifying starting values in all three channels. Here, the blue channel is initialized with 255, the green channel is initialized with 0, and red channel is initialized with 0. This will create an image of size 256 x 256 in blue. Different combinations of values in tuple will create different colors. The output of the preceding program is as follows:

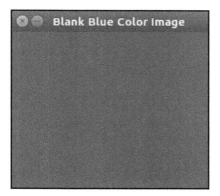

Drawing shapes on the blank image

To start drawing different shapes on an image, we will start by creating a blank black image of arbitrary size with the following command:

```
Mat img(512, 512, CV_8UC3, Scalar(0,0,0));
```

This command will create a black image of the size 512 x 512. Now, we will start by drawing different shapes on this image.

Drawing a line

A line can be specified by two points: the start point and end point. To draw a line on the image, these two points have to be specified. The function to draw a line on an image is as follows:

```
line(img,Point(0,0),Point(511,511),Scalar(0,255,0),7);
```

The line function has five arguments. The first argument specifies the image on which a line needs to be drawn, the second and third arguments define the start point and end points, respectively. The points are defined using the `Point` class constructor, which takes *x* and *y* coordinates of an image as argument. The fourth argument specifies the color of the line. It is specified as a tuple of B, G, and R values. Here, the value taken is (0,255,0), which specifies green. The fifth argument is the thickness of the line. Its value is taken as 7 pixels wide. This function also has an optional `linetype` argument. The preceding function will draw a diagonal green line of 7 pixels wide from (0,0) to (511,511).

Drawing a rectangle

A rectangle can be specified using two extreme diagonal points. OpenCV provides a function for drawing a rectangle on an image that has syntax as follows:

```
rectangle(img,Point(384,0),Point(510,128),Scalar(255,255,0),5);
```

The rectangle function has five arguments. The first argument is the image on which the rectangle is to be drawn. The second argument is the top-left point of the rectangle. The third argument is the bottom-right point of the rectangle. The fourth argument specifies the color of the border. It is specified as (255,255,0), which is a mix of blue and green, giving cyan. The fifth argument is the thickness of the border. If the fifth argument is specified as −1, the shape will be filled with color. So the preceding function will draw a rectangle with two extreme points, (384,0) and (510,128), in cyan with a border thickness of 5 pixels.

Drawing a circle

A circle can be specified by a center and its radius. OpenCV provides a function for drawing a circle on an image that has syntax as follows:

```
circle(img,Point(447,63), 63, Scalar(0,0,255), -1);
```

The circle function has five arguments. The first argument is the image on which a circle needs to be drawn. The second argument specifies the center point for that circle and the third argument specifies the radius. The fourth argument specifies the color of the circle. The value taken is (0,0,255), which is red. The fifth argument is the thickness of the border. Here, it is −1, which means the circle will be filled with red color.

Drawing an ellipse

OpenCV provides a function for drawing an ellipse on an image that has syntax as follows:

```
ellipse(img,Point(256,256),Point(100,100),0,0,180,255,-1);
```

The ellipse function has many arguments. The first argument specifies the image on which an ellipse needs to be drawn. The second argument specifies the center of the ellipse. The third argument specifies the box size under which the ellipse will be drawn. The fourth argument specifies the angle by which the ellipse needs to be rotated. It is taken as 0 degrees. The fifth and sixth argument specifies the range of angles for which the ellipse needs to be drawn. It is taken as 0 to 180 degrees. So only half the ellipse will be drawn. The next argument specifies the color of the ellipse, which is specified only as 255. It is the same as (255,0,0), which is blue. The final argument specifies the thickness of the border. It is taken as -1, so the ellipse will be filled with blue.

Writing text on an image

OpenCV provides a function for writing text on an image, which is putText. The syntax for the function is as follows:

```
putText( img, "OpenCV!", Point(10,500), FONT_HERSHEY_SIMPLEX, 3,Scalar(255,
255, 255), 5, 8 );
```

The putText function has many arguments. The first argument is the image on which text is to be written. The second argument is the text as a String data type, which we want to write on an image. The third argument specifies the bottom-left corner of the text. The fourth argument specifies the font type. There are many font types available in OpenCV, for which you can check OpenCV documentation. The fifth argument specifies the scale of the font. The sixth argument is the color of the text. It is taken as (255,255,255), which makes white. The seventh argument is the thickness of the text, which is taken as 5, and the last argument specifies linetype, which is taken as 8.

We have seen separate functions for drawing shapes on an empty black image. The following code shows the combination of all the functions previously discussed:

```
#include <opencv2/opencv.hpp>
#include <iostream>

using namespace cv;
using namespace std;

int main(int argc, char** argv)
{
```

```
    Mat img(512, 512, CV_8UC3, Scalar(0,0,0));
    line(img,Point(0,0),Point(511,511),Scalar(0,255,0),7);
    rectangle(img,Point(384,0),Point(510,128),Scalar(255,255,0),5);
    circle(img,Point(447,63),  63, Scalar(0,0,255), -1);
    ellipse(img,Point(256,256),Point(100,100),0,0,180,255,-1);
    putText( img, "OpenCV!", Point(10,500), FONT_HERSHEY_SIMPLEX,
3,Scalar(255, 255,  255), 5, 8 );
    String win_name = "Shapes on blank Image";
    namedWindow(win_name);
    imshow(win_name, img);
    waitKey(0);
    destroyWindow(win_name);
    return 0;
}
```

The output image for the preceding code is as follows:

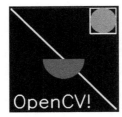

Saving an image to a file

Images can also be saved to a disk from the OpenCV program. This is helpful when we want to store our processed image to a disk on a computer. OpenCV provides the `imwrite` function to do this operation. The syntax of this function is as follows:

```
bool flag = imwrite("images/save_image.jpg", img);
```

The `imwrite` function takes two arguments. The first argument is the name of the file you want to save along with its path. The second argument is the `img` variable that you want to save. This function returns a Boolean value that indicates whether the file is saved successfully or not on a disk.

In this section, we have worked with images using OpenCV. In the next section, we will work with videos, which are nothing but a sequence of images, using OpenCV.

Working with videos in OpenCV

This section will show the process for reading videos from a file and webcam using OpenCV. It will also describe the process for saving videos to a file. This can also work with USB cameras attached to computers. Videos are nothing more than a sequence of images. Though OpenCV is not optimized for video processing applications, it does a decent job with it. OpenCV is not able to capture audio, so we have to use some other utilities with OpenCV to capture both audio and video.

Working with video stored on a computer

This section describes the process of reading a video file stored on a computer. All the frames from a video will be read one by one, operated upon, and displayed on the screen in all video processing applications using OpenCV.

The following code is for reading and displaying video—a line-by-line explanation is then given:

```cpp
#include <opencv2/opencv.hpp>
#include <iostream>
using namespace cv;
using namespace std;
int main(int argc, char* argv[])
{
  //open the video file from PC
  VideoCapture cap("images/rhinos.avi");
  // if not success, exit program
  if (cap.isOpened() == false)
  {
    cout << "Cannot open the video file" << endl;
    return -1;
  }
  cout<<"Press Q to Quit" << endl;
  String win_name = "First Video";
  namedWindow(win_name);
  while (true)
  {
    Mat frame;
    // read a frame
    bool flag = cap.read(frame);

    //Breaking the while loop at the end of the video
    if (flag == false)
    {
```

```
        break;
    }
    //display the frame
    imshow(win_name, frame);
    //Wait for 100 ms and key 'q' for exit
    if (waitKey(100) == 'q')
    {
        break;
    }
}
destroyWindow(win_name);
return 0;
}
```

After including libraries, the first thing that needs to be done inside the main function for processing video is to create an object of VideoCapture. The VideoCapture class has many constructors available for working with videos. When we want to work with video files stored on a computer, we need to provide the name of the video along with its path as an argument to the constructor while creating an object of VideoCapture.

This object provides many methods and properties that give information related to a video. We will see those as and when they are required. It provides the isopened property, which indicates whether the object creation was successful and whether or not video is available. It returns a Boolean value. If cap.isopened is false, the video is not available so there is no need to go any further in the program. So that is handled by an if loop, which exits the program after notifying the user when a video is not available.

The VideoCapture class provides a read method that captures the frames one by one. To process the entire video, we have to start a continuous loop that runs until the end of the video. The infinite while loop can do this job. Inside the while loop, the first frame is read using the read method. This method has one argument. It is a Mat object in which we want to store the frame. It returns a Boolean value that indicates whether the frame has been read successfully or not. When the loop has reached the end of video, this Boolean will return false, indicating there is no frame available. This flag is checked continuously in the loop for the end of the video; and if it is detected, we come out of the while loop using the break statement.

The frame is a single image, so displaying the process for that is the same as we saw earlier. In the preceding code, the waitKey function is used inside an if statement. It is waiting for 100 ms after every frame for a keystroke. The if statement is checking whether the keystroke is q or not. If it is q, it means that the user wants to quit the video so the break statement is included inside if.

This code will terminate display of the video either when the whole video is finished or the user presses q on the keyboard. Throughout this book, we will use this coding practice while processing videos. The output of the preceding program is as follows. The screenshot is a frame from a video:

We have used 100 ms delay between every frame. What do you think will happen when you decrease this value to, maybe, 10 ms? The answer is, each frame will be displayed faster. It does not mean the frame rate of the video changes. It just means that the delay between frames is reduced. If you want to see the actual frame rate of the video, you can use the CAP_PROP_FPS property of the cap object. It can be displayed with the following code:

```
double frames_per_second = cap.get(CAP_PROP_FPS);
cout << "Frames per seconds of the video is : " << frames_per_second ;
```

The cap object also has other properties, such as CAP_PROP_FRAME_WIDTH and CAP_PROP_FRAME_HEIGHT, which indicate the width and height of the frames. It can also be fetched with the get method. These properties can be set by using a set method of cap object. The set method has two arguments. The first argument is the name of the property and the second argument is the value we want to set.

This section described the method to read a video from a file. The next section will show the process for working with videos from either a webcam or USB camera.

Working with videos from a webcam

This section describes the process for capturing a video from a webcam or USB camera attached to a computer. The good part of OpenCV is that this same code will work for laptop and any embedded system that can run C/C++. This helps in deploying computer vision applications on any hardware platforms. The code for capturing video and displaying it is as follows:

```cpp
#include <opencv2/opencv.hpp>
#include <iostream>

using namespace cv;
using namespace std;

int main(int argc, char* argv[])
{
  //open the Webcam
  VideoCapture cap(0);
  // if not success, exit program
  if (cap.isOpened() == false)
  {
    cout << "Cannot open Webcam" << endl;
    return -1;
  }
  //get the frames rate of the video from webcam
  double frames_per_second = cap.get(CAP_PROP_FPS);
  cout << "Frames per seconds : " << frames_per_second << endl;
  cout<<"Press Q to Quit" <<endl;
  String win_name = "Webcam Video";
  namedWindow(win_name); //create a window
  while (true)
  {
    Mat frame;
    bool flag = cap.read(frame); // read a new frame from video
    //show the frame in the created window
    imshow(win_name, frame);
    if (waitKey(1) == 'q')
    {
      break;
    }
  }
  return 0;
}
```

While capturing video from a webcam or USB camera, the device ID for that camera needs to be provided as an argument to the constructor of the `VideoCapture` object. The primary camera connected will have a device ID zero. The webcam of a laptop or USB camera (when there is no webcam) will have device ID zero. If there are multiple cameras connected to a device, their device ID will be `(0,1)`, and so on. In the preceding code, zero indicates that the primary camera will be used by the code to capture the video.

The other code is more or less similar to the code for reading video from a file. Here, the frame rate of the video is also fetched and displayed. The frames will be read one by one at a 1 ms interval and displayed on the window created. You have to press `q` to terminate the operation. The output of video captured using the webcam is as follows:

Saving video to a disk

To save video from the OpenCV program, we need to create an object of the `VideoWriter` class. The code to save a video to a file is as follows:

```
Size frame_size(640, 640);
int frames_per_second = 30;

VideoWriter v_writer("images/video.avi", VideoWriter::fourcc('M', 'J', 'P',
'G'), frames_per_second, frame_size, true);
```

```
//Inside while loop
v_writer.write(frame);

//After finishing video write
v_writer.release();
```

While creating an object of the `VideoWriter` class, the constructor takes five arguments. The first argument is the name of the video file you want to save along with the absolute or relative path. The second argument is the four character code used for video codec. It is created using the `VideoWriter::fourcc` function. Here we are using motion JPEG codec, so the four character code for it is `'M'`, `'J'`, `'P'`, and `'G'`. There are other codecs that can be used depending on your requirements and operating system. The third argument is frames per second. It can be specified as an integer variable previously defined or an integer value directly in the function. In the preceding code, `30` frames per second is used. The fourth argument is the size of the frame. It is defined using the `size` keyword with two arguments, `frame_width` and `frame_height`. It is taken as 640 x 640 in the preceding code. The fifth argument specifies whether the frame to be stored is color or grayscale. If its true, the frame is saved as a color frame.

To start writing frames using the `VideoWriter` object, OpenCV provides a `write` method. This method is used to write frames into video one by one, so it is included inside an infinite `while` loop. This method takes only one argument, which is the name of the frame variable. The size of the frame should be the same as the size specified while creating the `VideoWriter` object. It is important to flush and close the video file created after writing is finished. This can be done by releasing the created `VideoWriter` object using the `release` method.

To summarize, in this section we looked at the process of reading video from a file or camera attached to a device. We have also seen the code for writing a video to a file. From the next section onward, we will see how we can operate on images or videos using OpenCV with CUDA acceleration.

Basic computer vision applications using the OpenCV CUDA module

In earlier chapters, we saw that CUDA provides an excellent interface to utilize the parallel computing capability of GPU to accelerate complex computing applications. In this section, we will see how we can utilize the capability of CUDA alongside OpenCV for computer vision applications.

Introduction to the OpenCV CUDA module

OpenCV has a CUDA module that has hundreds of functions that can utilize GPU capabilities. It is only supported on Nvidia GPUs because it uses Nvidia CUDA runtime in the background. OpenCV has to be compiled with the `WITH_CUDA` flag set to ON for using the CUDA module.

One great feature of using the CUDA module of OpenCV is that it provides a similar API to regular OpenCV API. It also does not require detailed knowledge of programming in CUDA, although knowledge of CUDA and GPU architecture will not do any harm. The researchers have shown that using functions with CUDA acceleration can provide 5x-100x speedup over similar CPU functions.

In the next section, we will see how to use the CUDA module along with OpenCV in various computer vision and image processing applications that operate on individual pixels of an image.

Arithmetic and logical operations on images

In this section, we will see how to perform various arithmetic and logical operations on images. We will use functions defined in the CUDA module of OpenCV to perform these operations.

Addition of two images

The addition of two images can be performed when two images are of the same size. OpenCV provides an `add` function inside the `cv::cuda` namespace for addition operation. It performs pixel-wise addition of two images. Suppose in two images, the pixel at `(0,0)` has intensity values 100 and 150 respectively. The intensity value in the resultant image will be 250, which is the addition of two intensity values. OpenCV addition is a saturated operation, which means that if an answer of addition goes above 255, it will be saturated at 255. The code to perform addition is as follows:

```
#include <iostream>
#include "opencv2/opencv.hpp"

int main (int argc, char* argv[])
{
  //Read Two Images
  cv::Mat h_img1 = cv::imread("images/cameraman.tif");
  cv::Mat h_img2 = cv::imread("images/circles.png");
  //Create Memory for storing Images on device
```

```
    cv::cuda::GpuMat d_result1,d_img1, d_img2;
    cv::Mat h_result1;
    //Upload Images to device
    d_img1.upload(h_img1);
    d_img2.upload(h_img2);

    cv::cuda::add(d_img1,d_img2, d_result1);
    //Download Result back to host
    d_result1.download(h_result1);
    cv::imshow("Image1 ", h_img1);
    cv::imshow("Image2 ", h_img2);
    cv::imshow("Result addition ", h_result1);
    cv::imwrite("images/result_add.png", h_result1);
    cv::waitKey();
    return 0;
}
```

When any computer vision operation needs to be performed on GPU, the images have to be stored on device memory. The memory for it can be allocated with the gpumat keyword, which is similar to the Mat type used for host memory. The images are read in the same way as earlier. Two images are read for addition and stored in host memory. These images are copied to device memory using the upload method of device memory variable. The host image variable is passed as a parameter to this method.

The function in the GPU CUDA module is defined in the cv::cuda namespace. It requires images on device memory as its arguments. The add function from the CUDA module is used for image addition. It requires three arguments. The first two arguments are two images that are to be added and the last argument is the destination in which the result will be stored. All three variables should be defined using gpumat.

The resultant image is copied back to the host using the download method of the device variable. The host img variable, in which the result will be copied, is provided as an argument to the download method. Then this image is displayed and stored on the disk using the same functions explained in the last section. The output of the program is as follows:

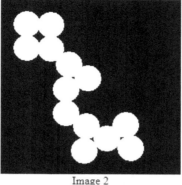

| Image 1 | Image 2 | Result after addition |

Subtracting two images

Other arithmetic operations can be performed on images using OpenCV and CUDA. The `subtract` function is provided by OpenCV to subtract two images. It is also a saturated operation, which means that when the answer of subtraction goes below zero, it will be saturated to zero. The syntax of the subtract command is as follows:

```
//d_result1 = d_img1 - d_img2
cv::cuda::subtract(d_img1, d_img2,d_result1);
```

Again, two images to be subtracted are provided as the first two arguments and the resultant image is provided as the third argument. The result of the subtraction between two images is as follows:

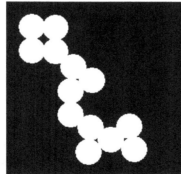

| Image 1 | Image 2 | Result after Subtraction |

Image blending

Sometimes there is a need to blend two images with different proportions, instead of directly adding two images. Image blending can be represented mathematically by the following equation:

```
result = α * img1 + β * img2 + γ
```

This can be easily accomplished with the `addWeighted` function inside OpenCV. The syntax of the function is as follows:

```
cv::cuda::addWeighted(d_img1,0.7,d_img2,0.3,0,d_result1)
```

The function has six arguments. The first argument is the first source image, the second argument is a weight of the first image for blending, the third argument is the second source image, the fourth argument is a weight of the second image for blending, and the fifth argument is the constant gamma to be added while blending. The final argument specifies the destination in which the result needs to be stored. The function given takes 70 percent of `img1` and 30 percent of `img2` for blending. The output for this function is as follows:

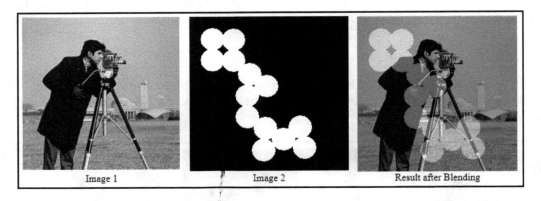

| Image 1 | Image 2 | Result after Blending |

Image inversion

Apart from arithmetic operations, OpenCV also provides Boolean operations that work on individual bits. It includes AND, OR, NOT, and so on. AND and OR are very useful for masking operations, as we will see later on. The NOT operation is used for inverting an image where black is converted to white and white is converted to black. It can be represented by the following equation:

```
result_image = 255 - input_image
```

In the equation, 255 indicates maximum intensity value for an 8-bit image. The program for doing image inversion is as follows:

```
#include <iostream>
#include "opencv2/opencv.hpp"

int main (int argc, char* argv[])
{
  cv::Mat h_img1 = cv::imread("images/circles.png");
  //Create Device variables
  cv::cuda::GpuMat d_result1,d_img1;
  cv::Mat h_result1;
  //Upload Image to device
  d_img1.upload(h_img1);

  cv::cuda::bitwise_not(d_img1,d_result1);
  //Download result back  to host
  d_result1.download(h_result1);
  cv::imshow("Result inversion ", h_result1);
  cv::imwrite("images/result_inversion.png", h_result1);
  cv::waitKey();
  return 0;
}
```

The program is similar to the program for arithmetic operations. The `bitwise_not` function is used for image inversion. The image should be a grayscale image. It takes two arguments. The first argument indicates the source image to be inverted and the second argument indicates the destination in which the inverted image is to be stored. The output of the `bitwise_not` operation is as follows:

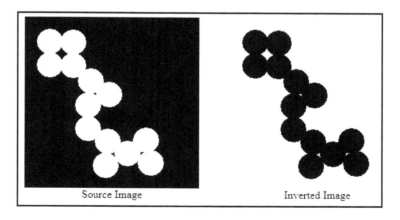

Source Image   Inverted Image

As can be seen, by doing an inversion, white is converted to black and black is converted to white.

To summarize, in this section, we have seen various arithmetic and logical operations using OpenCV and CUDA. In the next section, we will see some more computer vision operations that are widely used in computer vision applications.

Changing the color space of an image

As described earlier, OpenCV can read an image as a grayscale image or as a color image, with three channels green, blue, and red, which is called BGR format. Other image processing software and algorithms work on RGB images, where the red channel is followed by green and blue. There are many other color formats that can be used for certain applications. These include the HSV color space, where the three channels are Hue, Saturation, and Value. Hue represents color value, saturation indicates the gray level in the color, and value represents the brightness of the color. The other color space is YCrCb, which is also very useful. This system represents colors in an image in terms of one luminance component: luma (Y), and two chrominance components: chroma(Cb and Cr).

There are many other color spaces available that are supported by OpenCV, such as XYZ, HLS, Lab and so on. OpenCV supports more than 150 color conversion methods. The conversion from one color space to another can be accomplished by using the `cvtColor` function available in OpenCV. An example of using this function for changing between various color space is as follows:

```
#include <iostream>
#include "opencv2/opencv.hpp"

int main (int argc, char* argv[])
{
  cv::Mat h_img1 = cv::imread("images/autumn.tif");
  //Define device variables
  cv::cuda::GpuMat d_result1,d_result2,d_result3,d_result4,d_img1;
  //Upload Image to device
  d_img1.upload(h_img1);

  //Convert image to different color spaces
  cv::cuda::cvtColor(d_img1, d_result1,cv::COLOR_BGR2GRAY);
  cv::cuda::cvtColor(d_img1, d_result2,cv::COLOR_BGR2RGB);
  cv::cuda::cvtColor(d_img1, d_result3,cv::COLOR_BGR2HSV);
  cv::cuda::cvtColor(d_img1, d_result4,cv::COLOR_BGR2YCrCb);
  cv::Mat h_result1,h_result2,h_result3,h_result4;
  //Download results back to host
  d_result1.download(h_result1);
```

```
    d_result2.download(h_result2);
    d_result3.download(h_result3);
    d_result4.download(h_result4);

    cv::imshow("Result in Gray ", h_result1);
    cv::imshow("Result in RGB", h_result2);
    cv::imshow("Result in HSV ", h_result3);
    cv::imshow("Result in YCrCb ", h_result4);
    cv::waitKey();
    return 0;
}
```

The `imshow` function expects color images in BGR color format, so the output of other color formats using `imshow` might not be visually attractive. The output of the preceding program with the same image in different color formats is as follows:

Original Image   Grayscale Image   RGB Image

HSV Image   YCrCb Image

Image thresholding

Image thresholding is a very simple image segmentation technique used to extract important regions from a grayscale image based on certain intensity values. In this technique, if the pixel value is greater than a certain threshold value, it is assigned one value, otherwise it is assigned another value.

The function used for image thresholding in OpenCV and CUDA is `cv::cuda::threshold`. This function has many arguments. The first argument is the source image, which should be a grayscale image. The second argument is the destination in which the result is to be stored. The third argument is the threshold value, which is used to segment the pixel values. The fourth argument is the `maxVal` constant, which represents the value to be given if the pixel value is more than the threshold value. OpenCV provides different types of thresholding techniques and it is decided by the last argument of the function. These thresholding types are as follows:

- `cv:.THRESH_BINARY`: If the intensity of the pixel is greater than the threshold, set that pixel intensity equal to the `maxVal` constant. Otherwise set that pixel intensity to zero.
- `cv::THRESH_BINARY_INV`: If the intensity of the pixel is greater than the threshold, set that pixel intensity equal to zero. Otherwise set that pixel intensity to `maxVal` constant.
- `cv::THRESH_TRUNC`: This is basically a truncation operation. If the intensity of the pixel is greater than the threshold, set that pixel intensity equal to the threshold. Otherwise, keep the intensity value as it is.
- `cv::THRESH_TOZERO`: If the intensity of the pixel is greater than the threshold, keep the pixel intensity as it is. Otherwise set that pixel intensity to zero.
- `cv::THRESH_TOZERO_INV`: If the intensity of the pixel is greater than the threshold, set that pixel intensity equal to zero. Otherwise keep the pixel intensity as it is.

The program to implement all these thresholding techniques using OpenCV and CUDA is as follows:

```
#include <iostream>
#include "opencv2/opencv.hpp"

int main (int argc, char* argv[])
{
  cv::Mat h_img1 = cv::imread("images/cameraman.tif", 0);
  //Define device variables
  cv::cuda::GpuMat d_result1,d_result2,d_result3,d_result4,d_result5,
```

```
d_img1;
  //Upload image on device
  d_img1.upload(h_img1);

  //Perform different thresholding techniques on device
  cv::cuda::threshold(d_img1, d_result1, 128.0, 255.0, cv::THRESH_BINARY);
  cv::cuda::threshold(d_img1, d_result2, 128.0, 255.0,
cv::THRESH_BINARY_INV);
  cv::cuda::threshold(d_img1, d_result3, 128.0, 255.0, cv::THRESH_TRUNC);
  cv::cuda::threshold(d_img1, d_result4, 128.0, 255.0, cv::THRESH_TOZERO);
  cv::cuda::threshold(d_img1, d_result5, 128.0, 255.0,
cv::THRESH_TOZERO_INV);

  cv::Mat h_result1,h_result2,h_result3,h_result4,h_result5;
  //Copy results back to host
  d_result1.download(h_result1);
  d_result2.download(h_result2);
  d_result3.download(h_result3);
  d_result4.download(h_result4);
  d_result5.download(h_result5);
  cv::imshow("Result Threshhold binary ", h_result1);
  cv::imshow("Result Threshhold binary inverse ", h_result2);
  cv::imshow("Result Threshhold truncated ", h_result3);
  cv::imshow("Result Threshhold truncated to zero ", h_result4);
  cv::imshow("Result Threshhold truncated to zero inverse ", h_result5);
  cv::waitKey();

  return 0;
}
```

In the `cv::cuda::threshold` function for all thresholding techniques, 128 is taken as a threshold for pixel intensity, which is a midpoint between black (0) and white (255). The `maxVal` constant is taken as 255, which will be used to update pixel intensity when it exceeds the threshold. The other program is similar to other OpenCV programs seen earlier.

The output of the program is as follows, which displays the input image along with the output of all five thresholding techniques:

Original Image | Result of binary Threshold | Result of inverse binary Threshold

Result of Thresholding by truncating | Result of Thresholding by truncating to zero | Result of Thresholding by truncating to zero inverse

Performance comparison of OpenCV applications with and without CUDA support

The performance of image processing algorithms can be measured in terms of the time it takes to process a single image. When algorithms work on video, performance is measured in terms of frames per second, which indicates the number of frames it can process in a second. When the algorithm can process more than 30 frames per second, it can be considered to work in real time. We can also measure the performance of our algorithms implemented in OpenCV, which will be discussed in this section.

As we discussed earlier, when OpenCV is built with CUDA compatibility, it can increase the performance of algorithms drastically. OpenCV functions in the CUDA module are optimized to utilize GPU parallel processing capability. OpenCV also provides similar functions that only run on CPU. In this section, we will compare the performance of thresholding operations built in the last section with and without using GPU. We will compare the performance of the thresholding operation in terms of the time taken to process one image and frames per second. The code to implement thresholding on CPU and measure performance is as follows:

```
#include <iostream>
#include "opencv2/opencv.hpp"
using namespace cv;
using namespace std;

int main (int argc, char* argv[])
{
  cv::Mat src = cv::imread("images/cameraman.tif", 0);
  cv::Mat result_host1,result_host2,result_host3,result_host4,result_host5;

  //Get initial time in miliseconds
  int64 work_begin = getTickCount();
  cv::threshold(src, result_host1, 128.0, 255.0, cv::THRESH_BINARY);
  cv::threshold(src, result_host2, 128.0, 255.0,  cv::THRESH_BINARY_INV);
  cv::threshold(src, result_host3, 128.0, 255.0, cv::THRESH_TRUNC);
  cv::threshold(src, result_host4, 128.0, 255.0, cv::THRESH_TOZERO);
  cv::threshold(src, result_host5, 128.0, 255.0, cv::THRESH_TOZERO_INV);

  //Get time after work has finished
  int64 delta = getTickCount() - work_begin;
  //Frequency of timer
  double freq = getTickFrequency();
  double work_fps = freq / delta;
  std::cout<<"Performance of Thresholding on CPU: " <<std::endl;
  std::cout <<"Time: " << (1/work_fps) <<std::endl;
  std::cout <<"FPS: " <<work_fps <<std::endl;
  return 0;
}
```

In the preceding code, the threshold function from the cv namespace is used, which only uses CPU for execution, rather than the cv::cuda module. The performance of the algorithm is measured using the gettickcount and gettickfrequency functions. The gettickcount function returns the time, in milliseconds, that has passed after starting the system. We measured the time ticks before and after the execution of the code that operates on the image. The difference between the time ticks indicates the ticks passed during an execution of the algorithm to process an image. This time is measured in the delta variable. The gettickfrequncy function returns the frequency of the timer. Total time taken to process an image can be measured by dividing the time ticks by the frequency of the timer. The inverse of this time indicates **frames per second** (FPS). Both these performance measures are printed on the console for thresholding application on the CPU. The output on the console is as follows:

```
Performance of Thresholding on CPU:
Time: 0.169766
FPS: 5.89046
```

As can be seen from the output, the CPU takes 0.169766 seconds to process one image, which is equal to 5.89046 FPS. Now we will implement the same algorithm on GPU and try to measure the performance of the code. As per the discussion earlier, this should increase the performance of the algorithm drastically. The code for GPU implementation is as follows:

```
#include <iostream>
#include "opencv2/opencv.hpp"

int main (int argc, char* argv[])
{
  cv::Mat h_img1 = cv::imread("images/cameraman.tif", 0);
  cv::cuda::GpuMat d_result1,d_result2,d_result3,d_result4,d_result5,
d_img1;
  //Measure initial time ticks
  int64 work_begin = getTickCount();
  d_img1.upload(h_img1);
  cv::cuda::threshold(d_img1, d_result1, 128.0, 255.0,
cv::THRESH_BINARY);
  cv::cuda::threshold(d_img1, d_result2, 128.0, 255.0,
cv::THRESH_BINARY_INV);
  cv::cuda::threshold(d_img1, d_result3, 128.0, 255.0, cv::THRESH_TRUNC);
  cv::cuda::threshold(d_img1, d_result4, 128.0, 255.0, cv::THRESH_TOZERO);
  cv::cuda::threshold(d_img1, d_result5, 128.0, 255.0,
cv::THRESH_TOZERO_INV);

  cv::Mat h_result1,h_result2,h_result3,h_result4,h_result5;
```

```
d_result1.download(h_result1);
d_result2.download(h_result2);
d_result3.download(h_result3);
d_result4.download(h_result4);
d_result5.download(h_result5);
//Measure difference in time ticks
int64 delta = getTickCount() - work_begin;
double freq = getTickFrequency();
//Measure frames per second
double work_fps = freq / delta;
std::cout <<"Performance of Thresholding on GPU: " <<std::endl;
std::cout <<"Time: " << (1/work_fps) <<std::endl;
std::cout <<"FPS: " <<work_fps <<std::endl;
return 0;
}
```

In the code, the functions are used from the cv::cuda module, which is optimized for GPU parallel processing capabilities. The images are copied to device memory, operated upon on GPU, and copied back to host. The performance measures are calculated in a similar way as preceding and printed on the console. The output of the program is as follows:

```
Performance of Thresholding on GPU:
Time: 0.000550593
FPS: 1816.22
```

As can be seen, ,GPU implementation only takes 0.55 ms to process a single image, which is equal to 1816 FPS. This is a drastic improvement over a CPU implementation, though it must be kept in mind that this is a very simple application and not ideal for performance comparison between CPU and GPU. This application was shown simply to make you familiar with how one can measure the performance of any code in OpenCV.

A more realistic comparison of CPU and GPU performance can be made by running the example codes provided in the OpenCV installation in the `samples/gpu` directory. One of the codes, `hog.cpp`, calculates the **histogram of oriented (HoG)** features from an image and classifies it using **Support Vector Machine** (**SVM**). Though details of algorithms are out of the scope of this book, it gives you an idea about performance improvement while using GPU implementations. The performance comparison on webcam video is as follows:

| CPU Performance | GPU Performance |

As can be seen, while we use only CPU, the performance of the code is around 13 FPS, and if we use GPU, it increases to 24 FPS, which is almost double the CPU performance. This will give you an idea about the importance of using CUDA with OpenCV.

To summarize, in this section we looked at a comparison between the performance of OpenCV using CUDA (GPU) and without using CUDA (CPU). It reemphasizes the notion that use of CUDA will improve the performance of computer vision applications drastically.

Summary

In this chapter, we started with the introduction of computer vision and image processing. We described OpenCV library, which is specifically made for computer vision applications, and how it is different from other computer vision software. OpenCV can leverage the parallel processing capability of GPU by using CUDA. We looked at the installation procedure for OpenCV with CUDA in all operating systems. We described the process to read an image from disk, display it on screen, and save it back to disk. Videos are nothing more than a sequence of images. We learned to work with videos from disk as well as videos captured from camera. We developed several image processing applications that do different operations on images, such as arithmetic operations, logical operations, color space conversions, and thresholding. In the last section, we compared the performance of the same algorithm on CPU and GPU in terms of time taken to process an image and FPS. So at the end of this chapter, you have an idea of the usefulness of OpenCV with CUDA in computer vision applications and how to write simple code using it. In the next chapter, we will build upon this knowledge and try to develop some more useful computer vision applications, such as filtering, edge detection, and morphological operations using OpenCV.

Questions

1. State the difference between terms computer vision and image processing
2. Why is OpenCV ideal for deploying computer vision applications on embedded systems
3. Write an OpenCV command to initialize 1960 x 1960 color image with red color
4. Write a program to capture frames from a webcam and save it to disk
5. Which color format is used by OpenCV to read and display a color image
6. Write a program to capture video from webcam, convert it to grayscale and display on the screen
7. Write a program to measure the performance of add and subtract operation on GPU
8. Write a program for bitwise AND and OR operation on images and explain how it can be used for masking

6
Basic Computer Vision Operations Using OpenCV and CUDA

The last chapter described the process of working with images and videos using OpenCV and CUDA. We looked at the code for some basic image and video processing applications and compared the performance of OpenCV code with and without CUDA acceleration. In this chapter, we will build on this knowledge and try to develop some more computer vision and image processing applications using OpenCV and CUDA. This chapter describes the method for accessing individual pixel intensities in color and grayscale images. A histogram is a very useful concept for image processing. This chapter describes the method for calculating histograms and how histogram equalization can improve the visual quality of images. This chapter will also describe how different geometric transformations can be performed using OpenCV and CUDA. Image filtering is a very important concept, which is useful in image preprocessing and feature extraction. This is described in detail in this chapter. The last part of this chapter describes different morphological operations, such as erosion, dilation, and opening and closing images.

The following topics will be covered in this chapter:

- Accessing individual pixel intensities in OpenCV
- Histogram calculation and histogram equalization
- Image transformation
- Filtering operations on images
- Morphological operations on images

Technical requirements

This chapter requires a basic understanding of image processing and computer vision. It needs familiarity with basic C or C++ programming language, CUDA, and all of the codes sample explained in previous chapters. All of the code used in this chapter can be downloaded from the following GitHub link: `https://github.com/PacktPublishing/` `Hands-On-GPU-Accelerated-Computer-Vision-with-OpenCV-and-CUDA`. The code can be executed on any operating system, though it has only been tested on Ubuntu 16.04.

Check out the following video to see the code in action:
`http://bit.ly/2xERUDL`

Accessing the individual pixel intensities of an image

Sometimes there is a need to access pixel intensity value at a particular location when we are working with images. This is very useful when we want to change the brightness or contrast of a group of pixels or we want to perform some other pixel-level operations. For an 8-bit grayscale image, this intensity value at a point will be in a range of 0 to 255, while for a color image there will be three different intensity values for the blue, green, and red channels with all having values between 0 to 255.

OpenCV provides a `cv::Mat::at<>` method for accessing intensity values at a particular location for any channel images. It needs one argument, which is the location of the point at which the intensity is to be accessed. The point is passed using the `Point` class with row and column values as arguments. For a grayscale image, the method will return a scalar object while, for a color image, it will return a vector of three intensities. The code for accessing pixel intensities at a particular location for a grayscale as well as a color image is as follows:

```
#include <iostream>
#include "opencv2/opencv.hpp"
int main ()
{
  //Gray Scale Image
  cv::Mat h_img1 = cv::imread("images/cameraman.tif",0);
  cv::Scalar intensity = h_img1.at<uchar>(cv::Point(100, 50));
  std::cout<<"Pixel Intensity of gray scale Image at (100,50) is:"
<<intensity.val[0]<<std::endl;
  //Color Image
  cv::Mat h_img2 = cv::imread("images/autumn.tif",1);
```

```
   cv::Vec3b intensity1 = h_img1.at<cv::Vec3b>(cv::Point(100, 50));
   std::cout<<"Pixel Intensity of color Image at (100,50)
is:"<<intensity1<<std::endl;
   return 0;
}
```

The grayscale image is read first and the at method is called on this image object. The intensity value is measured at the (100,50) point, which indicates the pixel at the 100th row and 50th column. It returns a scalar, which is stored in the intensity variable. The value is printed on the console. The same procedure is followed for a color image but the return value for it will be a vector of three intensities, which is stored in the Vec3b object. The intensity values are printed on the console. The output of the above program is as follows:

```
bhaumik@bhaumik-Lenovo-ideapad-520-15IKB:~/Desktop/opencv/Chapter 6$ g++ -std=c+
+11 individual_pixel.cpp `pkg-config --libs --cflags opencv` -o pixel
bhaumik@bhaumik-Lenovo-ideapad-520-15IKB:~/Desktop/opencv/Chapter 6$ ./pixel
Pixel Intensity of gray scale Image at (100,50) is:9
Pixel Intensity of color Image at (100,50) is:[175, 179, 177]
```

As can be seen, pixel intensity for a grayscale image at (100,50) is 9 while for a color image it is [175,179,177], which indicates the blue intensity is 175, the green intensity is 179, and red intensity is 177. The same method is used to modify pixel intensity at a particular location. Suppose, you want to change the pixel intensity at the (100,50) location to 128, then you can write:

```
   h_img1.at<uchar>(100, 50) = 128;
```

To summarize, in this section we have seen a method to access and change intensity values at a particular location. In the next section, we will see the method to calculate the histogram in OpenCV.

Histogram calculation and equalization in OpenCV

A histogram is a very important property of an image as it provides a global description of the appearance of that image. An enormous amount of information can be obtained from the histogram. It represents the relative frequency of occurrence of gray levels in an image. It is basically a plot of gray levels on the X-axis and the number of pixels in each gray level on the Y-axis. If the histogram is concentrated on the left side then the image will be very dark and if it is concentrated on the right side, then the image will be very bright. It should be evenly distributed for good visual quality of an image.

The following image demonstrates histograms for dark, bright, and normal images:

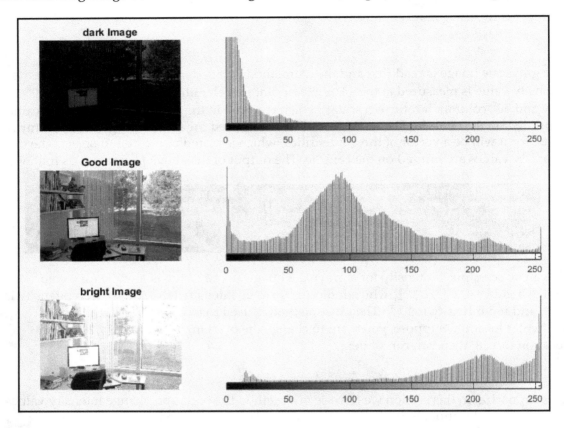

OpenCV provides a function to calculate the histogram of an Image. The syntax of the function is as follows:

```
void cv::cuda::calcHist ( InputArray src, OutputArray hist)
```

The function needs two arrays as an argument. The first array is the input image for which the histogram needs to be calculated. The second argument is an output array in which the histogram will be stored. The output can be plotted to get a histogram like what is shown in the preceding screenshot. As described earlier, a flat histogram improves the visual quality of an Image. OpenCV and CUDA provide a function to flatten the histogram, which is described in the following section.

Histogram equalization

A perfect image has an equal number of pixels in all its gray levels. So a histogram should have a large dynamic range and an equal number of pixels in the entire range. This can be accomplished by a technique called histogram equalization. It is a very important preprocessing step in any computer vision application. In this section, we will see how histogram equalization can be performed for grayscale and color images using OpenCV and CUDA.

Grayscale images

Grayscale images are normally 8-bit single channel images that have 256 different gray levels. If the histogram is not evenly distributed, the image is too dark or the image is too light, and histogram equalization should be performed to improve the visual quality of the image. The following code describes the process for histogram equalization on a grayscale image:

```
#include <iostream>
#include "opencv2/opencv.hpp"
int main ()
{
  cv::Mat h_img1 = cv::imread("images/cameraman.tif",0);
  cv::cuda::GpuMat d_img1,d_result1;
  d_img1.upload(h_img1);
  cv::cuda::equalizeHist(d_img1, d_result1);
  cv::Mat h_result1;
  d_result1.download(h_result1);
  cv::imshow("Original Image ", h_img1);
  cv::imshow("Histogram Equalized Image", h_result1);
  cv::waitKey();
  return 0;
}
```

The image read is uploaded to the device memory for histogram equalization. It is a mathematically intensive step so CUDA acceleration will help in improving the performance of the program. OpenCV provides the `equalizeHist` function for histogram equalization. It needs two arguments. The first argument is the source image and the second argument is the destination image. The destination image is downloaded back to the host and displayed on the console. The output after histogram equalization is as follows:

As can be seen, the image after histogram equalization has a better visual quality than the original image. The same operation for color images is described next.

Color image

Histogram equalization can also be done on color images. It has to be performed on separate channels. So the color image has to be split into three channels. The histogram of each channel is equalized independently and then channels are merged to reconstruct the image. The code for histogram equalization on a color image is as follows:

```
#include <iostream>
#include "opencv2/opencv.hpp"
int main ()
{
  cv::Mat h_img1 = cv::imread("images/autumn.tif");
  cv::Mat h_img2,h_result1;
  cvtColor(h_img1, h_img2, cv::COLOR_BGR2HSV);
  //Split the image into 3 channels; H, S and V channels respectively and
store it in a std::vector
  std::vector< cv::Mat > vec_channels;
  cv::split(h_img2, vec_channels);
```

```
    //Equalize the histogram of only the V channel
    cv::equalizeHist(vec_channels[2], vec_channels[2]);
    //Merge 3 channels in the vector to form the color image in HSV color
space.
    cv::merge(vec_channels, h_img2);
    //Convert the histogram equalized image from HSV to BGR color space again
    cv::cvtColor(h_img2,h_result1, cv::COLOR_HSV2BGR);
    cv::imshow("Original Image ", h_img1);
    cv::imshow("Histogram Equalized Image", h_result1);
    cv::waitKey();
    return 0;
}
```

A histogram is not normally equalized in the BGR color space; HSV and YCrCb color spaces are used for it. So, in the code, the BGR color space is converted in to the HSV color space. Then, it is split into three separate channels using the `split` function. Now, hue and saturation channels contain the color information so there is no point in equalizing those channels. Histogram equalization is performed only on the value channel. Three channels are merged back to reconstruct the color image using the `merge` function. The HSV color image is converted back into the BGR color space for display using `imshow`. The output of the program is as follows:

To summarize, histogram equalization improves the visual quality of an image so it is a very important preprocessing step for any computer vision application. The next section describes the geometric transformation of images.

Geometric transformation on images

Sometimes, there is a need for resizing an image, the translation of images, and the rotation of images for larger computer vision applications. These kinds of geometric transformation is explained in this section.

Image resizing

images need to be of specific sizes in some computer vision applications. So there is a need to convert the image of arbitrary size into the specific size. OpenCV provides a function to resize an image. The code for image resizing is as follows:

```
#include <iostream>
#include "opencv2/opencv.hpp"
int main ()
{
  cv::Mat h_img1 = cv::imread("images/cameraman.tif",0);
  cv::cuda::GpuMat d_img1,d_result1,d_result2;
  d_img1.upload(h_img1);
  int width= d_img1.cols;
  int height = d_img1.size().height;
  cv::cuda::resize(d_img1,d_result1,cv::Size(200, 200),    cv::INTER_CUBIC);
  cv::cuda::resize(d_img1,d_result2,cv::Size(0.5*width, 0.5*height),
cv::INTER_LINEAR);
  cv::Mat h_result1,h_result2;
  d_result1.download(h_result1);
  d_result2.download(h_result2);
  cv::imshow("Original Image ", h_img1);
  cv::imshow("Resized Image", h_result1);
  cv::imshow("Resized Image 2", h_result2);
  cv::waitKey();
  return 0;
}
```

The height and width of an image can be obtained using two different functions, as shown in the code. The rows and cols properties of the Mat object describes the height and width of an image respectively. The Mat object also has the size() method, which has height and width properties which are used to find the size of an image. The image is resized in two ways. In the first way, the image is resized to a specific size of (200,200) and, in the second, it is resized to half of its original dimensions. OpenCV provides the resize function for this operation. It has four arguments.

The first two arguments are the source and destination images respectively. The third argument is the size of the destination image. It is defined using the `Size` object. When images are resized, then pixel values have to be interpolated on the destination image from the source image. There are various interpolation methods such as, bilinear interpolation, bicubic interpolation, area interpolation which are available for interpolating pixel values. This interpolation method is provided as the fourth argument to the `resize` function. It can be `cv::INTER_LINEAR` (bilinear), `cv::INTER_CUBIC` (bicubic), or `cv::INTER_AREA` (Area). The output of the image resizing code is as follows:

Image translation and rotation

Image translation and rotation are important geometric transformations that are needed in some computer vision applications. OpenCV provides an easy API to perform these transformations on images. The code to perform translation and rotation is as follows:

```
#include <iostream>
#include "opencv2/opencv.hpp"

int main ()
{
  cv::Mat h_img1 = cv::imread("images/cameraman.tif",0);
  cv::cuda::GpuMat d_img1,d_result1,d_result2;
  d_img1.upload(h_img1);
  int cols= d_img1.cols;
  int rows = d_img1.size().height;
  //Translation
```

```
cv::Mat trans_mat = (cv::Mat_<double>(2,3) << 1, 0, 70, 0, 1, 50);
cv::cuda::warpAffine(d_img1,d_result1,trans_mat,d_img1.size());
//Rotation
cv::Point2f pt(d_img1.cols/2., d_img1.rows/2.);
cv::Mat rot_mat = cv::getRotationMatrix2D(pt, 45, 1.0);
cv::cuda::warpAffine(d_img1, d_result2, rot_mat, cv::Size(d_img1.cols,
d_img1.rows));
cv::Mat h_result1,h_result2;
d_result1.download(h_result1);
d_result2.download(h_result2);
cv::imshow("Original Image ", h_img1);
cv::imshow("Translated Image", h_result1);
cv::imshow("Rotated Image", h_result2);
cv::waitKey();
return 0;
}
```

A translation matrix needs to be created, which specifies the image translation in horizontal and vertical directions. It is a 2 x 3 matrix as shown here:

$$\begin{bmatrix} 1 & 0 & tx \\ 0 & 1 & ty \end{bmatrix}$$

`tx` and `ty` are translation offset in the x and y directions. In the code, this matrix is created using the `Mat` object with 70 as an offsets in the X-direction and 50 as an offset in the Y-direction. This matrix is passed as an argument to the `warpAffine` function for Image translation. The other arguments for the `warpAffine` function are the source image, destination image, and size of the output image respectively.

A rotation matrix should be created for Image rotation at a particular degree centered at a particular point. OpenCV provides the `cv::getRotationMatrix2D` function to construct this rotation matrix. It needs three arguments. The first argument is the point for rotation; the center of the image is used for this. The second argument is the angle of rotation in degrees, which is specified as 45 degrees. The last argument is the scale, which is specified as 1. The constructed rotation matrix is again passed as an argument to the `warpAffine` function for Image rotation.

The output of the Image translation and Image rotation code is as follows:

To summarize, this section described various geometric transformations such as Image resizing, image translation, and Image rotation using OpenCV and CUDA.

Filtering operations on images

The methods described till this point worked on a single pixel intensity, and are called point processing methods. Sometimes it is helpful to look at the neighborhood of a pixel rather than only single pixel intensity. This are called neighborhood processing techniques. The neighborhood can be 3 x 3, 5 x 5, 7 x 7, and so on and are matrix-centered at a particular pixel. Image filtering is an important neighborhood processing technique.

Filtering is an important concept in signal processing where we reject a certain band of frequencies and allow a certain band of frequency to pass. How is frequency measured in images? If gray levels change slowly over a region, then it is a low-frequency region. If gray levels changes drastically, then it is a high-frequency region. Normally the background of an image is considered a low-frequency region and the edges are high-frequency regions. Convolution is a very important mathematical concept for neighborhood processing and Image filtering in particular. It is explained in the following section.

Convolution operations on an image

The basic idea of convolutions evolved from a similar idea in biology called receptive fields, where it is sensitive to some parts in an image and insensitive to other parts. It can be mathematically represented as the following:

$$g(x,y) = f(x,y)*h(x,y) = \sum\sum f(n,m)h(x-n,y-m)$$

In simplified form, this equation is a dot product between a filter, *h*, and a sub-image of the image, *f*, centered around the *(x,y)* point. The answer to this product is equal to the *(x,y)* point in the image, *g*. To illustrate the working of the convolution operation on an image, an example of a 3 x 3 filter applied to an image of a size of 6 x 6 is shown in the following diagram:

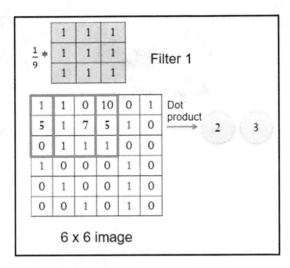

A dot product is taken between the leftmost window shown in red with the filter to find a point in the destination image. The answer of the dot product will be *2 ((1*1 + 1*1 + 1*0 + 1*5 + 1*1 +1*7 +1*0 +1*1 + 1*1)/9)*. The same operation is repeated after moving this window by 1 pixel to the right and answer the will be *3*. This is repeated for all windows in an image to construct the destination image. Different low pass and high-pass filters can be constructed by changing the values of the 3 x 3 filter matrix. This is explained in the next two sections.

Low pass filtering on an image

A low pass filter removes high-frequency content from an Image. Generally, noise is considered high-frequency content so a low pass filter removes noise from an image. There are many types of noise, such as Gaussian noise, uniform noise, exponential noise, and salt-and-pepper noise, which can effect an image. Low pass filters are used to eliminate this kind of noise. There are many types of low pass filters available:

- Averaging or box filters
- Gaussian filters

- Median filters

These filters and implementation of them using OpenCV is explained in this section.

Averaging filters

An averaging filters as the name suggests, performs averaging operations on neighborhood pixels. If a Gaussian noise is present in an image then the low pass averaging filter can be used to remove the noise. It will also blur the edges of an Image, because of the averaging operation. The neighborhood can be 3 x 3, 5 x 5, 7 x 7, and so on. The bigger the size of the filter window, the more blurring of the image will take place. The 3 x 3 and 5 x 5 averaging mask is as follows:

$$
\text{Averaging Filter 3x3} \qquad \text{Averaging Filter 5x5}
$$

$$
\frac{1}{9} * \begin{bmatrix} 1 & 1 & 1 \\ 1 & 1 & 1 \\ 1 & 1 & 1 \end{bmatrix} \qquad \frac{1}{25} * \begin{bmatrix} 1 & 1 & 1 & 1 & 1 \\ 1 & 1 & 1 & 1 & 1 \\ 1 & 1 & 1 & 1 & 1 \\ 1 & 1 & 1 & 1 & 1 \\ 1 & 1 & 1 & 1 & 1 \end{bmatrix}
$$

OpenCV provides a simple interface to apply many kinds of filters on an image. The code to apply an averaging filter with a different mask is as follows:

```
#include <iostream>
#include "opencv2/opencv.hpp"
int main ()
{
    cv::Mat h_img1 = cv::imread("images/cameraman.tif",0);
    cv::cuda::GpuMat d_img1,d_result3x3,d_result5x5,d_result7x7;
    d_img1.upload(h_img1);
    cv::Ptr<cv::cuda::Filter> filter3x3,filter5x5,filter7x7;
    filter3x3 = cv::cuda::createBoxFilter(CV_8UC1,CV_8UC1,cv::Size(3,3));
    filter3x3->apply(d_img1, d_result3x3);
    filter5x5 = cv::cuda::createBoxFilter(CV_8UC1,CV_8UC1,cv::Size(5,5));
    filter5x5->apply(d_img1, d_result5x5);
    filter7x7 = cv::cuda::createBoxFilter(CV_8UC1,CV_8UC1,cv::Size(7,7));
    filter7x7->apply(d_img1, d_result7x7);

    cv::Mat h_result3x3,h_result5x5,h_result7x7;
    d_result3x3.download(h_result3x3);
    d_result5x5.download(h_result5x5);
    d_result7x7.download(h_result7x7);
    cv::imshow("Original Image ", h_img1);
    cv::imshow("Blurred with kernel size 3x3", h_result3x3);
    cv::imshow("Blurred with kernel size 5x5", h_result5x5);
```

```
      cv::imshow("Blurred with kernel size 7x7", h_result7x7);
      cv::waitKey();
      return 0;
}
```

cv::Ptr, which is a template class for smart pointers, is used to store a filter of the cv::cuda::Filter type. Then, the createBoxFilter function is used to create an averaging filter of different window sizes. It requires three mandatory and three optional arguments. The first and second arguments are datatypes for the source and destination images. They are taken as CV_8UC1, which indicates an 8-bit unsigned grayscale image. The third argument defines the size of the filter window. It can be 3 x 3, 5 x 5, 7 x 7, and so on. The fourth argument is the anchor point, which has a default value of (-1,-1) which indicates the anchor is at the center point of the kernel. The final two optional arguments are related to the pixel interpolation method and border value, which are omitted here.

The created filter pointer has an apply method, which is used to apply the created filter on any image. It has three arguments. The first argument is the source image, the second argument is the destination image, and the third optional argument is, CUDA stream, which is used for multitasking, as explained earlier in this book. In the code, three averaging filters of different sizes are applied on an Image. The result is as follows:

As can be seen from the output, as the size of the filter increases, more pixels are used for averaging, which introduces more blurring on an image. Though a large filter will eliminate more noise.

Gaussian filters

A Gaussian filter uses a mask that has a Gaussian distribution to filter an Image instead of a simple averaging mask. This filter also introduces smooth blurring on an Image and is widely used to eliminate noise from an image. A 5 x 5 Gaussian filter with an approximate standard deviation of 1 is as follows:

$$\text{Gaussian Filter 5x5}$$

$$\frac{1}{273} * \begin{bmatrix} 1 & 4 & 7 & 4 & 1 \\ 4 & 16 & 26 & 16 & 4 \\ 7 & 26 & 41 & 26 & 7 \\ 4 & 16 & 26 & 16 & 4 \\ 1 & 4 & 7 & 4 & 1 \end{bmatrix}$$

OpenCV provides a function to implement the Gaussian filter. The code for it is as follows:

```cpp
#include <iostream>
#include "opencv2/opencv.hpp"

int main ()
{
  cv::Mat h_img1 = cv::imread("images/cameraman.tif",0);
  cv::cuda::GpuMat d_img1,d_result3x3,d_result5x5,d_result7x7;
  d_img1.upload(h_img1);
  cv::Ptr<cv::cuda::Filter> filter3x3,filter5x5,filter7x7;
  filter3x3 =
cv::cuda::createGaussianFilter(CV_8UC1,CV_8UC1,cv::Size(3,3),1);
  filter3x3->apply(d_img1, d_result3x3);
  filter5x5 =
cv::cuda::createGaussianFilter(CV_8UC1,CV_8UC1,cv::Size(5,5),1);
  filter5x5->apply(d_img1, d_result5x5);
  filter7x7 =
cv::cuda::createGaussianFilter(CV_8UC1,CV_8UC1,cv::Size(7,7),1);
  filter7x7->apply(d_img1, d_result7x7);

  cv::Mat h_result3x3,h_result5x5,h_result7x7;
  d_result3x3.download(h_result3x3);
  d_result5x5.download(h_result5x5);
  d_result7x7.download(h_result7x7);
  cv::imshow("Original Image ", h_img1);
```

```
    cv::imshow("Blurred with kernel size 3x3", h_result3x3);
    cv::imshow("Blurred with kernel size 5x5", h_result5x5);
    cv::imshow("Blurred with kernel size 7x7", h_result7x7);
    cv::waitKey();
    return 0;
}
```

The createGaussianFilter function is used to create a mask for the Gaussian filter. The datatype of the source and destination images, size of the filter, and standard deviation in the horizontal direction are provided as arguments to the function. We can also provide a standard deviation in the vertical direction as an argument; if it is not provided, then its default value is equal to standard deviation in the horizontal direction. The created Gaussian mask of a different size is applied to the image using an apply method. The output of the program is as follows:

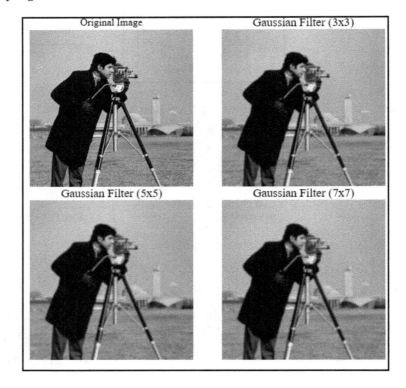

Again as the size of the Gaussian filter increases, more blurring is introduced in the image. The Gaussian filter is used to eliminate noise and introduce smooth blurring on an image.

Median filtering

When an image is affected by salt and pepper noise, it will not be eliminated by the averaging or Gaussian filter. It needs a nonlinear filter. Median operations on a neighborhood instead of averaging can help in eliminating salt and pepper noise. In this filter, the median of 9-pixel values in the neighborhood is placed at the center pixel. It will eliminate extreme high or low values introduced by salt and pepper noise. Though OpenCV and CUDA provide a function for median filtering, it is slower than regular functions in OpenCV, so this function is used to implement median filter as shown in the following code:

```
#include <iostream>
#include "opencv2/opencv.hpp"

int main ()
{
  cv::Mat h_img1 = cv::imread("images/saltpepper.png",0);
  cv::Mat h_result;
  cv::medianBlur(h_img1,h_result,3);
  cv::imshow("Original Image ", h_img1);
  cv::imshow("Median Blur Result", h_result);
  cv::waitKey();
  return 0;
}
```

The `medianBlur` function in OpenCV is used to implement a median filter. It needs three arguments. The first argument is the source image, the second argument is the destination image, and the third argument is the window size for the median operation. The output of the median filtering is as follows:

The source image is affected by salt and pepper noise, as can be seen in the screenshot. This noise is eliminated completely by the median filter of a size of 3x3 without introducing extreme blurring. So median filtering is a very important preprocessing step when images applications are affected by salt and pepper noise.

To summarize, we have seen three types of low pass filter, which are widely used in various computer vision applications. Averaging and Gaussian filters are used to eliminate Gaussian noise, but they will also blur the edges of an Image. A median filter is used to remove salt-and-pepper noise.

High-pass filtering on an image

High-pass filters remove low-frequency components from images and enhance high-frequency components. So, when a high-pass filter is applied to an Image, it will remove the background, as it is a low-frequency region, and enhances the edges, which are high-frequency components. So, high-pass filters can also be called edge detectors. The coefficients of the filter will change, otherwise it is similar to the filters seen in the last section. There are many high-pass filters available such as following:

- Sobel filters
- Scharr filters
- Laplacian filters

We will see each one of them separately in this section.

Sobel filters

The Sobel operator or Sobel filter is a widely used image processing and computer vision algorithm for edge detection applications. It is a 3 x 3 filter that approximates the gradient of the image intensity function. It provides a separate filter to compute the gradient in a horizontal and vertical direction. The filter is convolved with the image in a similar way as described earlier in this chapter. The horizontal and vertical 3 x 3 Sobel filter is as follows:

$$Sx = \begin{bmatrix} 1 & 0 & -1 \\ 2 & 0 & -2 \\ 1 & 0 & -1 \end{bmatrix} \qquad Sy = \begin{bmatrix} 1 & 2 & 1 \\ 0 & 0 & 0 \\ -1 & -2 & -1 \end{bmatrix}$$

The code for implementing this Sobel filter is as follows:

```
#include <iostream>
#include "opencv2/opencv.hpp"

int main ()
{
  cv::Mat h_img1 = cv::imread("images/blobs.png",0);
  cv::cuda::GpuMat d_img1,d_resultx,d_resulty,d_resultxy;
  d_img1.upload(h_img1);
  cv::Ptr<cv::cuda::Filter> filterx,filtery,filterxy;
  filterx = cv::cuda::createSobelFilter(CV_8UC1,CV_8UC1,1,0);
  filterx->apply(d_img1, d_resultx);
  filtery = cv::cuda::createSobelFilter(CV_8UC1,CV_8UC1,0,1);
  filtery->apply(d_img1, d_resulty);
  cv::cuda::add(d_resultx,d_resulty,d_resultxy);
  cv::Mat h_resultx,h_resulty,h_resultxy;
  d_resultx.download(h_resultx);
  d_resulty.download(h_resulty);
  d_resultxy.download(h_resultxy);
  cv::imshow("Original Image ", h_img1);
  cv::imshow("Sobel-x derivative", h_resultx);
  cv::imshow("Sobel-y derivative", h_resulty);
  cv::imshow("Sobel-xy derivative", h_resultxy);
  cv::waitKey();
  return 0;
}
```

OpenCV provides the `createSobelFilter` function for implementing a Sobel filter. It requires many arguments. The first two arguments are data types of the source and destination images. The third and fourth arguments are the order of the x and y derivatives respectively. For computing the x derivative or vertical edges, 1 and 0 are provided, and for computing the y derivative or horizontal edges, 0 and 1 are provided. The fifth argument which indicates the size of the kernel, is optional. The default value is 3. The scale for derivatives can also be provided.

To see both horizontal and vertical edges simultaneously, the result of the x-derivative and the y-derivative are summed. The result is as follows:

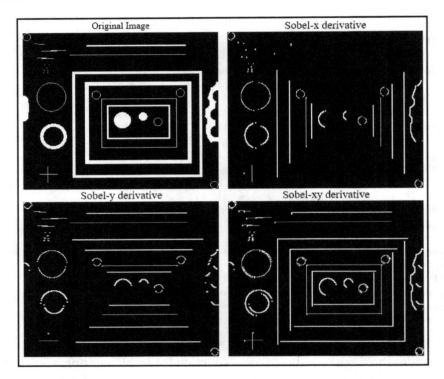

The Sobel operator provides a very inaccurate approximation of derivative but still, it is quite useful in computer vision applications for edge detection. It does not have rotation symmetry; to overcome that, the Scharr operator is used.

Scharr filters

As Sobel does not provide rotation symmetry, a Scharr operator is used to overcome that by using different filter masks as follows:

$$Sx = \begin{bmatrix} 3 & 0 & -3 \\ 10 & 0 & -10 \\ 3 & 0 & -3 \end{bmatrix} \qquad Sy = \begin{bmatrix} 3 & 10 & 3 \\ 0 & 0 & 0 \\ -3 & -10 & -3 \end{bmatrix}$$

As can be seen from the mask, the Scharr operator gives more weight to central rows or central columns to find edges. The program to implement a Scharr filter is as follows:

```
#include <iostream>
#include "opencv2/opencv.hpp"
int main ()
{
    cv::Mat h_img1 = cv::imread("images/blobs.png",0);
    cv::cuda::GpuMat d_img1,d_resultx,d_resulty,d_resultxy;
    d_img1.upload(h_img1);
    cv::Ptr<cv::cuda::Filter> filterx,filtery;
    filterx = cv::cuda::createScharrFilter(CV_8UC1,CV_8UC1,1,0);
    filterx->apply(d_img1, d_resultx);
    filtery = cv::cuda::createScharrFilter(CV_8UC1,CV_8UC1,0,1);
    filtery->apply(d_img1, d_resulty);
    cv::cuda::add(d_resultx,d_resulty,d_resultxy);
    cv::Mat h_resultx,h_resulty,h_resultxy;
    d_resultx.download(h_resultx);
    d_resulty.download(h_resulty);
    d_resultxy.download(h_resultxy);
    cv::imshow("Original Image ", h_img1);
    cv::imshow("Scharr-x derivative", h_resultx);
    cv::imshow("Scharr-y derivative", h_resulty);
    cv::imshow("Scharr-xy derivative", h_resultxy);
    cv::waitKey();
        return 0;
}
```

OpenCV provides the `createScharrFilter` function for implementing the Scharr filter. It requires many arguments. The first two arguments are datatypes of the source and destination images. The third and fourth arguments are the order of the x and y derivatives respectively. For computing the x derivative or vertical edges, 1 and 0 are provided, and for computing the y derivative or horizontal edges, 0 and 1 are provided. The fifth argument, which indicate the size of the kernel, is optional. The default value is 3.

To see both horizontal and vertical edges simultaneously, the result of the x-derivative and the y-derivative are summed. The result is as follows:

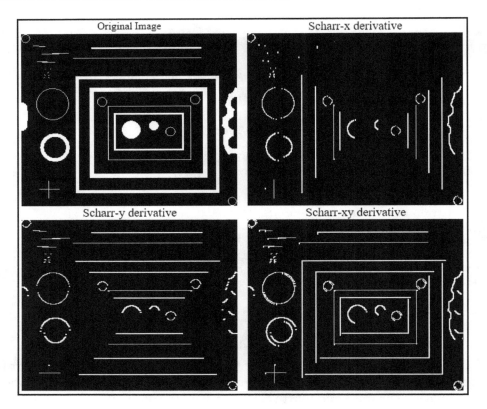

Laplacian filters

The Laplacian filters is also a derivative operator to find out edges in an Image. The difference is that Sobel and Scharr are first-order derivative operators, while Laplacian is a second-order derivative operator. It also finds out edges in both horizontal and vertical directions simultaneously, which is different than Sobel and Scharr operators. The Laplacian filter is computes the second derivative, so it is very sensitive to noise in an image, it is desirable to blur the image and remove noise before applying the Laplacian filter. The code for implementing a Laplacian filter is as follows:

```
#include <iostream>
#include "opencv2/opencv.hpp"

int main ()
```

```
{
  cv::Mat h_img1 = cv::imread("images/blobs.png",0);
  cv::cuda::GpuMat d_img1,d_result1,d_result3;
  d_img1.upload(h_img1);
  cv::Ptr<cv::cuda::Filter> filter1,filter3;
  filter1 = cv::cuda::createLaplacianFilter(CV_8UC1,CV_8UC1,1);
  filter1->apply(d_img1, d_result1);
  filter3 = cv::cuda::createLaplacianFilter(CV_8UC1,CV_8UC1,3);
  filter3->apply(d_img1, d_result3);
  cv::Mat h_result1,h_result3;
  d_result1.download(h_result1);
  d_result3.download(h_result3);
  cv::imshow("Original Image ", h_img1);
  cv::imshow("Laplacian filter 1", h_result1);
  cv::imshow("Laplacian filter 3", h_result3);
  cv::waitKey();
  return 0;
}
```

Two Laplacian filters with kernel sizes of 1 and 3 are applied on an image using the `createLaplacianFilter` function. Along with the size of the kernel, the function also requires datatypes of the source and destination images as arguments. The created Laplacian filter is applied to an image using the `apply` method. The output of the Laplacian filter is as follows:

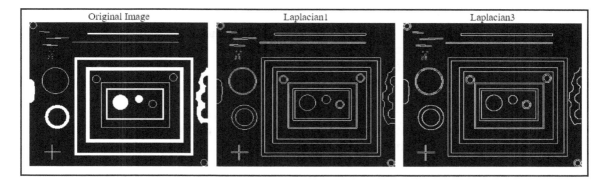

To summarize, in this section, we have described different high-pass filters such as Sobel, Scharr, and Laplacian filters. Sobel and Scharr are first-order derivative operators used to compute edges and they are less sensitive to noise. Laplacian is a second-order derivative operator used to compute edges and it is very sensitive to noise.

Morphological operations on images

Image morphology deals with the regions and shapes of an image. It is used to extract image components that are useful to represent shapes and regions. Image morphology treats the image as an ensemble of sets unlike, other Image processing operations seen earlier. The image interacts with a small template, which is called a structuring element, and which defines the region of interest or neighborhood in the image morphology. There are various morphological operations that can be performed on images, which are explained one by one in this section:

- **Erosion**: Erosion sets a center pixel to the minimum over all pixels in the neighborhood. The neighborhood is defined by the structuring element, which is a matrix of 1s and 0s. Erosion is used to enlarge holes in the object, shrink the boundary, eliminate the island, and get rid of narrow peninsulas that might exist on the image boundary.

- **Dilation**: Dilation sets a center pixel to the maximum over all pixels in the neighborhood. The dilation increases the size of a white block and reduces the size of the black region. It is used to fill holes in the object and expand the boundary of the object.

- **Opening**: Image opening is basically a combination of erosion and dilation. Image opening is defined as erosion followed by dilation. Both operations are performed using the same structuring elements. It is used to smooth the contours of the image, break down narrow bridges and isolate objects that are touching one another. It is used in the analysis of wear particles in engine oils, ink particles in recycled paper, and so on.

- **Closing**: Image closing is defined as dilation followed by erosion. Both operations are performed using the same structuring elements. It is used to fuse narrow breaks and eliminate small holes.

The morphological operators can be easily understood by applying them on binary images that only contain black and white. OpenCV and CUDA provide an easy API to apply a morphological transformation on images. The code for it is as follows:

```
#include <iostream>
#include "opencv2/opencv.hpp"
int main ()
{
  cv::Mat h_img1 = cv::imread("images/blobs.png",0);
  cv::cuda::GpuMat d_img1,d_resulte,d_resultd,d_resulto, d_resultc;
  cv::Mat element =
cv::getStructuringElement(cv::MORPH_RECT,cv::Size(5,5));
  d_img1.upload(h_img1);
  cv::Ptr<cv::cuda::Filter> filtere,filterd,filtero,filterc;
```

```
    filtere =
cv::cuda::createMorphologyFilter(cv::MORPH_ERODE,CV_8UC1,element);
    filtere->apply(d_img1, d_resulte);
    filterd =
cv::cuda::createMorphologyFilter(cv::MORPH_DILATE,CV_8UC1,element);
    filterd->apply(d_img1, d_resultd);
    filtero =
cv::cuda::createMorphologyFilter(cv::MORPH_OPEN,CV_8UC1,element);
    filtero->apply(d_img1, d_resulto);
    filterc =
cv::cuda::createMorphologyFilter(cv::MORPH_CLOSE,CV_8UC1,element);
    filterc->apply(d_img1, d_resultc);
    cv::Mat h_resulte,h_resultd,h_resulto,h_resultc;
    d_resulte.download(h_resulte);
    d_resultd.download(h_resultd);
    d_resulto.download(h_resulto);
    d_resultc.download(h_resultc);
    cv::imshow("Original Image ", h_img1);
    cv::imshow("Erosion", h_resulte);
    cv::imshow("Dilation", h_resultd);
    cv::imshow("Opening", h_resulto);
    cv::imshow("closing", h_resultc);
    cv::waitKey();
    return 0;
}
```

A structuring element that defines the neighborhood for the morphological operation needs to be created first. This can be done by using the getStructuringElement function in OpenCV. The shape and size of the structuring element need to be provided as an argument to this function. In the code, a rectangular structuring element of a size of 5 x 5 is defined.

The filter for morphological operations is created using the createMorphologyFilter function. It needs three mandatory arguments. The first argument defines the operation to be performed. cv::MORPH_ERODE is used for erosion, cv::MORPH_DILATE for dilation, cv::MORPH_OPEN for opening, and cv::MORPH_CLOSE for closing. The second argument is the datatype of an image, and the third argument is the structuring element created earlier. The apply method is used to apply these filters on an image.

The output of morphological operations on an image is as follows:

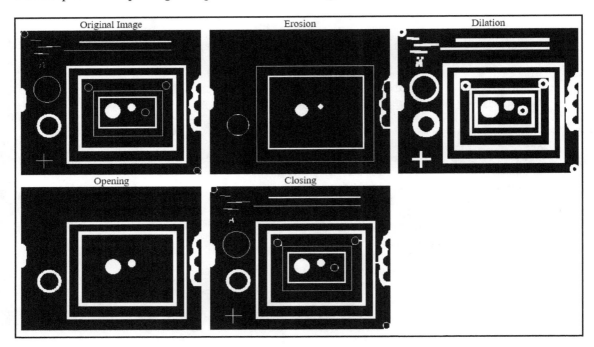

As can be seen from the output, erosion reduces the boundary of an object while dilation thickens it. We consider the white part an object and the black part is the background. Opening smooths the contours of the image. Closing eliminates small holes in an image. If the size of the structuring element is increased to 7 x 7 from 5 x 5, then the erosion of the boundary will be more pronounced in an erosion operation and the boundary will get thicker in a dilation operation. The small circles on the left side, which were visible in an eroded image of 5 x 5, are removed when it is eroded with a size of 7 x 7.

The output of morphological operations using a 7 x 7 structuring element is as follows:

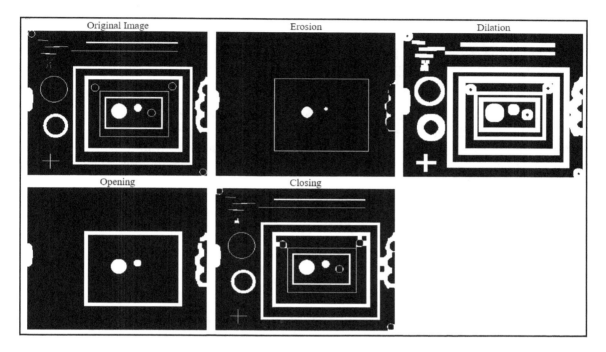

To summarize, morphological operations are important to find out components used to define the shape and regions of an image. It can be used to fill holes in an image and smoothen the contours of an image.

Summary

This chapter described the method to access pixel intensities at a particular location in an image. It is very useful when we are performing a pointwise operation on an image. A histogram is a very important global feature used to describe an image. This chapter described the method to compute a histogram and the process of histogram equalization, which improves the visual quality of an image. Various geometric transformations such as image resizing, rotation, and translation were explained in detail. Image filtering is a useful neighborhood processing technique used to eliminate noise and extract edge features of an image and was described in detail. A low pass filter is used to remove noise but it will also blur out the edges of an image. A high-pass filter removes the background, which is a low-frequency region while enhancing edges, which are high-frequency regions. The last part of this chapter described different morphological operations such as erosion, dilation, opening, and closing, which can be used to describe the shape of an image and fill holes in an image. In the next chapter, we will use these concepts to build some useful computer vision applications using OpenCV and CUDA.

Questions

1. Write an OpenCV function to print pixel intensity at the location (200,200) of any color image on the console.
2. Write an OpenCV function to resize an image to (300,200) pixels. Use the bilinear interpolation method.
3. Write an OpenCV function to upsample an Image by 2. Use the area interpolation method.
4. State true or false: blurring decreases as we increase the size of the averaging filter.
5. State true or false: median filters can remove gaussian noise.
6. What steps can be taken to reduce noise sensitivity of Laplacian operator?
7. Write an OpenCV function to implement top hat and black hat morphological operation.

Object Detection and Tracking Using OpenCV and CUDA

The last chapter described basic computer vision operations using OpenCV and CUDA. In this chapter, we will see how to use these basic operations along with OpenCV and CUDA to develop complex computer vision applications. We will use the example of object detection and tracking to demonstrate this concept. Object detection and tracking is a very active area of research in computer vision. It deals with identifying the location of an object in an image and tracking it in a sequence of frames. Many algorithms are proposed for this task based on color, shape, and the other salient features of an image. In this chapter, these algorithms are implemented using OpenCV and CUDA. We start with an explanation of detecting an object based on color, then describe the methods to detect an object with a particular shape. All objects have salient features that can be used to detect and track objects. This chapter describes the implementation of different feature detection algorithms and how they can be used to detect objects. The last part of the chapter will demonstrate the use of a background subtraction technique that separates the foreground from the background for object detection and tracking.

The following topics will be covered in this chapter:

- Introduction to object detection and tracking
- Object detection and tracking based on color
- Object detection and tracking based on a shape
- Feature-based object detection
- Object detection using Haar cascade
- Background subtraction methods

Technical requirements

This chapter requires a good understanding of image processing and computer vision. It also requires some basic knowledge of algorithms used for object detection and tracking. It needs familiarity with the basic C or C++ programming language, CUDA, and all the codes explained in previous chapters. All the code used in this chapter can be downloaded from the following GitHub link: `https://github.com/PacktPublishing/Hands-On-GPU-Accelerated-Computer-Vision-with-OpenCV-and-CUDA`. The code can be executed on any operating system, though it has only been tested on Ubuntu 16.04.

Check out the following video to see the code in action:
`http://bit.ly/2PSRqkU`

Introduction to object detection and tracking

Object detection and tracking is an active research topic in the field of computer vision that makes efforts to detect, recognize, and track objects through a series of frames. It has been found that object detection and tracking in the video sequence is a challenging task and a very time-consuming process. Object detection is the first step in building a larger computer vision system. A large amount of information can be derived from the detected object, as follows:

- The detected object can be classified into a particular class
- It can be tracked in an image sequence
- More information about the scene or other object inferences can be derived from the detected object

Object tracking is defined as the task of detecting objects in every frame of the video and establishing the correspondence between the detected objects from one frame to the other.

Applications of object detection and tracking

Object detection and tracking can be used to develop video surveillance systems to track suspicious activities, events, and persons. It can be used for developing an intelligent traffic system to track vehicles and detect traffic rule violations. Object detection is essential in autonomous vehicles to give them information about the surroundings and planning for their navigation. It is also useful for pedestrian detection or vehicle detection in automatic driver assistance systems. It can be used in the medical field for applications like breast cancer detection or brain tumor detection and so on. It can be used for face and hand gesture recognition. It has a wide application in industrial assembly and quality control in production lines. It is vital for image retrieval from search engines and for photo management.

Challenges in object detection

Object detection is a challenging task because images in real life are affected by noise, illumination variation, dynamic backgrounds, shadowing effect, camera jitter, and motion blur. Object detection is difficult when an object to be detected is rotated, scaled, or under occlusion. Many applications require detecting more than one object class. If a large number of classes are being detected then the processing speed becomes an important issue along with the kinds of classes that the system can handle without accuracy loss.

There are many algorithms that overcome some of these challenges. They are discussed in this chapter. The chapter does not describe the algorithms in detail, but more focus is given on how it can be implemented using CUDA and OpenCV.

Object detection and tracking based on color

An object has many global features like color and shape, which describe the object as a whole. These features can be utilized for the detection of an object and tracking it in a sequence of frames. In this section, we will use color as a feature to detect an object with a particular color. This method is useful when an object to be detected is of a specific color and this color is different to the color of the background. If the object and background have the same color, then this method for detection will fail. In this section, we will try to detect any object with a blue color from a webcam stream using OpenCV and CUDA.

Blue object detection and tracking

The first question that should come to your mind is which color space should be used for segmenting blue color. A **Red Green Blue** (**RGB**) color space does not separate color information from intensity information. The color spaces that separate color information from intensity, like **Hue Saturation Value** (HSV) and **YCrCb** (where Y' is the luma component and CB and CR are the blue-difference and red-difference chroma components), are ideal for this kind of task. Every color has a specific range in the hue channel that can be utilized for detection of that color. The boilerplate code for starting the webcam, capturing frames, and uploading on-device memory for a GPU operation is as follows:

```cpp
#include <iostream>
#include "opencv2/opencv.hpp"

using namespace cv;
using namespace std;

int main()
{
  VideoCapture cap(0); //capture the video from web cam
  // if webcam is not available then exit the program
  if ( !cap.isOpened() )
  {
    cout << "Cannot open the web cam" << endl;
    return -1;
  }
  while (true)
  {
    Mat frame;
    // read a new frame from webcam
    bool flag = cap.read(frame);
    if (!flag)
    {
      cout << "Cannot read a frame from webcam" << endl;
      break;
    }
    cuda::GpuMat d_frame, d_frame_hsv,d_intermediate,d_result;
    cuda::GpuMat d_frame_shsv[3];
    cuda::GpuMat d_thresc[3];
    Mat h_result;
    d_frame.upload(frame);

    d_result.download(h_result);
    imshow("Thresholded Image", h_result);
    imshow("Original", frame);

    if (waitKey(1) == 'q')
```

```
    {
      break;
    }
  }
  return 0;
}
}
```

To detect the blue color, we need to find a range for blue color in the HSV color space. If a range is accurate then the detection will be accurate. The range of blue color for three channels, hue, saturation, and value, is as follows:

```
lower_range = [110,50,50]
upper_range = [130,255,255]
```

This range will be used to threshold an image in a particular channel to create a mask for the blue color. If this mask is again ANDed with the original frame, then only a blue object will be there in the resultant image. The code for this is as follows:

```
//Transform image to HSV
cuda::cvtColor(d_frame, d_frame_hsv, COLOR_BGR2HSV);

//Split HSV 3 channels
cuda::split(d_frame_hsv, d_frame_shsv);

//Threshold HSV channels for blue color according to range
cuda::threshold(d_frame_shsv[0], d_thresc[0], 110, 130, THRESH_BINARY);
cuda::threshold(d_frame_shsv[1], d_thresc[1], 50, 255, THRESH_BINARY);
cuda::threshold(d_frame_shsv[2], d_thresc[2], 50, 255, THRESH_BINARY);

//Bitwise AND the channels
cv::cuda::bitwise_and(d_thresc[0], d_thresc[1],d_intermediate);
cv::cuda::bitwise_and(d_intermediate, d_thresc[2], d_result);
```

The frame from the webcam is converted to an HSV color space. The blue color has a different range in three channels, so each channel has to be thresholded individually. The channels are split using the split method and thresholded using the threshold function. The minimum and maximum ranges for each channel are used as lower and upper thresholds. The channel value inside this range will be converted to white and others are converted to black. These three thresholded channels are logically ANDed to get a final mask for a blue color. This mask can be used to detect and track an object with a blue color from a video.

The output of two frames, one without the blue object and the other with the blue object, is as follows:

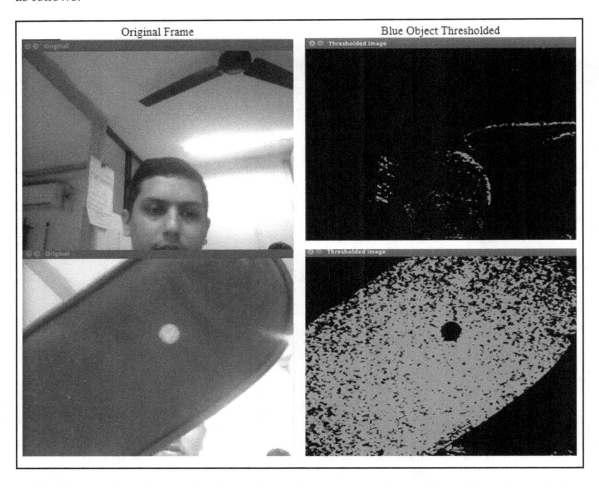

As can be seen from the result, when a frame does not contain any blue object, the mask is almost black; whereas in the frame below, when the blue object comes into frame, that part turns white. This method will only work when the background does not contain the color of an object.

Object detection and tracking based on shape

The shape of an object can also be utilized as a global feature to detect an object with a distinct shape. This shape can be a straight line, polygons, circles, or any other irregular shapes. Object boundaries, edges, and contours can be utilized to detect an object with a particular shape. In this section, we will use the Canny edge detection algorithm and Hough transform to detect two regular shapes, which are a line and a circle.

Canny edge detection

In the last chapter, we saw various high pass filters, which can be used as edge detectors. In this section, the Canny edge detection algorithm, which combines Gaussian filtering, gradient finding, non-maximum suppression, and hysteresis thresholding, is implemented using OpenCV and CUDA. High pass filters, as explained in the last chapter, are very sensitive to noise. In Canny edge detection, Gaussian smoothing is done before detecting edges, which makes it less sensitive to noises. It also has a non-maximum suppression stage after detecting edges to remove unnecessary edges from the result.

Canny edge detection is a computationally intensive task, which is hard to use in real-time applications. The CUDA version of the algorithm can be used to accelerate it. The code for implementing a Canny edge detection algorithm is described below:

```cpp
#include <cmath>
#include <iostream>
#include "opencv2/opencv.hpp"

using namespace std;
using namespace cv;
using namespace cv::cuda;


int main()
{
  Mat h_image = imread("images/drawing.JPG",0);
  if (h_image.empty())
  {
    cout << "can not open image"<< endl;
    return -1;
  }
  GpuMat d_edge,d_image;
  Mat h_edge;
  d_image.upload(h_image);
```

```
cv::Ptr<cv::cuda::CannyEdgeDetector> Canny_edge =
cv::cuda::createCannyEdgeDetector(2.0, 100.0, 3, false);
Canny_edge->detect(d_image, d_edge);
d_edge.download(h_edge);
imshow("source", h_image);
imshow("detected edges", h_edge);
waitKey(0);

return 0;
}
```

OpenCV and CUDA provides the `createCannyEdgeDetector` class for Canny edge detection. The object of this class is created, and many arguments can be passed while creating it. The first and second arguments are the low and high thresholds for hysteresis thresholding. If the intensity gradient at a point is greater then the maximum threshold, then it is categorized as an edge point. If the gradient is less than the low threshold, then the point is not an edge point. If the gradient is in between thresholds, then whether the point is an edge or not is decided based on connectivity. The third argument is the aperture size for the edge detector. The final argument is the Boolean argument, which indicates whether to use `L2_norm` or `L1_norm` for gradient magnitude calculation. `L2_norm` is computationally expensive but it is more accurate. The true value indicates the use of `L2_norm`. The output of the code is shown below:

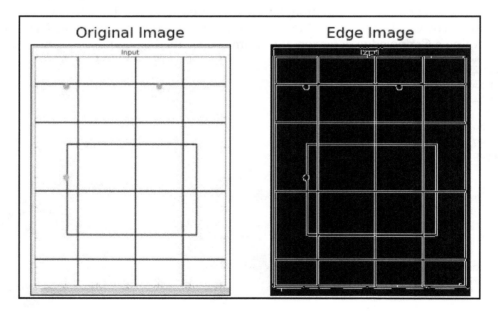

You can play around with the values of the lower and upper thresholds to detect edges more accurately for a given image. Edge detection is a very important preprocessing step for many computer vision applications and Canny edge detection is widely used for that.

Straight line detection using Hough transform

The detection of straight lines is important in many computer vision applications, like lane detection. It can also be used to detect lines that are part of other regular shapes. Hough transform is a popular feature extraction technique used in computer vision to detect straight lines. We will not go into detail about how Hough transform detects lines, but we will see how it can be implemented in OpenCV and CUDA. The code for implementing Hough transform for line detection is as follows:

```
#include <cmath>
#include <iostream>
#include "opencv2/opencv.hpp"

using namespace std;
using namespace cv;
using namespace cv::cuda;


int main()
{
  Mat h_image = imread("images/drawing.JPG",0);
  if (h_image.empty())
  {
    cout << "can not open image"<< endl;
    return -1;
  }

  Mat h_edge;
  cv::Canny(h_image, h_edge, 100, 200, 3);

  Mat h_imagec;
  cv::cvtColor(h_edge, h_imagec, COLOR_GRAY2BGR);
  Mat h_imageg = h_imagec.clone();
  GpuMat d_edge, d_lines;
  d_edge.upload(h_edge);
  {
    const int64 start = getTickCount();
    Ptr<cuda::HoughSegmentDetector> hough =
cuda::createHoughSegmentDetector(1.0f, (float) (CV_PI / 180.0f), 50, 5);
    hough->detect(d_edge, d_lines);
```

```
        const double time_elapsed = (getTickCount() - start) /
    getTickFrequency();
        cout << "GPU Time : " << time_elapsed * 1000 << " ms" << endl;
        cout << "GPU FPS : " << (1/time_elapsed) << endl;
    }
    vector<Vec4i> lines_g;
    if (!d_lines.empty())
    {
        lines_g.resize(d_lines.cols);
        Mat h_lines(1, d_lines.cols, CV_32SC4, &lines_g[0]);
        d_lines.download(h_lines);
    }
    for (size_t i = 0; i < lines_g.size(); ++i)
    {
        Vec4i line_point = lines_g[i];
        line(h_imageg, Point(line_point[0], line_point[1]),
    Point(line_point[2], line_point[3]), Scalar(0, 0, 255), 2, LINE_AA);
    }

    imshow("source", h_image);
    imshow("detected lines [GPU]", h_imageg);
    waitKey(0);
    return 0;
}
```

OpenCV provides the `createHoughSegmentDetector` class for implementing Hough transform. It needs an edge map of an image as input. So edges are detected from an image using a Canny edge detector. The output of the Canny edge detector is uploaded to the device memory for GPU computation. The edges can also be computed on GPU as discussed in the last section.

The object of `createHoughSegmentDetector` is created. It requires many arguments. The first argument indicates the resolution of parameter r used in Hough transform, which is taken as 1 pixel normally. The second argument is the resolution of parameter theta in radians, which is taken as 1 radian or pi/180. The third argument is the minimum number of points that are needed to form a line, which is taken as 50 pixels. The final argument is the maximum gap between two points to be considered as the same line, which is taken as 5 pixels.

The detect method of the created object is used to detect straight lines. It needs two arguments. The first argument is the image on which the edges are to be detected, and the second argument is the array in which detected line points will be stored. The array contains the starting and ending (x,y) points of the detected lines. This array is iterated using the `for` loop to draw individual lines on an image using the line function from OpenCV. The final image is displayed using the `imshow` function.

Hough transform is a mathematically intensive step. Just to show an advantage of CUDA, we will implement the same algorithm for CPU and compare the performance of it with a CUDA implementation. The CPU code for Hough transform is as follows:

```
Mat h_imagec;
vector<Vec4i> h_lines;
{
  const int64 start = getTickCount();
  HoughLinesP(h_edge, h_lines, 1, CV_PI / 180, 50, 60, 5);
  const double time_elapsed = (getTickCount() - start) /
getTickFrequency();
  cout << "CPU Time : " << time_elapsed * 1000 << " ms" << endl;
  cout << "CPU FPS : " << (1/time_elapsed) << endl;
}

for (size_t i = 0; i < h_lines.size(); ++i)
{
  Vec4i line_point = h_lines[i];
  line(h_imagec, Point(line_point[0], line_point[1]), Point(line_point[2],
line_point[3]), Scalar(0, 0, 255), 2, LINE_AA);
}
imshow("detected lines [CPU]", h_imagec);
```

The `HoughLinesP` function is used for detecting lines on a CPU using probabilistic Hough transform. The first two arguments are the source image and the array to store output line points. The third and fourth arguments are a resolution for r and theta. The fifth argument is the threshold that indicates the minimum number of intersection points for a line. The sixth argument indicates the minimum number of points needed to form a line. The last argument indicates the maximum gap between points to be considered on the same line.

The array returned by the function is iterated using the `for` loop for displaying detected lines on the original image. The output for both the GPU and CPU function is as follows:

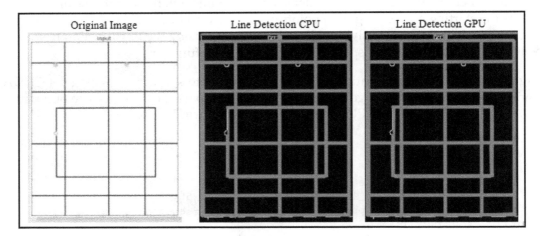

The comparison between the performance of the GPU and CPU code for the Hough transform is shown in the following screenshot:

```
bhaumik@bhaumik-Lenovo-ideapad-520-15IKB:~/Desktop/opencv/chapter 7$ ./hough_lin
e
CPU Time : 4.01799 ms
CPU FPS : 248.88
GPU Time : 1.5828 ms
GPU FPS : 631.791
```

It takes around 4 ms for a single image to process on the CPU and 1.5 ms on the GPU, which is equivalent to 248 FPS on the CPU, and 632 FPS on the GPU, which is almost 2.5 times an improvement on the GPU.

Circle detection

Hough transform can also be used for circle detection. It can be used in many applications, like ball detection and tracking and coin detection, and so on, where objects are circular. OpenCV and CUDA provide a class to implement this. The code for coin detection using Hough transform is as follows:

```
#include "opencv2/opencv.hpp"
#include <iostream>

using namespace cv;
using namespace std;

int main(int argc, char** argv)
{
  Mat h_image = imread("images/eight.tif", IMREAD_COLOR);
  Mat h_gray;
  cvtColor(h_image, h_gray, COLOR_BGR2GRAY);
  cuda::GpuMat d_gray,d_result;
  std::vector<cv::Vec3f> d_Circles;
cv::Ptr<cv::cuda::HoughCirclesDetector> detector =
cv::cuda::createHoughCirclesDetector(1, 100, 122, 50, 1,
max(h_image.size().width, h_image.size().height));
  d_gray.upload(h_gray);
  detector->detect(d_gray, d_result);
  d_Circles.resize(d_result.size().width);
  if (!d_Circles.empty())
    d_result.row(0).download(cv::Mat(d_Circles).reshape(3, 1));

  cout<<"No of circles: " <<d_Circles.size() <<endl;
  for( size_t i = 0; i < d_Circles.size(); i++ )
  {
    Vec3i cir = d_Circles[i];
    circle( h_image, Point(cir[0], cir[1]), cir[2], Scalar(255,0,0), 2,
LINE_AA);
  }
  imshow("detected circles", h_image);
  waitKey(0);

  return 0;
}
```

There is a `createHoughCirclesDetector` class for detecting the circular object. The object of that class is created. Many arguments can be provided while creating an object of this class. The first argument is `dp` that signifies an inverse ratio of the accumulator resolution to the image resolution, which is mostly taken as 1. The second argument is the minimum distance between the centers of the detected circle. The third argument is a Canny threshold and the fourth argument is the accumulator threshold. The fifth and sixth arguments are the minimum and maximum radiuses of the circles to be detected.

The minimum distance between the centers of the circle is taken as `100` pixels. You can play around with this value. If this is decreased, then many circles are detected falsely on the original image, while if it is increased then some true circles may be missed. The last two arguments, which are the minimum and maximum radiuses, can be taken as 0 if you don't know the exact dimension. In the preceding code, it is taken as 1 and maximum dimension of an image to detect all circles in an image. The output of the program is as follows:

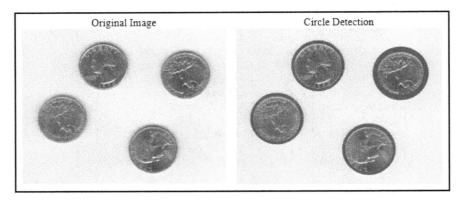

The Hough transform is very sensitive to Gaussian and salt-pepper noise. So, sometimes it is better to preprocess the image with Gaussian and median filters before applying Hough transform. It will give more accurate results.

To summarize, we have used the Hough line and circle transforms to detect objects with regular shapes. Contours and convexity can also be used for shape detection. The functions for this are available in OpenCV, but they are not available with CUDA implementation. You will have to develop your own versions of these functions.

Key-point detectors and descriptors

Till this point, we have used global features like color and shape to detect an object. These features are easy to compute, are quick, and require a small amount of memory, but they can only be used when some information regarding the object is already available. If that is not the case then local features are used, which require more computation and memory, but they are more accurate. In this section, various algorithms that find local features are explained. They are also called key point detectors. Key-points are the points that characterize the image and can be used to define an object accurately.

Features from Accelerated Segment Test (FAST) feature detector

The FAST algorithm is used to detect corner points as key-points from an image. It detects the corners by applying a segment test to every pixel. It considers a circle of 16 pixels around the pixel. If there are n continuous points in a circle of radius 16, which have the intensity of pixel greater than $Ip +t$ or less than $Ip- t$, then that pixel is considered a corner. Ip is intensity at pixel p, and t is the selected threshold.

Sometimes instead of checking all points in the radius, a few selected points are checked for intensity values to determine corner points. It accelerates the performance of the FAST algorithm. FAST provides corner points that can be utilized as key-points to detect an object. It is rotation-invariant, as corners of an object will remain the same even if the object is rotated. FAST is not scale-invariant, as the increase in dimension may result in a smooth transition of intensity values rather than a sharp transition at corners.

OpenCV and CUDA provide an efficient way of implementing the FAST algorithm. The program to detect key-points using the FAST algorithm is shown below:

```
#include <iostream>
#include "opencv2/opencv.hpp"

using namespace cv;
using namespace std;

int main()
{
  Mat h_image = imread( "images/drawing.JPG", 0 );

  //Detect the key-points using FAST Detector
  cv::Ptr<cv::cuda::FastFeatureDetector> detector =
cv::cuda::FastFeatureDetector::create(100,true,2);
```

```
std::vector<cv::key point> key-points;
cv::cuda::GpuMat d_image;
d_image.upload(h_image);
detector->detect(d_image, key-points);
cv::drawkey-points(h_image,key-points,h_image);
//Show detected key-points
imshow("Final Result", h_image );
waitKey(0);
return 0;
}
```

OpenCV and CUDA provide a `FastFeatureDetector` class for implementing the FAST algorithm. The object of this class is created using the create method of the class. It needs three arguments. The first argument is the intensity threshold to be used for the FAST algorithm. The second argument specifies whether to use non-maximum suppression or not. It is a Boolean value, which can be specified as `true` or `false`. The third argument indicates which FAST method is used for calculating the neighborhood. Three methods, `cv2.FAST_FEATURE_DETECTOR_TYPE_5_8`, `cv2.FAST_FEATURE_DETECTOR_TYPE_7_12`, and `cv2.FAST_FEATURE_DETECTOR_TYPE_9_16`, are available, which can be specified as flags 0, 1, or 2.

The detect method of the created object is used to detect key-points. It needs an input image and vector to store key-points as an argument. The calculated key-points can be drawn on an original image using the `drawkey-points` function. It requires source image, the vector of the key-points and the destination image as an argument.

The intensity threshold can be changed to detect the different number of key-points. If the threshold is low, then more key-points will pass the segment test and will be categorized as key-points. As this threshold is increased, the number of key-points detected will gradually decrease. In the same way, if non-maximum suppression is false then more than one key point is detected at a single corner point. The output of the code is as follows:

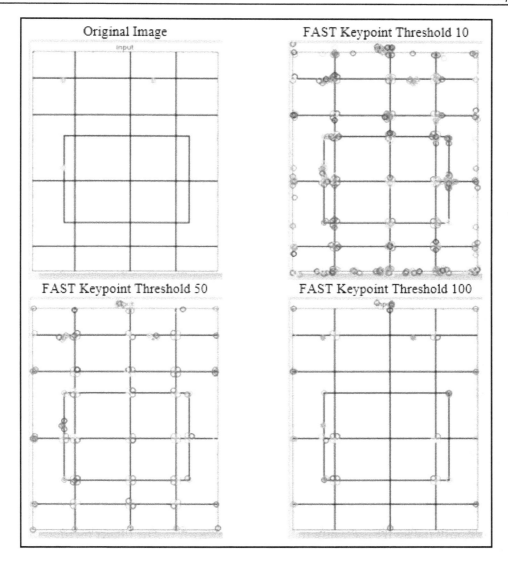

As can be seen from the output, as the threshold increases from 10 to 50 and 100, the number of key-points decreases. These key-points can be used to detect an object in a query image.

Oriented FAST and Rotated BRIEF (ORB) feature detection

ORB is a very efficient feature detection and description algorithm. It is a combination of the FAST algorithm for feature detection and the **Binary Robust Independent Elementary Features (BRIEF)** algorithm for feature description. It provides an efficient alternative to the SURF and SIFT algorithms, which are widely used for object detection. As they are patented, their use should be paid for. ORB matches the performance of SIFT and SURF at no cost.

OpenCV and CUDA provide an easy API for implementing the ORB algorithm. The code for implementing the ORB algorithm is as follows:

```
#include <iostream>
#include "opencv2/opencv.hpp"

using namespace cv;
using namespace std;

int main()
{
  Mat h_image = imread( "images/drawing.JPG", 0 );
  cv::Ptr<cv::cuda::ORB> detector = cv::cuda::ORB::create();
  std::vector<cv::key point> key-points;
  cv::cuda::GpuMat d_image;
  d_image.upload(h_image);
  detector->detect(d_image, key-points);
  cv::drawkey-points(h_image,key-points,h_image);
  imshow("Final Result", h_image );
  waitKey(0);
  return 0;
}
```

The object of the ORB class is created using the create method. All the arguments to this method are optional so we are using the default values for it. The detect method of the created object is used to detect key-points from an image. It requires an input image and the vector of key-points in which the output will be stored as arguments. The detected key-points are drawn on the image using the drawkey-points function. The output of the preceding code is as follows:

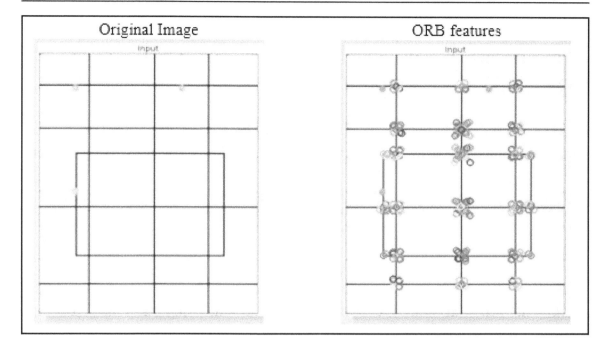

The ORB class also provides a method to calculate descriptors for all the key-points. These descriptors can accurately describe the object and can be used to detect objects from an image. These descriptors can also be used to classify an object.

Speeded up robust feature detection and matching

SURF approximates Laplacian of Gaussian with computation based on a simple two-dimensional box filter as described in the last chapter. The convolution with the box filter can be easily calculated with the help of integral images, which improves the performance of the algorithm. SURF relies on the determinant of the Hessian matrix for both scale and location. The approximated determinant of Hessian can be expressed as:

$$| H_a | = D_x D_y - (wDxy)^2$$

Where w is a relative weight for the filter response and used to balance the expression for the determinant. The Dx, Dy are the result of the Laplacian operator in X- and Y-direction.

SURF uses wavelet responses in horizontal and vertical directions, using an integral image approach for orientation assignment. Adequate Gaussian weights are also applied to it. The dominant orientation is estimated by calculating the sum of all responses within a sliding orientation window of angle 60 degrees.

For feature description, SURF uses Haar wavelet responses in horizontal and vertical directions. This is computed for all subregions in an image, resulting in a SURF feature descriptor with a total of 64 dimensions. The lower the dimensions, the higher the speed of computation and matching will be. For more precision, the SURF feature descriptor has an extended 128-dimension version. SURF is rotation-invariant and scale-invariant.

SURF has a higher processing speed than SIFT because it uses a 64-directional feature vector compared to SIFT, which uses a 128-dimensional feature vector. SURF is good at handling images with blurring and rotation, but not good at handling a viewpoint change and illumination change.

OpenCV and CUDA provide an API to calculate SURF key-points and descriptors. We will also see how these can be used to detect an object in the query image. The code for SURF feature detection and matching is as follows:

```
#include <stdio.h>
#include <iostream>
#include "opencv2/opencv.hpp"
#include "opencv2/features2d.hpp"
#include "opencv2/xfeatures2d.hpp"
#include "opencv2/xfeatures2d/nonfree.hpp"
#include "opencv2/xfeatures2d/cuda.hpp"

using namespace cv;
using namespace cv::xfeatures2d;
using namespace std;

int main( int argc, char** argv )
{
  Mat h_object_image = imread( "images/object1.jpg", 0 );
  Mat h_scene_image = imread( "images/scene1.jpg", 0 );
  cuda::GpuMat d_object_image;
  cuda::GpuMat d_scene_image;
  cuda::GpuMat d_key-points_scene, d_key-points_object;
  vector< key point > h_key-points_scene, h_key-points_object;
  cuda::GpuMat d_descriptors_scene, d_descriptors_object;
  d_object_image.upload(h_object_image);
  d_scene_image.upload(h_scene_image);
  cuda::SURF_CUDA surf(150);
  surf( d_object_image, cuda::GpuMat(), d_key-points_object,
d_descriptors_object );
```

```
surf( d_scene_image, cuda::GpuMat(), d_key-points_scene,
d_descriptors_scene );

Ptr< cuda::DescriptorMatcher > matcher =
cuda::DescriptorMatcher::createBFMatcher();
vector< vector< DMatch> > d_matches;
matcher->knnMatch(d_descriptors_object, d_descriptors_scene, d_matches, 3);
surf.downloadkey-points(d_key-points_scene, h_key-points_scene);
surf.downloadkey-points(d_key-points_object, h_key-points_object);
std::vector< DMatch > good_matches;
for (int k = 0; k < std::min(h_key-points_object.size()-1,
d_matches.size()); k++)
{
  if ( (d_matches[k][0].distance < 0.75*(d_matches[k][1].distance)) &&
      ((int)d_matches[k].size() <= 2 && (int)d_matches[k].size()>0) )
  {
    good_matches.push_back(d_matches[k][0]);
  }
}
std::cout << "size:" <<good_matches.size();
Mat h_image_result;
drawMatches( h_object_image, h_key-points_object, h_scene_image, h_key-
points_scene,
      good_matches, h_image_result, Scalar::all(-1), Scalar::all(-1),
      vector<char>(), DrawMatchesFlags::DEFAULT );
imshow("Good Matches & Object detection", h_image_result);
waitKey(0);
return 0;
}
```

Two images are read from the disk. The first image contains the object to be detected. The second image is the query image in which the object is to be searched. We will calculate SURF features from both the images, and then these features will be matched for detecting an object from a query image.

OpenCV provides the SURF_CUDA class for calculating SURF features. The object of this class is created. It requires the Hessian threshold as an argument. It is taken as 150. This threshold determines how large the output from the Hessian determinant calculation must be in order for a point to be considered as a key point. A larger threshold value will result in fewer but more salient interest points, and a smaller value will result in more numerous but less salient points. It can be chosen according to the application.

This `surf` object is used to calculate key-points and descriptors from both the object and query image. The image, data type of the image, vectors to store key-points, and descriptors are passed as an argument. To match the object in the query image, descriptors from both the images need to be matched. OpenCV provides the different type of matching algorithms for this purpose, like the Brute-Force matcher and the **Fast Library for Approximate Nearest Neighbors (FLANN)** matcher.

The Brute-Force matcher is used in the program; it is a simple method. It takes the descriptor of one feature in an object that is matched with all other features in the query image, using some distance calculation. It returns the best match key point, or best k matches using the nearest neighbor algorithm when using the `knnMatch` method of the `matcher` class. The `knnMatch` method requires two sets of descriptors along with the number of nearest neighbors. It is taken as 3 in the code.

The good, matching key-points are extracted from the matching points returned by the `knnMatch` method. These good matches are found out by using the ratio test method, described in the original paper. These good matches are used to detect an object from a scene.

The `drawMatches` function is used to draw a line between matched good points from both the images. It requires many arguments. The first argument is the source image, the second image is the key-points of the source image, the third argument is the second image, the fourth argument is the key-points of the second image, and the fifth argument is the output image. The sixth argument is the color of the lines and key-points. It is taken as `Scalar::all(-1)` , which indicates that a color will be taken randomly. The seventh argument is the color of the key-points, which do not have any matches. It is also taken as `Scalar::all(-1)` , which indicates that a color will be taken randomly. The last two arguments specify a mask to draw matches and flag settings. The empty mask is taken so that all matches are drawn.

These matches can be used to draw a bounding box around the detected object, which will localize the object from the scene. The code for drawing a bounding box is as follows:

```
std::vector<Point2f> object;
std::vector<Point2f> scene;
for (int i = 0; i < good_matches.size(); i++) {
   object.push_back(h_key-points_object[good_matches[i].queryIdx].pt);
   scene.push_back(h_key-points_scene[good_matches[i].trainIdx].pt);
}
Mat Homo = findHomography(object, scene, RANSAC);
std::vector<Point2f> corners(4);
std::vector<Point2f> scene_corners(4);
corners[0] = Point(0, 0);
corners[1] = Point(h_object_image.cols, 0);
```

```
corners[2] = Point(h_object_image.cols, h_object_image.rows);
corners[3] = Point(0, h_object_image.rows);
perspectiveTransform(corners, scene_corners, Homo);
line(h_image_result, scene_corners[0] + Point2f(h_object_image.cols,
0),scene_corners[1] + Point2f(h_object_image.cols, 0), Scalar(255, 0, 0),
4);
line(h_image_result, scene_corners[1] + Point2f(h_object_image.cols,
0),scene_corners[2] + Point2f(h_object_image.cols, 0),Scalar(255, 0, 0),
4);
line(h_image_result, scene_corners[2] + Point2f(h_object_image.cols,
0),scene_corners[3] + Point2f(h_object_image.cols, 0),Scalar(255, 0, 0),
4);
line(h_image_result, scene_corners[3] + Point2f(h_object_image.cols,
0),scene_corners[0] + Point2f(h_object_image.cols, 0),Scalar(255, 0, 0),
4);
```

OpenCV provides the findHomography function to search for the position, orientation, and scale of the object in the scene, based on the good matches. The first two arguments are good, matching key-points from the object and scene images. The **random sample consensus** (**RANSAC**) method is passed as one of the arguments that is used to find the best translation matrix.

After finding this translation matrix, the perspectiveTransform function is used to find an object. It requires four corner points and a translation matrix as an argument. These transformed points are used to draw a bounding box around the detected object. The output of the SURF program for finding features and matching objects is as follows:

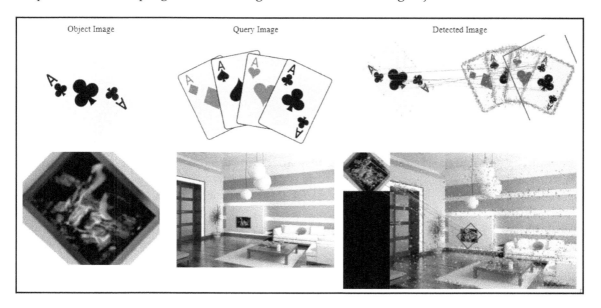

The figure contains the object image, query image, and detected image. As can be seen from the preceding image, SURF can accurately determine the position of the object even if the object is rotated. Though sometimes it may detect the wrong features. The Hessian threshold and test ratio can be varied to find the optimum matches.

So to summarize, in this section we have seen FAST, ORB, and SURF key point detection algorithms. We have also seen how these points can be used to match and localize an object in an image by using SURF features as an example. You can try using FAST and ORB features to do the same. In the next section, we discuss Haar cascades in detail for detecting faces and eyes from an image.

Object detection using Haar cascades

A Haar cascade uses rectangular features to detect an object. It uses rectangles of different sizes to calculate different line and edge features. The rectangle contains some black and white regions, as shown in the following figure, and they are centered at different positions in an image:

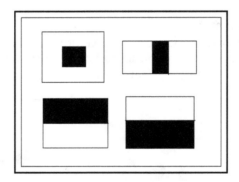

The idea behind the Haar-like feature selection algorithm is to compute the difference between the sum of white pixels and the sum of black pixels inside the rectangle.

The main advantage of this method is the fast sum computation using the integral image. This makes a Haar cascade ideal for real-time object detection. It requires less time for processing an image than algorithms like SURF described previously. This algorithm can also be implemented on embedded systems, like Raspberry Pi, because it is less computationally intensive and has less memory footprint. It is called Haar-like because it is based on the same principle as Haar wavelets. Haar cascades are widely used in human body detection, along with its parts like face and eye detection. It can also be used for expression analysis. The Haar cascade can be utilized for detecting vehicles like a car.

In this section, the Haar cascade is described for detecting faces and eyes from an image and webcam. Haar cascade is a machine learning algorithm, which needs to be trained to do a particular task. It is difficult to train a Haar cascade from scratch for a particular application, so OpenCV provides some trained XML files, which can be used to detect objects. These XML files are provided in the `opencv\data\haarcascades_cuda` folder of an OpenCV or CUDA installation.

Face detection using Haar cascades

We will use the Haar cascade for detecting faces from an image and live webcam in this section. The code for detecting faces from an image using the Haar cascade is as follows:

```
#include "opencv2/objdetect/objdetect.hpp"
#include "opencv2/highgui/highgui.hpp"
#include "opencv2/imgproc/imgproc.hpp"
#include "opencv2/cudaobjdetect.hpp"
#include <iostream>
#include <stdio.h>

using namespace std;
using namespace cv;

int main( )
{
  Mat h_image;
  h_image = imread("images/lena_color_512.tif", 0);
  Ptr<cuda::CascadeClassifier> cascade =
cuda::CascadeClassifier::create("haarcascade_frontalface_alt2.xml");
  cuda::GpuMat d_image;
  cuda::GpuMat d_buf;
  d_image.upload(h_image);
  cascade->detectMultiScale(d_image, d_buf);
  std::vector<Rect> detections;
  cascade->convert(d_buf, detections);
  if (detections.empty())
    std::cout << "No detection." << std::endl;
  cvtColor(h_image,h_image,COLOR_GRAY2BGR);
  for(int i = 0; i < detections.size(); ++i)
  {
    rectangle(h_image, detections[i], Scalar(0,255,255), 5);
  }
  imshow("Result image", h_image);
  waitKey(0);
  return 0;
}
```

OpenCV and CUDA provide the `CascadeClassifier` class that can be used for implementing the Haar cascade. The create method is used to create an object of that class. It requires the filename of the trained XML file to be loaded. There is the `detectMultiScale` method of the created object, which detects an object at multiple scales from an image. It requires an image file and a `Gpumat` array to store the output results as arguments. This `gpumat` vector is converted to a standard rectangle vector by using the convert method of the `CascadeClassifier` object. This converted vector contains the coordinates for drawing a rectangle on the detected object.

The `detectMultiScale` function has many parameters that can be modified before invoking the function. These include `scaleFactor` that is used to specify how much the image size will be reduced at each image scale, and `minNeighbors` specifies the value of the minimum neighbors each rectangle should have for retention; `minSize` specifies the minimum object size and `maxSize` the maximum object size. All these parameters have their default values, so in normal scenarios there is no need for modification. If we want to change them, then we can use the following code before invoking the `detectMultiscale` function:

```
cascade->setMinNeighbors(0);
cascade->setScaleFactor(1.01);
```

This first function will set minimum neighbors to 0 and the second function will reduce the image size by a factor of 1.01 after every scale. The scale factor is very important for detecting objects with a different size. If it is large then the algorithm will take less time to complete, but some faces might not be detected. If it is small then the algorithm will take more time to complete, and it will be more accurate. The output of the preceding code is as follows:

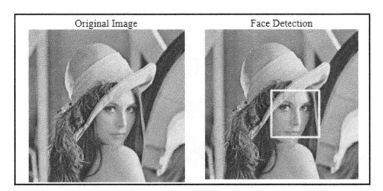

From video

The same concept of the Haar cascade can be used to detect faces from videos. The code for detecting a face is included inside the `while` loop so that the face is detected in every frame of a video. The code for face detection from a webcam is as follows:

```cpp
#include <iostream>
#include <opencv2/opencv.hpp>
using namespace cv;
using namespace std;

int main()
{
  VideoCapture cap(0);
  if (!cap.isOpened()) {
    cerr << "Can not open video source";
    return -1;
  }
  std::vector<cv::Rect> h_found;
  cv::Ptr<cv::cuda::CascadeClassifier> cascade =
cv::cuda::CascadeClassifier::create("haarcascade_frontalface_alt2.xml");
  cv::cuda::GpuMat d_frame, d_gray, d_found;
  while(1)
  {
    Mat frame;
    if ( !cap.read(frame) ) {
      cerr << "Can not read frame from webcam";
      return -1;
    }
    d_frame.upload(frame);
    cv::cuda::cvtColor(d_frame, d_gray, cv::COLOR_BGR2GRAY);

    cascade->detectMultiScale(d_gray, d_found);
    cascade->convert(d_found, h_found);
    for(int i = 0; i < h_found.size(); ++i)
    {
      rectangle(frame, h_found[i], Scalar(0,255,255), 5);
    }

    imshow("Result", frame);
    if (waitKey(1) == 'q') {
      break;
    }
  }

  return 0;
}
```

The webcam is initialized and frames from the webcam are captured one by one. This frame is uploaded to the device memory for processing on GPU. The object of the `CascadeClassifier` class is created by using the `create` method of the class. The XML file for face detection is provided as an argument while creating an object. Inside the `while` loop, the `detectMultiscale` method is applied to every frame so that faces of different sizes can be detected in each frame. The detected location is converted to a rectangle vector using the `convert` method. Then this vector is iterated using the `for` loop so that the bounding box can be drawn using the `rectangle` function on all the detected faces. The output of the program is as follows:

Eye detection using Haar cascades

This section will describe the use of Haar cascades in detecting the eyes of humans. The XML file for a trained Haar cascade for eye detection is provided in the OpenCV installation directory. This file is used to detect eyes. The code for it is as follows:

```
#include <iostream>
#include <stdio.h>
 #include <opencv2/opencv.hpp>
```

```
using namespace std;
using namespace cv;

int main( )
{
  Mat h_image;
  h_image = imread("images/lena_color_512.tif", 0);
  Ptr<cuda::CascadeClassifier> cascade =
cuda::CascadeClassifier::create("haarcascade_eye.xml");
  cuda::GpuMat d_image;
  cuda::GpuMat d_buf;
  d_image.upload(h_image);
  cascade->setScaleFactor(1.02);
  cascade->detectMultiScale(d_image, d_buf);
  std::vector<Rect> detections;
  cascade->convert(d_buf, detections);
  if (detections.empty())
    std::cout << "No detection." << std::endl;
    cvtColor(h_image,h_image,COLOR_GRAY2BGR);
    for(int i = 0; i < detections.size(); ++i)
    {
      rectangle(h_image, detections[i], Scalar(0,255,255), 5);
    }

    imshow("Result image", h_image);
    waitKey(0);
    return 0;
  }
}
```

The code is similar to the code for face detection. This is the advantage of using Haar cascades. If an XML file for a trained Haar cascade on a given object is available then the same code will work on all applications. Just the name of the XML file needs to change when creating an object of the CascadeClassifier class. In the preceding code, haarcascade_eye.xml, which is a trained XML file for eye detection, is used. The other code is self-explanatory. The scale factor is set at 1.02 so that the image size will be reduced by 1.02 at every scale.

The output of the eye detection program is as follows:

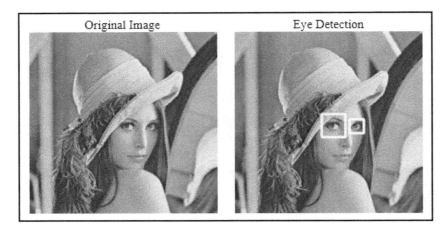

The sizes of eyes are different because of the viewpoint taken to capture the image, but still the Haar cascade is able to localize both eyes efficiently. The performance of the code can also be measured to see how quickly it can work.

To summarize, in this section we demonstrated the use of Haar cascades for face and eye detection. It is very simple to implement once the trained file is available, and it is a very powerful algorithm. It is widely used in embedded or mobile environments where memory and processing power are limited.

Object tracking using background subtraction

Background subtraction is the process of separating out foreground objects from the background in a sequence of video frames. It is widely used in object detection and tracking applications to remove the background part. Background subtraction is performed in four steps:

1. Image preprocessing
2. Modeling of background
3. Detection of foreground
4. Data validation

Image preprocessing is always performed to remove any kind of noise present in the image. The second step is to model the background so that it can be separated from the foreground. In some applications, the first frame of the video is taken as the background and it is not updated. The absolute difference between each frame and the first frame is taken to separate foreground from background.

In other techniques, the background is modeled by taking an average or median of all the frames that have been seen by the algorithm, and that background is separated from the foreground. It will be more robust for illumination changes and will produce a more dynamic background than the first method. Even more statistically intensive models, like Gaussian models and support vector models that use a history of frames, can be used for modeling a background.

The third step is to segregate the foreground from the modeled background by taking the absolute difference between the current frame and the background. This absolute difference is compared with the set threshold, and if it is greater than the threshold then the objects are considered moving, and if it is less than the threshold then the objects are stationary.

Mixture of Gaussian (MoG) method

MoG is a widely used background subtraction method used for separating foregrounds from backgrounds, based on Gaussian mixtures. The background is continuously updated from the sequence of frames. A mixture of K Gaussian distribution is used to categorize pixels as being foreground or background. The time sequence of the frame is also weighted to improve background modeling. The intensities that are continuously changing are categorized as foreground, and the intensities that are static are categorized as background.

OpenCV and CUDA provide an easy API to implement MoG for background subtraction. The code for this is as follows:

```cpp
#include <iostream>
#include <string>
#include "opencv2/opencv.hpp"
using namespace std;
using namespace cv;
using namespace cv::cuda;
int main()
{
  VideoCapture cap("abc.avi");
  if (!cap.isOpened())
  {
    cerr << "can not open camera or video file" << endl;
    return -1;
```

```
   }
  Mat frame;
  cap.read(frame);
  GpuMat d_frame;
  d_frame.upload(frame);
  Ptr<BackgroundSubtractor> mog = cuda::createBackgroundSubtractorMOG();
  GpuMat d_fgmask,d_fgimage,d_bgimage;
  Mat h_fgmask,h_fgimage,h_bgimage;
  mog->apply(d_frame, d_fgmask, 0.01);
  while(1)
  {
    cap.read(frame);
    if (frame.empty())
      break;
    d_frame.upload(frame);
    int64 start = cv::getTickCount();
    mog->apply(d_frame, d_fgmask, 0.01);
    mog->getBackgroundImage(d_bgimage);
    double fps = cv::getTickFrequency() / (cv::getTickCount() - start);
    std::cout << "FPS : " << fps << std::endl;
    d_fgimage.create(d_frame.size(), d_frame.type());
    d_fgimage.setTo(Scalar::all(0));
    d_frame.copyTo(d_fgimage, d_fgmask);
    d_fgmask.download(h_fgmask);
    d_fgimage.download(h_fgimage);
    d_bgimage.download(h_bgimage);
    imshow("image", frame);
    imshow("foreground mask", h_fgmask);
    imshow("foreground image", h_fgimage);
    imshow("mean background image", h_bgimage);
    if (waitKey(1) == 'q')
      break;
  }

  return 0;
}
```

The `createBackgroundSubtractorMOG` class is used to create an object for MoG implementation. It can be provided with some optional arguments while creating an object. The parameters include `history`, `nmixtures`, `backgroundRatio`, and `noiseSigma`. The `history` parameter signifies the number of previous frames used for modeling the background. Its default value is 200. The `nmixture` parameter specifies the number of Gaussian mixtures used to segregate pixels. Its default value is 5. You can play around with these values according to an application.

The `apply` method of the created object is used to create a foreground mask from the first frame. It requires an input image and an image array to store the foreground mask and learning rate as the input. This foreground mask and the background image are continuously updated after every frame inside the `while` loop.
The `getBackgroundImage` function is used to fetch the current background model.

The foreground mask is used to create a foreground image that indicates which objects are currently moving. It is basically logical and operates between the original frame and foreground mask. The foreground mask, foreground image, and the modeled background are downloaded to host memory after every frame for displaying on the screen.

The MoG model is applied to a video from the PETS 2009 dataset, which is widely used for pedestrian detection. It has a static background and persons are moving around in the video. The output of two different frames from the video is as follows:

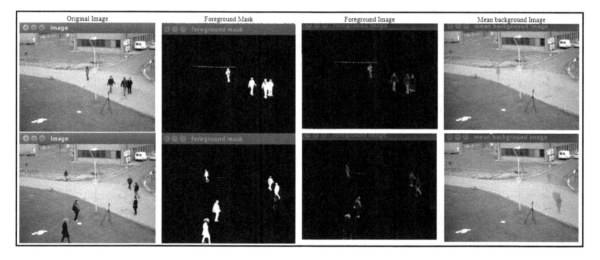

As can be seen, MoG models the background very efficiently. Only the persons who are moving are present in the foreground mask and foreground image. This foreground image can be used for further processing of the detected objects. If a human stops walking, then he will start being part of the background, as can be seen from the result of the second frame. So this algorithm can only be used to detect moving objects. It will not consider static objects. The performance of MoG in terms of frame rate is as follows:

```
FPS : 333.944
FPS : 332.342
FPS : 331.221
FPS : 330.282
```

The frame rate is updated after every frame. It can be seen that it is around 330 frames per second, which is very high and easily used in real-time applications. OpenCV and CUDA also provide the second version of MoG, which can be invoked by the `createBackgroundSubtractorMOG2` class.

GMG for background subtraction

The name of the algorithm GMG is derived from the initials of the inventors who proposed the algorithm. The algorithm is a combination of background estimation and Bayesian segmentation per pixel. It uses Bayesian inference to separate the background from the foreground. It also uses the history of frames for modeling the background. It is again weighted based on the time sequence of the frame. The new observation is weighted more than the old observations.

OpenCV and CUDA provide a similar API to MoG for implementation of the GMG algorithm. The code for implementing the GMG algorithm for background subtraction is as follows:

```
#include <iostream>
#include <string>
#include "opencv2/opencv.hpp"
#include "opencv2/core.hpp"
#include "opencv2/core/utility.hpp"
#include "opencv2/cudabgsegm.hpp"
#include "opencv2/cudalegacy.hpp"
#include "opencv2/video.hpp"
#include "opencv2/highgui.hpp"

using namespace std;
using namespace cv;
using namespace cv::cuda;

int main()
{
  VideoCapture cap("abc.avi");
  if (!cap.isOpened())
  {
    cerr << "can not open video file" << endl;
    return -1;
  }
  Mat frame;
  cap.read(frame);
  GpuMat d_frame;
  d_frame.upload(frame);
  Ptr<BackgroundSubtractor> gmg = cuda::createBackgroundSubtractorGMG(40);
```

```
GpuMat d_fgmask,d_fgimage,d_bgimage;
Mat h_fgmask,h_fgimage,h_bgimage;
gmg->apply(d_frame, d_fgmask);
while(1)
{
  cap.read(frame);
  if (frame.empty())
    break;
  d_frame.upload(frame);
  int64 start = cv::getTickCount();
  gmg->apply(d_frame, d_fgmask, 0.01);
  double fps = cv::getTickFrequency() / (cv::getTickCount() - start);
  std::cout << "FPS : " << fps << std::endl;
  d_fgimage.create(d_frame.size(), d_frame.type());
  d_fgimage.setTo(Scalar::all(0));
  d_frame.copyTo(d_fgimage, d_fgmask);
  d_fgmask.download(h_fgmask);
  d_fgimage.download(h_fgimage);
  imshow("image", frame);
  imshow("foreground mask", h_fgmask);
  imshow("foreground image", h_fgimage);
  if (waitKey(30) == 'q')
    break;
}
return 0;
}
```

The createBackgroundSubtractorGMG class is used to create an object for GMG implementation. It can be provided with two arguments while creating an object. The first argument is the number of previous frames used for modeling the background. It is taken as 40 in the code above. The second argument is the decision threshold, which is used to categorize pixels as foreground. Its default value is 0.8.

The `apply` method of the created object is used on the first frame to create a foreground mask. The foreground mask and foreground image are continuously updated inside the `while` loop by using the history of frames. The foreground mask is used to create a foreground image in a similar way as shown for MoG. The output of the GMG algorithm on the same video and two frames is as follows:

The output of GMG is noisy compared to MoG. The morphological opening and closing operation can be applied to the result of GMG to remove shadowing noise present in the result. The performance of the GMG algorithm in terms of FPS is as follows:

```
FPS : 112.059
FPS : 113.165
FPS : 111.566
FPS : 113.295
FPS : 113.228
```

As it is more computationally intensive than MoG, the FPS rate is less, but still the FPS performance is 120, which is more than 30 FPS for real-time performance.

To summarize, in this section we have seen two methods for background modeling and background subtraction. MoG is faster and less noisy compared to the GMG algorithm. The GMG algorithm requires morphological operations to remove noise present in the result.

Summary

This chapter described the role of OpenCV and CUDA in real-time object detection and tracking applications. It started with the introduction of object detection and tracking, along with challenges encountered in that process and the applications of it. Different features like color, shape, histograms, and other distinct key-points, like corners, can be used to detect and track objects in an image. Color-based object detection is easier to implement, but it requires that the object should have a distinct color from the background. For shape-based object detection, the Canny edge detection technique has been described to detect edges, and Hough transform has been described for straight line and circle detection. It has many applications, such as land detection, ball tracking, and so on. The color and shape are global features, which are easier to compute and require less memory. They are more susceptible to noise. Other algorithms like FAST, ORB, and SURF have been described in detail, which can be used to detect key-points from the image, and these key-points can be used to describe an image accurately, which in turn can be used to detect an object in the image. ORB is open source and gives a comparable result to SURF at no cost. SURF is patented but it is faster, scale-invariant, and rotation-invariant. The Haar cascade has been described, which is a simple algorithm used to detect objects like faces, eyes, and the human body from an image. It can be used in embedded systems for real-time applications. The last part of the chapter described background subtraction algorithms in detail, such as MoG and GMG, which can separate foregrounds from backgrounds. The output of these algorithms can be used for object detection and tracking. The next chapter will describe how these applications can be deployed on embedded development boards.

Questions

1. Write an OpenCV code for detecting objects of yellow color from the video.
2. In which situations will the object detection using color fail?
3. Why is the Canny edge detection algorithm better than the other edge detection algorithm seen in the last chapter?
4. What can be done to reduce the noise sensitivity of Hough transform?
5. What is the importance of the threshold in the FAST key point detector?
6. What is the importance of the Hessian threshold in the SURF detector?
7. If the scale factor in a Haar cascade is changed from 1.01 to 1.05 then what effect will it have on output?
8. Compare the MoG and GMG background subtraction methods. What can be done to remove noise from GMG outputs?

8
Introduction to the Jetson TX1 Development Board and Installing OpenCV on Jetson TX1

The last chapter described various computer vision applications that use OpenCV and CUDA. When these applications need to be deployed in real-life situations, there is the need for an embedded development board that can process images at high speed by taking advantage of OpenCV and CUDA. Nvidia provides several GPU-based development boards, such as Jetson TK1, TX1, and TX2, which are ideal for high-end computing tasks such as computer vision. One of these development boards, the Jetson TX1, will be introduced in this chapter. The features and applications with which this board can be used are also discussed in detail. CUDA and OpenCV are essential for computer vision applications, so steps to install them on the Jetson TX1 are discussed in detail.

The following topics will be covered in this chapter:

- Introduction to the Jetson TX1 Development Board
- Features and applications of the Jetson TX1 Development Board
- Basic requirements and steps to install JetPack on the Jetson TX1 Development Board

Technical requirements

This chapter requires a good understanding of the Linux operating system (OS) and networking. It also requires any Nvidia GPU development board, such as Jetson TK1, TX1, or TX2. The JetPack installation file used in this chapter can be downloaded from the following link: `https://developer.nvidia.com/embedded/jetpack`.

Introduction to Jetson TX1

When high-end visual computing and computer vision applications need to be deployed in real-life scenarios, then embedded development platforms are required, which can do computationally intensive tasks efficiently. Platforms such as Raspberry Pi can use OpenCV for computer vision applications and camera-interfacing capability, but it is very slow for real-time applications. Nvidia, which specializes in GPU manufacturing, has developed modules that use GPUs for computationally intensive tasks. These modules can be used to deploy computer vision applications on embedded platforms and include Jetson TK1, Jetson TX1, and Jetson TX2.

Jetson TK1 is the preliminary board and contains 192 CUDA cores with the Nvidia Kepler GPU. It is the cheapest of the three. Jetson TX1 is intermediate in terms of processing speed, with 256 CUDA cores with Maxwell architecture, operating at 998 MHz along with ARM CPU. Jetson TX2 is highest in terms of processing speed and price. It comprises 256 CUDA cores with Pascal architecture operating at 1,300 MHz. This chapter will describe Jetson TX1 in detail.

Jetson TX1 is a small system on a module developed specifically for demanding embedded applications. It is Linux-based and offers super-computing performance at the level of teraflops, which can be utilized for computer vision and deep learning applications. The Jetson TX1 module is shown in the following photograph:

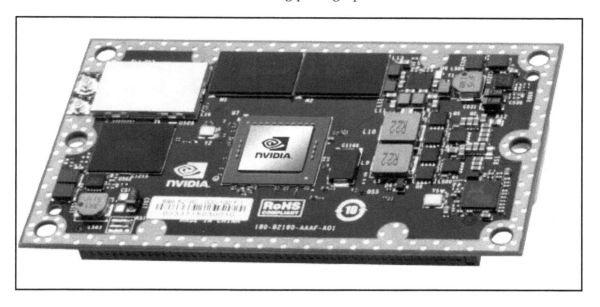

The size of the module is 50 x 87 mm, which makes it easy to integrate into any system. Nvidia also offers the Jetson TX1 Development Board, which houses this GPU for prototyping applications in a short amount of time. The whole development kit is shown in the following photograph:

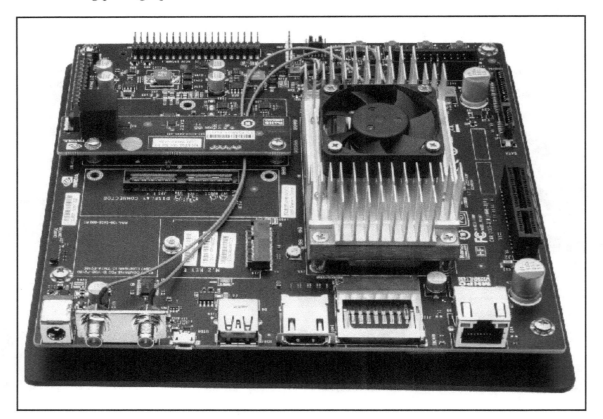

As can be seen from the photograph, apart from the GPU module, the development kit contains a camera module, USB ports, an Ethernet port, a heat sink, fan, and antennas. It is backed by a software ecosystem including JetPack, Linux for Tegra, CUDA Toolkit, cuDNN, OpenCV, and VisionWorks. This makes it ideal for developers who are doing research into deep learning and computer vision for rapid prototyping. The features of the Jetson TX1 development kit are explained in detail in the following section.

Important features of the Jetson TX1

The Jetson TX1 development kit has many features that make it ideal for super-computing tasks:

- It is a system on a chip built using 20 nm technology, and comprises an ARM Cortex A57 quad-core CPU operating at 1.73 GHz and a 256 core Maxwell GPU operating at 998 Mhz.
- It has 4 GB of DDR4 memory with a data bus of 64 bits working at a speed of 1,600 MHz, which is equivalent to 25.6 GB/s.
- It contains a 5 MP MIPI CSI-2 camera module. It supports up to six two lane or three four lane cameras at 1,220 MP/s.
- The development kit also has a normal USB 3.0 type A port and micro USB port for connecting a mouse, a keyboard, and USB cameras to the board.
- It also has an Ethernet port and Wi-Fi connectivity for network connection.
- It can be connected to an HDMI display device via the HDMI port.
- The kit contains a heat sink and a fan for cooling down the GPU device at its peak performance.
- It draws as little as 1 watt of power in an idle condition, around 8-10 watts under normal load, and up to 15 watts when the module is fully utilized. It can process 258 images/second with a power dissipation of 5.7 watts, which is equivalent to the performance/watt value of 45. A normal i7 CPU processor has a performance of 242 images/second at 62.5 watts, which is equivalent to a performance/watt value of 3.88. So Jetson TX1 is 11.5 times better than an i7 processor.

Applications of Jetson TX1

Jetson TX1 can be used in many deep learning and computer vision applications that require computationally intensive tasks. Some of the areas and applications in which Jetson TX1 can be used are as follows:

- It can be used in building autonomous machines and self-driving cars for various computationally intensive tasks.
- It can be used in various computer vision applications such as object detection, classification, and segmentation. It can also be used in medical imaging for the analysis of MRI images and **computed tomography (CT)** images.
- It can be used to build smart video surveillance systems that can help in crime monitoring or traffic monitoring.

- It can be used in bioinformatics and computational chemistry for simulating DNA genes, sequencing, protein docking, and so on.
- It can be used in various defense equipment where fast computing is required.

Installation of JetPack on Jetson TX1

The Jetson TX1 comes with a preinstalled Linux OS. The Nvidia drivers for it should be installed when it is booted for the first time. The commands to do it are as follows:

```
cd ${HOME}/NVIDIA-INSTALLER
sudo ./installer.sh
```

When TX1 is rebooted after these two commands, the Linux OS with user interface will start. Nvidia offers a **software development kit (SDK)**, which contains all of the software needed for building computer vision and deep learning applications, along with the target OS to flash the development board. This SDK is called **JetPack**. The latest JetPack contains Linux for Tegra (L4T) board support packages; TensorRT, which is used for deep learning inference in computer vision applications; the latest CUDA toolkit, cuDNN, which is a CUDA deep neural network library; VisionWorks, which is also used for computer vision and deep learning applications; and OpenCV.

All of the packages will be installed by default when you install JetPack. This section describes the procedure to install JetPack on the board. The procedure is long, tedious, and a little bit complex for a newcomer to Linux. So, just follow the steps and screenshots given in the following section carefully.

Basic requirements for installation

There are a few basic requirements for the installation of JetPack on TX1. JetPack can't be installed directly on the board, so a PC or virtual machine that runs Ubuntu 14.04 is required as a host PC. The installation is not checked with the latest version of Ubuntu, but you are free to play around with it. The Jetson TX1 board needs peripherals such as a mouse, keyboard, and monitor, which can be connected to the USB and HDMI ports. The Jetson TX1 board should be connected to the same router as the host machine via an Ethernet cable. The installation will also require a micro USB to USB cable to connect the board with a PC for transferring packages on the board via serial transfer. Note down the IP address of the board by checking the router configuration. If all requirements are satisfied, then move to the following section for the installation of JetPack.

Steps for installation

This section describes the steps to install the latest JetPack version, accompanied by screenshots. All of the steps need to be executed on the host machine, which is running Ubuntu 14.04:

1. Download the latest JetPack version from the official Nvidia site by following the link, `https://developer.nvidia.com/embedded/jetpack`, and clicking on the download button, as shown in the following screenshot:

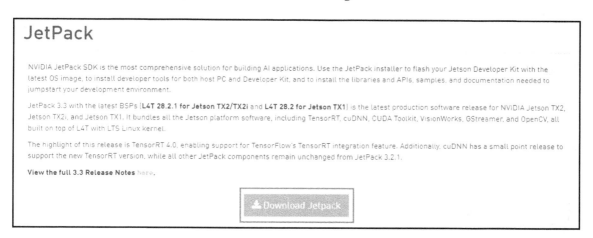

2. JetPack 3.3, which is the latest version at the time of the writing of this book, is used to demonstrate the installation procedure. The name of the downloaded file is **JetPack-L4T-3.3-linux-x64_b39.run**.
3. Create a folder on **Desktop** named **jetpack** and copy this file in that folder, as shown in the following screenshot:

4. Start a Terminal in that folder by right-clicking and selecting the **Open** option. The file needs to be executed, so it should have an execute permission. If that is not the case, change the permission and then start the installer, as shown in the screenshot:

```
bhaumik@bhaumik-VirtualBox:~$ cd Desktop/jetpack
bhaumik@bhaumik-VirtualBox:~/Desktop/jetpack$ chmod +x JetPack-L4T-3.3-linux-x64
_b39.run
bhaumik@bhaumik-VirtualBox:~/Desktop/jetpack$ ./JetPack-L4T-3.3-linux-x64_b39.ru
n
Creating directory _installer
Verifying archive integrity... All good.
Uncompressing JetPack     57%
```

5. It will start an installation wizard for JetPack 3.3 as shown in the following screenshot. Just click on **Next** in this window:

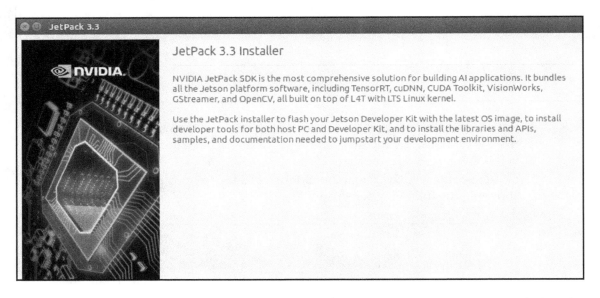

6. The wizard will ask for directories where the packages will be downloaded and installed. You can choose the current directory for installation and create a new folder in this directory for saving downloaded packages, as shown in the following screenshot. Then click on **Next**:

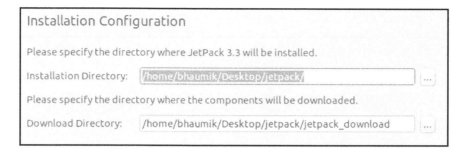

7. The installation wizard will ask you to choose the development board on which the JetPack packages are to be installed. Select **Jetson TX1,** as shown in the following screenshot, and click on **Next**:

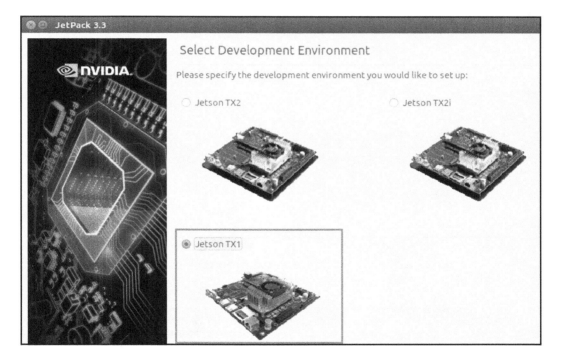

8. The components manager window will be displayed, which shows which packages will be downloaded and installed. It will show packages such as **CUDA Toolkit**, **cuDNN**, **OpenCV**, and **VisionWorks**, along with the OS image, as shown in the following screenshot:

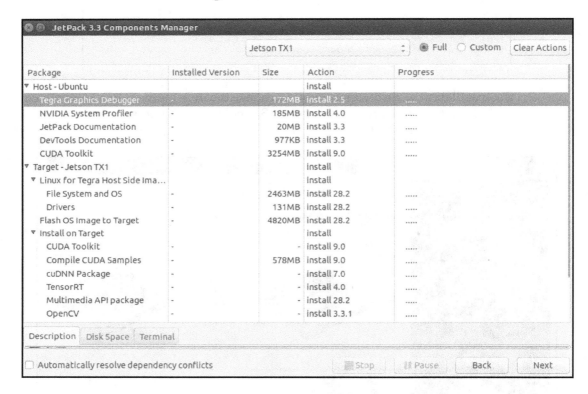

9. It will ask to accept the license agreement. So click on **Accept all**, as shown in the following screenshot, and click on **Next**:

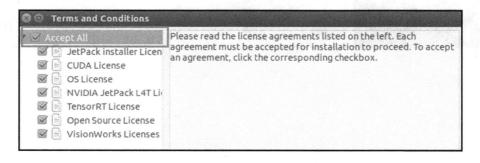

10. It will start to download the packages, as shown in the following screenshot:

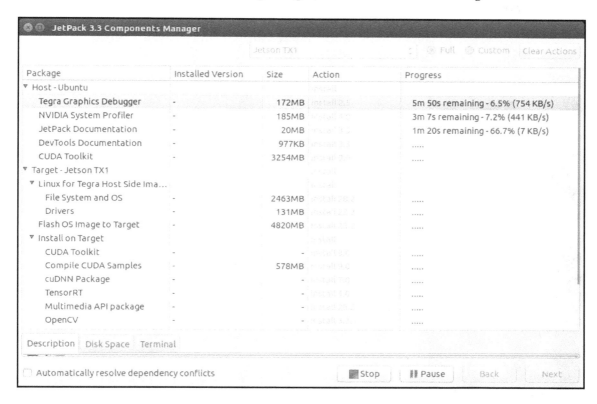

11. When all of the packages are downloaded and installed, click on **Next** to complete the installation on the host. It will display the following window:

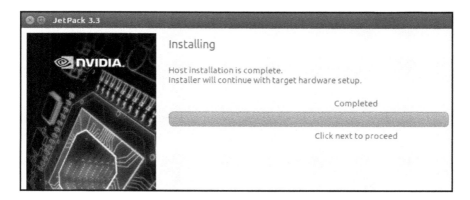

12. It will ask you to select a network layout of how the board is connected to the host PC. The board and host PC are connected to the same router, so the first option, which tells the device to access the internet via the same router or switch, is selected, as shown in the following screenshot, and then click **Next**:

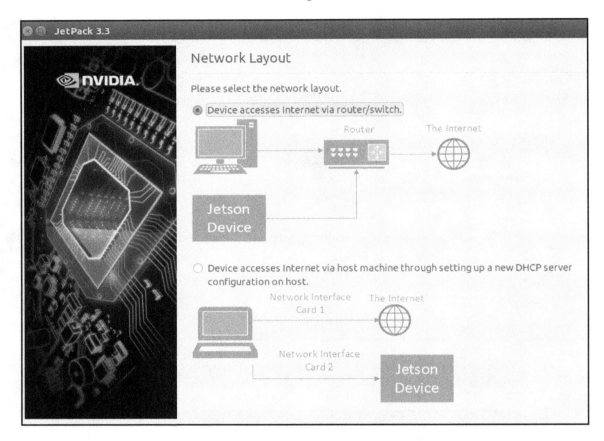

13. It will ask for the interface used to connect the board to the network. We have to use an Ethernet cable to connect the router to the board, so we will select the **eth0** interface, as shown in the following screenshot:

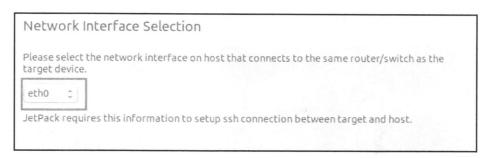

14. This will finish the installation on the host and it will show the summary of the packages that will be transferred and installed on the board. When you click **Next** in the window, it will show you the steps to connect the board to the PC via the micro USB to USB cable and to boot the board in **Force USB Recovery Mode**. The window with the steps are shown as follows:

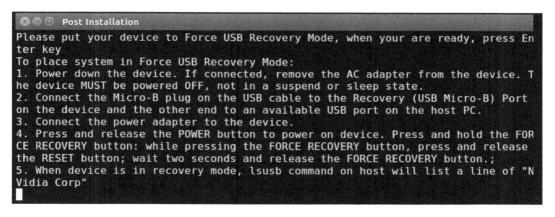

15. To go into force recovery mode, after pressing the **POWER** button, press the **FORCE RECOVERY** button and, while pressing it, press and release the **RESET** button. Then release the **FORCE RECOVERY** button. The device will boot in force recovery mode.

16. Type the **lsusb** command in the window; it will start transferring packages on to the device if it is correctly connected. If you are using a virtual machine, then you have to enable the device from the USB settings of the virtual machine. Also, select **USB 3.0** controller if it's not selected. The process that starts after typing the **lsusb** command is shown as follows:

```
☒ ☒ ☒   Post Installation
         populating extlinux.conf.emmc to rootfs... done.
         populating /home/bhaumik/Desktop/jetpack/64_TX1/Linux_for_Tegra/kernel/d
tb/tegra210-jetson-tx1-p2597-2180-a01-devkit.dtb to rootfs... done.
done.
Making Boot image... done.
copying bcffile(/home/bhaumik/Desktop/jetpack/64_TX1/Linux_for_Tegra/bootloader/
t210ref/cfg/board_config_p2597-devkit.xml)... done.
Existing sosfile(/home/bhaumik/Desktop/jetpack/64_TX1/Linux_for_Tegra/bootloader
/nvtboot_recovery.bin) reused.
copying tegraboot(/home/bhaumik/Desktop/jetpack/64_TX1/Linux_for_Tegra/bootloade
r/t210ref/nvtboot.bin)... done.
Existing bpffile(/home/bhaumik/Desktop/jetpack/64_TX1/Linux_for_Tegra/bootloader
/bpmp.bin) reused.
copying wb0boot(/home/bhaumik/Desktop/jetpack/64_TX1/Linux_for_Tegra/bootloader/
t210ref/warmboot.bin)... done.
Existing tosfile(/home/bhaumik/Desktop/jetpack/64_TX1/Linux_for_Tegra/bootloader
/tos.img) reused.
Existing eksfile(/home/bhaumik/Desktop/jetpack/64_TX1/Linux_for_Tegra/bootloader
/eks.img) reused.
copying dtbfile(/home/bhaumik/Desktop/jetpack/64_TX1/Linux_for_Tegra/kernel/dtb/
tegra210-jetson-tx1-p2597-2180-a01-devkit.dtb)... done.
Making system.img...
         populating rootfs from /home/bhaumik/Desktop/jetpack/64_TX1/Linux_for_Te
gra/rootfs ... █
```

17. The process will flash the OS on the device. This process can take a long time, up to an hour to complete. It will ask for resetting the device after the flashing has completed an IP address for **ssh**. Write down the IP address noted earlier, along with the default username and password, which is ubuntu, and click **Next**. The following window will be displayed after that:

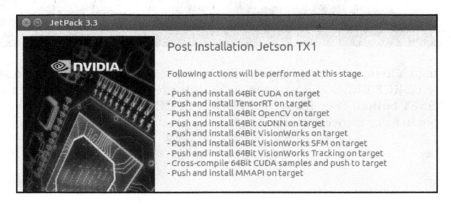

18. Click on **Next** and it will push all packages, such as **CUDA Toolkit**, **VisionWorks**, **OpenCV,** and **Multimedia**, onto the device. The following window will be displayed:

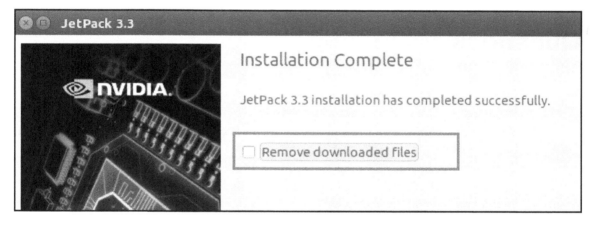

19. After the process is completed, it will ask whether to delete all the downloaded packages during the process. If you want to delete, then tick on the checkbox or keep it as it is, as shown in the following screenshot:

20. Click on **Next** and the installation process will be finished.
21. Reboot the Jetson TX1 Development Board and it will boot in the normal Ubuntu OS. You will also observe sample examples of all the packages that are installed. We will see how to use CUDA and OpenCV on the board in the next chapter.

Summary

This chapter introduced the Jetson TX1 Development Board for deploying computer vision and deep learning applications on embedded platforms. It is a small credit card-sized module, which can be used for computationally intensive applications. It has a better performance per power dissipation value than the latest i7 processors. It can be used in many domains where computer vision and deep learning is used for performance improvement and embedded deployment. Nvidia provides a development kit that houses this module along with other peripherals, which can be used for rapid prototyping of all applications. Nvidia also provides an SDK called JetPack, which is a collection of many software packages, such as `OpenCV`, `CUDA`, and `Visionworks`. This chapter described the process of installing JetPack on a Jetson TX1 in detail. The next chapter will describe the process of using OpenCV and CUDA to deploy computer vision applications on a Jetson TX1.

Questions

1. What is the advantage of using a Jetson Tx1 over Raspberry Pi?
2. How many cameras can be interfaced with Jetson TX1 ?
3. What can be done to connect more than two USB devices with Jetson TX1 ?
4. True or false: Jetson TX1 has better performance in terms of power than the latest i7 processor.
5. True or false: Jetson TX1 does not contain a CPU.
6. What are the JetPack installation requirements when a Jetson TX1 comes preflashed with the Ubuntu OS?

9

Deploying Computer Vision Applications on Jetson TX1

The previous chapter described the installation of OpenCV and CUDA on a Jetson TX1 development board. This chapter will describe how to use these features on the board. The properties of the Jetson TX1 GPU that make it useful for parallel processing will be described in detail. The chapter will also describe how we can execute the CUDA and C++ codes, seen earlier in this book, on Jetson TX1. It will also demonstrate the performance of the Jetson TX1 GPU in executing CUDA code. The primary motive of this chapter will be to demonstrate the use of Jetson TX1 in deploying image- and video-processing applications. Basic image-processing applications such as image reading, displaying, addition, thresholding, and filtering are taken as examples to demonstrate the use of Jetson TX1 for computer vision applications. Moreover, camera interfacing is important for the deployment of the board in real-life scenarios. This chapter will describe the procedure to use the onboard camera or USB camera for video-capturing and processing applications. How to deploy some advanced applications, like face detection and background subtraction, will be explained in the last part of the chapter.

The following topics will be covered in this chapter:

- Device properties of a Jetson TX1 board
- Running CUDA programs on a Jetson TX1 board
- Image processing on a Jetson TX1 board
- Interfacing cameras with a Jetson TX1 development board
- Advanced applications such as face detection, eye detection, and background subtraction on a Jetson TX1 development board

Technical requirements

This chapter requires a good understanding of the OpenCV, CUDA, and any programming language. It also requires any Nvidia GPU development board, like Jetson TK1, TX1, or TX2. The code files used in this chapter can be downloaded from the following GitHub link: `https://github.com/PacktPublishing/Hands-On-GPU-Accelerated-Computer-Vision-with-OpenCV-and-CUDA`.

Check out the following video to see the Code in Action:
`http://bit.ly/2xDtHhm`

Device properties of Jetson TX1 GPU

CUDA provides a simple interface to determine the capabilities of a GPU device, which is Tegra X1 present on a Jetson TX1 board. It is important to find out the properties of the device that will help in writing optimal programs for it. The program to find the properties of the device is available in the CUDA sample programs installed with JetPack in the home folder. You can also run the program we developed in the second chapter to find out the device properties.

The output of the program on an Nvidia Tegra X1 GPU is as follows:

```
ubuntu@tegra-ubuntu:~/Desktop/opencv/Chapter  9$ nvcc kernel.cu -o device
ubuntu@tegra-ubuntu:~/Desktop/opencv/Chapter  9$ ./device
./device Starting...

 CUDA Device Query (Runtime API) version (CUDART static linking)

Detected 1 CUDA Capable device(s)

Device 0: "NVIDIA Tegra X1"
  CUDA Driver Version / Runtime Version          9.0 / 9.0
  CUDA Capability Major/Minor version number:    5.3
  Total amount of global memory:                 3984 MBytes (4177342464 bytes)
  ( 2) Multiprocessors  GPU Max Clock rate:                998 MHz (1.00 GHz)
  Memory Clock rate:                             13 Mhz
  Memory Bus Width:                              64-bit
  L2 Cache Size:                                 262144 bytes
  Maximum Texture Dimension Size (x,y,z)         1D=(65536), 2D=(65536, 65536), 3D=(4096, 4096, 4096)
  Maximum Layered 1D Texture Size, (num) layers  1D=(16384), 2048 layers
  Maximum Layered 2D Texture Size, (num) layers  2D=(16384, 16384), 2048 layers
  Total amount of constant memory:               65536 bytes
  Total amount of shared memory per block:       49152 bytes
  Total number of registers available per block: 32768
  Warp size:                                     32
  Maximum number of threads per multiprocessor:  2048
  Maximum number of threads per block:           1024
  Max dimension size of a thread block (x,y,z): (1024, 1024, 64)
  Max dimension size of a grid size    (x,y,z): (2147483647, 65535, 65535)
  Maximum memory pitch:                          2147483647 bytes
  Texture alignment:                             512 bytes
  Concurrent copy and kernel execution:          Yes with 1 copy engine(s)
  Run time limit on kernels:                     Yes
  Integrated GPU sharing Host Memory:            Yes
  Support host page-locked memory mapping:       Yes
  Alignment requirement for Surfaces:            Yes
  Device has ECC support:                        Disabled
  Device supports Unified Addressing (UVA):      Yes
  Supports Cooperative Kernel Launch:            No
  Supports MultiDevice Co-op Kernel Launch:      No
  Device PCI Domain ID / Bus ID / location ID:   0 / 0 / 0
  Compute Mode:
     < Default (multiple host threads can use ::cudaSetDevice() with device simultaneously) >
ubuntu@tegra-ubuntu:~/Desktop/opencv/Chapter  9$ █
```

The JetPack 3.3 installs the CUDA 9.0 runtime version. The global memory for the GPU device is around 4 GB, with a GPU clock speed of around 1 GHz. This clock speed is slower than the GeForce 940 GPU mentioned earlier in this book. The memory clock speed is only 13 MHz compared to 2.505 GHz on GeForce 940, which makes Jetson TX1 slower. The L2 cache is 256 KB compared to 1 MB on GeForce 940. Most of the other properties are similar to GeForce 940.

The maximum number of threads that can be launched per block in X, Y, and Z directions are 1,024, 1,024, and 64 respectively. These numbers should be used while determining the number of parallel threads to be launched from a program. The same care should be taken while launching the number of parallel blocks per grid.

To summarize, we have seen the device properties of the Tegra X1 GPU available on a Jetson TX1 development board. It is an embedded board so memory is available and the clock rate is comparatively slower than for GPU devices like GeForce 940 that comes with a laptop. Still, it is way faster than embedded platforms like Arduino and Raspberry Pi. It can be easily used in deploying computer vision applications that require high computational power. Now that we have seen the device properties, we will start by developing the first program using CUDA on Jetson TX1.

Basic CUDA program on Jetson TX1

In this section, the example of adding two large arrays is taken to demonstrate the use of a Jetson TX1 development board in executing CUDA programs. The performance of the program is also measured using CUDA events.

The kernel function for adding two large arrays with 50,000 elements is as follows:

```
#include<iostream>
#include <cuda.h>
#include <cuda_runtime.h>
//Defining number of elements in Array
#define N 50000
//Defining Kernel function for vector addition
__global__ void gpuAdd(int *d_a, int *d_b, int *d_c) {
 //Getting Thread index of current kernel
 int tid = threadIdx.x + blockIdx.x * blockDim.x;
 while (tid < N)
 {
 d_c[tid] = d_a[tid] + d_b[tid];
 tid += blockDim.x * gridDim.x;
 }
}
```

The kernel function takes two device pointers, which point to input arrays as input, and one device pointer, which points to output arrays in the device memory as arguments. The thread ID of the current kernel execution is calculated and array elements indexed by the thread index are added by the kernel. If the number of kernels launched is less than the number of array elements, then the same kernel will add `Array` elements offset by the block dimension as shown in the `while` loop. The `main` function for adding two arrays is as follows:

```
int main(void)
{
 //Defining host arrays
 int h_a[N], h_b[N], h_c[N];
```

```
//Defining device pointers
int *d_a, *d_b, *d_c;
cudaEvent_t e_start, e_stop;
cudaEventCreate(&e_start);
cudaEventCreate(&e_stop);
cudaEventRecord(e_start, 0);
// allocate the memory
cudaMalloc((void**)&d_a, N * sizeof(int));
cudaMalloc((void**)&d_b, N * sizeof(int));
cudaMalloc((void**)&d_c, N * sizeof(int));
//Initializing Arrays
for (int i = 0; i < N; i++) {
h_a[i] = 2 * i*i;
h_b[i] = i;
}
// Copy input arrays from host to device memory
cudaMemcpy(d_a, h_a, N * sizeof(int), cudaMemcpyHostToDevice);
cudaMemcpy(d_b, h_b, N * sizeof(int), cudaMemcpyHostToDevice);
//Calling kernels passing device pointers as parameters
gpuAdd << <1024, 1024 >> >(d_a, d_b, d_c);
//Copy result back to host memory from device memory
cudaMemcpy(h_c, d_c, N * sizeof(int), cudaMemcpyDeviceToHost);
cudaDeviceSynchronize();
cudaEventRecord(e_stop, 0);
cudaEventSynchronize(e_stop);
float elapsedTime;
cudaEventElapsedTime(&elapsedTime, e_start, e_stop);
printf("Time to add %d numbers: %3.1f ms\n",N, elapsedTime);
```

Two host arrays are defined and memory is allocated to them using the `cudaMalloc` function. They are initialized to some random values and uploaded to the device memory. Two CUDA events are created to measure the performance of the CUDA program. The kernel is launched with 1,024 blocks in parallel, with each block having 1,024 threads. These numbers are taken from the device properties, as explained in the last section. The result from the kernel function is transferred to the host memory. The time taken by the kernel function is recorded by the `e_start` and `e_stop` events, before and after the kernel launch. The time taken by the function is displayed on the console.

The following code is added to verify the correctness of the result, computed by the GPU, and to clean up the memory used by the program:

```
int Correct = 1;
printf("Vector addition on GPU \n");
//Printing result on console
for (int i = 0; i < N; i++) {
if ((h_a[i] + h_b[i] != h_c[i]))
{
```

```
 Correct = 0;
 }


 }
 if (Correct == 1)
 {
 printf("GPU has computed Sum Correctly\n");
 }
 else
 {
 printf("There is an Error in GPU Computation\n");
 }
 //Free up memory
 cudaFree(d_a);
 cudaFree(d_b);
 cudaFree(d_c);
 return 0;
 }
```

The same array addition operation is performed on the CPU and compared with the result obtained from the GPU to verify whether the GPU has computed the result correctly or not. This is also displayed on the console. All the memory used by the program is freed up by using the cudaFree function.

The following two commands need to be run from the Terminal to execute the program. The program should be in the current working directory:

```
$ nvcc 01_performance_cuda_events.cu -o gpu_add
$ ./gpu_add
```

The nvcc command is used to compile CUDA code with an Nvidia CUDA compiler. The file name is passed as an argument to the command. The name of the object file, which will be created by the compiler, is specified with the -o option. This filename will be used to execute the program. This is done by the second command. The output of the program is as follows:

```
ubuntu@tegra-ubuntu:~/Desktop/opencv/Chapter 9$ nvcc 01_performance_cuda_events
.cu -o gpu_add
ubuntu@tegra-ubuntu:~/Desktop/opencv/Chapter 9$ ./gpu_add
Time to add 50000 numbers: 3.4 ms
Vector addition on GPU
GPU has computed Sum Correctly
```

As can be seen from the result, Jetson TX1 takes 3.4ms to compute the sum of two arrays with 50,000 elements, which is slower than GeForce 940 used in the third chapter of this book, but still it is faster than sequential execution on a CPU.

To summarize, this section demonstrated the use of a Jetson TX1 development board in the execution of CUDA programs. The syntax is the same as we have seen earlier in this book. So all CUDA programs developed earlier in the book can be executed on Jetson TX1 without much modification. The procedure to execute the program is also described. The next section will describe the use of Jetson TX1 for image-processing applications.

Image processing on Jetson TX1

This section will demonstrate the use of Jetson TX1 in the deployment of image-processing applications. We will again use OpenCV and CUDA for accelerating computer vision applications on Jetson TX1. In the last chapter, we saw the installation procedure for JetPack 3.3, which contains OpenCV and CUDA. But in the latest JetPack, OpenCV is not compiled with CUDA support nor has it GStreamer support, which is needed for accessing the camera from the code. So, it is a good idea to remove the OpenCV installation that comes with JetPack and to compile the new version of OpenCV with CUDA and GStreamer support. The next section will demonstrate the procedure to do that.

Compiling OpenCV with CUDA support (if necessary)

Though OpenCV which comes with JetPack, can work with a new OpenCV installation, it is a good idea to remove the old installation first and then start a new one. This will avoid unnecessary confusion. To accomplish that, the following steps have to be performed:

1. Run the following command from the Terminal:

   ```
   $ sudo apt-get purge libopencv*
   ```

2. Make sure that all the packages installed are the latest versions. If that is not the case, then you can update them by running the following two commands:

   ```
   $ sudo apt-get update
   $ sudo apt-get dist-upgrade
   ```

3. The latest versions of cmake and gcc compiler are needed to compile OpenCV from the source so they can be installed by running the following two commands:

   ```
   $ sudo apt-get install --only-upgrade gcc-5 cpp-5 g++-5
   $ sudo apt-get install build-essential make cmake cmake-curses-gui
   libglew-dev libgtk2.0-dev
   ```

4. There are some dependencies that need to be installed to compile OpenCV with GStreamer support. This can be done by the following command:

```
sudo apt-get install libdc1394-22-dev libxine2-dev libgstreamer1.0-
dev libgstreamer-plugins-base1.0-dev
```

5. Download the source for the latest version of OpenCV and extract it in a folder by executing the following commands:

```
$ wget https://github.com/opencv/opencv/archive/3.4.0.zip -O
opencv.zip
$ unzip opencv.zip
```

6. Now go inside the `opencv` folder and create the `build` directory. Then go inside this newly created `build` directory. These can be done by executing the following commands from Command Prompt.

```
$ cd opencv
$ mkdir build
$ cd build
```

7. The `cmake` command is used to compile `opencv` with CUDA support. Make sure the `WITH_CUDA` flag is set to `ON` in this command. Note `CUDA_ARCH_BIN` should be set to `5.3` for a Jetson TX1 development board and `6.2` for Jetson TX2. The examples are not built to save time and space. The entire `cmake` command is as follows:

```
cmake -D CMAKE_BUILD_TYPE=RELEASE -D
CMAKE_INSTALL_PREFIX=/usr/local \
   -D WITH_CUDA=ON -D CUDA_ARCH_BIN="5.3" -D CUDA_ARCH_PTX="" \
   -D WITH_CUBLAS=ON -D ENABLE_FAST_MATH=ON -D CUDA_FAST_MATH=ON \
   -D ENABLE_NEON=ON -D WITH_LIBV4L=ON -D BUILD_TESTS=OFF \
   -D BUILD_PERF_TESTS=OFF -D BUILD_EXAMPLES=OFF \
   -D WITH_QT=ON -D WITH_OPENGL=ON ..
```

8. It will start the configuration and creation of `makefile`. The `cmake` command will create `makefile` in the `build` directory after successful configuration.

9. To compile OpenCV using `makefile` execute the `make -j4` command from the command window.

10. After successful compilation, to install OpenCV you have to execute the command `sudo make install` from the command line.

If these steps are executed successfully then OpenCV 3.4.0 will be installed with CUDA and GStreamer support on Jetson TX1, and any computer vision application made using OpenCV can be deployed on it. The next section will demonstrate simple image-processing operations on the board.

Reading and displaying images

The first basic operation needed for any computer vision application is that of reading and displaying images that are stored on the disk. This section will demonstrate a simple code to do this operation on Jetson TX1. The OpenCV syntax will not change much as we move from the GPU on the computer to the Jetson TX1 development board. A few minor changes will be there. The code for reading and displaying images on Jetson TX1 is as follows:

```
#include <opencv2/opencv.hpp>
#include <iostream>

using namespace cv;
using namespace std;

int main()
{
 Mat img = imread("images/cameraman.tif",0);
 if (img.empty())
 {
 cout << "Could not open an image" << endl;
 return -1;
 }
 imshow("Image Read on Jetson TX1"; , img);
 waitKey(0);
 return 0;
}
```

The necessary OpenCV libraries are included in the code. The image is read using the imread function inside the Main function. The image is read as a grayscale image because the second argument to the imread command is specified as 0. To read an image as a color image, it can be specified as 1. The if statement checks whether the image is read or not, and if it is not then the code is terminated after displaying an error on the console. When the name of the image is incorrect or the image is not stored in the specified path, then an error in reading an image can happen. This error is handled by the if statement. The image is displayed using the imshow command. The waitKey function is used to display the image until any key is pressed on the keyboard.

The preceding code shown can be saved as the `image_read.cpp` file and executed using the following command from the Terminal. Make sure that the program file is stored in the current working directory of the Terminal:

```
For compilation:
$ g++ -std = c++11 image_read.cpp 'pkg_config --libs --cflags opencv' -o
image_read
For execution:
$ ./image_read
```

The output of the program is as follows:

This section demonstrated the procedure to read and display an image on Jetson TX1. In the next section, we will see some more image-processing operations and also try to measure the performance of them on Jetson TX1.

Image addition

This section will demonstrate the use of Jetson TX1 for simple image-processing applications like image addition. The intensities of pixels at the same location are added to construct the new image after addition. Suppose in two images, the pixel at (0,0) has intensity values 50 and 150 respectively, then the intensity value in the resultant image will be 200, which is the addition of the two intensity values. OpenCV addition is a saturated operation, which means that if an answer of addition goes above 255 then it will be saturated at 255. The code to perform addition on Jetson TX1 is as follows:

```
#include <iostream>
#include "opencv2/opencv.hpp"
```

```
#include "opencv2/core/cuda.hpp"

int main (int argc, char* argv[])
{
 //Read Two Images
 cv::Mat h_img1 = cv::imread("images/cameraman.tif");
 cv::Mat h_img2 = cv::imread("images/circles.png");
 int64 work_begin = cv::getTickCount();
 //Create Memory for storing Images on device
 cv::cuda::GpuMat d_result1,d_img1, d_img2;
 cv::Mat h_result1;
 //Upload Images to device
 d_img1.upload(h_img1);
 d_img2.upload(h_img2);

 cv::cuda::add(d_img1,d_img2, d_result1);
 //Download Result back to host
 d_result1.download(h_result1);
 cv::imshow("Image1 ", h_img1);
 cv::imshow("Image2 ", h_img2);
 cv::imshow("Result addition ", h_result1);
 int64 delta = cv::getTickCount() - work_begin;
 //Frequency of timer
 double freq = cv::getTickFrequency();
 double work_fps = freq / delta;
 std::cout<<"Performance of Addition on Jetson TX1: " <<std::endl;
 std::cout <<"Time: " << (1/work_fps) <<std::endl;
 std::cout <<"FPS: " <<work_fps <<std::endl;

 cv::imshow("result_add.png", h_result1);
 cv::waitKey();
 return 0;
}
```

One thing to be kept in mind while doing image addition is that both the images should be of the same size. If it is not the case, then they should be resized before addition. In the preceding code, two images of the same size are read from the disk and uploaded to the device memory for addition on a GPU. The add function from the cv::cuda module is used to perform image addition on the device. The resultant image is downloaded to the host and displayed on the console.

The output of the program is as follows:

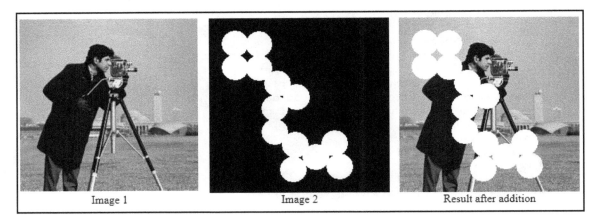

| Image 1 | Image 2 | Result after addition |

The performance of image addition is also measured using the `cv::getTickCount()` and `cv::getTickFrequency()` functions. The time taken by the addition operation is displayed on the console as shown in the following screenshot:

```
ubuntu@tegra-ubuntu:~/Desktop/opencv/Chapter 9$ ./image_add
Performance of Addition on Jetson TX!:
Time: 0.000262104
FPS: 3815.28
```

As can be seen from the preceding screenshot, it takes around 0.26ms to add two images of the size 256 x 256 on Jetson TX1. This is a very good performance for an embedded platform. It should be noted that performance should be measured before the `imshow` function to measure the accurate time for the addition operation. The `imshow` function takes more time to display an image, so the time measured will not be an accurate estimation of time taken to do an add operation.

Image thresholding

This section will demonstrate the use of Jetson TX1 for more computationally intensive computer vision applications, like image thresholding. Image thresholding is a very simple image segmentation technique used to extract important regions from a grayscale image, based on certain intensity values. In this technique, if the pixel value is greater than a certain threshold value then it is assigned one value, or else it is assigned another value.

OpenCV provides different types of thresholding techniques, and it is decided by the last argument of the function. These thresholding types are:

- `cv:.THRES H_BINARY`: If the intensity of the pixel is greater than the threshold, then set the pixel intensity equal to the `maxVal` constant, or else set the pixel intensity to zero.

- `cv::THRESH_BINARY_INV`: If the intensity of the pixel is greater than the threshold, then set the pixel intensity equal to zero, or else set the pixel intensity to the `maxVal` constant.

- `cv::THRESH_TRUNC`: This is basically a truncation operation. If the intensity of the pixel is greater than the threshold, then set the pixel intensity equal to the threshold, or else keep the intensity value as it is.

- `cv::THRESH_TOZERO`: If the intensity of the pixel is greater than the threshold, then keep the pixel intensity as it is, or else set the pixel intensity to zero.

- `cv::THRESH_TOZERO_INV`: If the intensity of the pixel is greater than the threshold, then set that pixel intensity equal to zero, or else keep the pixel intensity as it is.

The program to implement all these thresholding techniques using OpenCV and CUDA on Jetson TX1 is shown as follows:

```
#include <iostream>
#include "opencv2/opencv.hpp"
using namespace cv;
int main (int argc, char* argv[])
{
 cv::Mat h_img1 = cv::imread("images/cameraman.tif", 0);
 cv::cuda::GpuMat d_result1,d_result2,d_result3,d_result4,d_result5,
d_img1;
 //Measure initial time ticks
 int64 work_begin = getTickCount();
 d_img1.upload(h_img1);
 cv::cuda::threshold(d_img1, d_result1, 128.0, 255.0, cv::THRESH_BINARY);
 cv::cuda::threshold(d_img1, d_result2, 128.0, 255.0,
cv::THRESH_BINARY_INV);
 cv::cuda::threshold(d_img1, d_result3, 128.0, 255.0, cv::THRESH_TRUNC);
 cv::cuda::threshold(d_img1, d_result4, 128.0, 255.0, cv::THRESH_TOZERO);
 cv::cuda::threshold(d_img1, d_result5, 128.0, 255.0,
cv::THRESH_TOZERO_INV);

 cv::Mat h_result1,h_result2,h_result3,h_result4,h_result5;
 d_result1.download(h_result1);
 d_result2.download(h_result2);
 d_result3.download(h_result3);
```

```
d_result4.download(h_result4);
d_result5.download(h_result5);
//Measure difference in time ticks
int64 delta = getTickCount() - work_begin;
double freq = getTickFrequency();
//Measure frames per second
double work_fps = freq / delta;
std::cout <<"Performance of Thresholding on GPU: " <<std::endl;
std::cout <<"Time: " << (1/work_fps) <<std::endl;
std::cout <<"FPS: " <<work_fps <<std::endl;
return 0;
}
```

The function used for image thresholding in OpenCV and CUDA on a GPU is `cv::cuda::threshold`. This function has many arguments. The first argument is the source image, which should be a grayscale image. The second argument is the destination at which the result is to be stored. The third argument is the threshold value, which is used to segment the pixel values. The fourth argument is the `maxVal` constant, which represents the value to be given if the pixel value is more than the threshold value. The final argument is the thresholding methods discussed earlier. The output of the program that shows the original image and the output of five thresholding techniques is as follows:

Original Image | Result of binary Threshold | Result of inverse binary Threshold

Result of Thresholding by truncating | Result of Thresholding by truncating to zero | Result of Thresholding by truncating to zero inverse

The performance of image thresholding is also measured using the `cv::getTickCount()` and `cv::getTickFrequency()` functions. The time taken by five thresholding operations is displayed on the console, as shown in the following screenshot:

```
Performance of Thresholding
Time:  0.000326671
FPS:  3061.18
```

It takes `0.32ms` to do five thresholding operations on Jetson TX1, which is again a very good performance for an image segmentation task on embedded platforms. The next section will describe the filtering operations on Jetson TX1.

Image filtering on Jetson TX1

Image filtering is a very important step in image preprocessing and feature extractions. Low pass filters, like averaging, Gaussian, and median filters, are used to remove different types of noise in an image, while high pass filters, like Sobel, Scharr, and Laplacian, are used to detect edges in an image. Edges are important features that can be used for computer vision tasks like object detection and classification. Image filtering is explained in detail earlier in this book.

This section describes the procedure to apply low pass and high pass filters on an image on Jetson TX1. The code for this is as follows:

```
#include <iostream>
#include <string>
#include "opencv2/opencv.hpp"

using namespace std;
using namespace cv;
using namespace cv::cuda;

int main()
{
 Mat h_img1;
 cv::cuda::GpuMat d_img1,d_blur,d_result3x3;
 h_img1 = imread("images/blobs.png",1);

 int64 start = cv::getTickCount();
 d_img1.upload(h_img1);
 cv::cuda::cvtColor(d_img1,d_img1,cv::COLOR_BGR2GRAY);
 cv::Ptr<cv::cuda::Filter> filter3x3;
 filter3x3 =
```

```
cv::cuda::createGaussianFilter(CV_8UC1,CV_8UC1,cv::Size(3,3),1);
filter3x3->apply(d_img1, d_blur);
cv::Ptr<cv::cuda::Filter> filter1;
filter1 = cv::cuda::createLaplacianFilter(CV_8UC1,CV_8UC1,1);
filter1->apply(d_blur, d_result3x3);
cv::Mat h_result3x3,h_blur;
d_result3x3.download(h_result3x3);
d_blur.download(h_blur);
double fps = cv::getTickFrequency() / (cv::getTickCount() - start);
std::cout << "FPS : " << fps << std::endl;
imshow("Laplacian", h_result3x3);
imshow("Blurred", h_blur);
cv::waitKey();
return 0;
}
```

Laplacian is a second-order derivative used to extract both vertical and horizontal images from an image. It is highly sensitive to noise so sometimes it is necessary to remove noise using a low pass filter, like the Gaussian blur, and then apply a Laplacian filter. So in the code, the Gaussian filter of size 3 x 3 is applied to an input image with a standard deviation equal to 1. The filter is created using the `cv::cuda::createGaussianFilter` function of OpenCV. The Laplacian filter is then applied to the Gaussian blurred image. The Laplacian filter is created using the `cv::cuda::createLaplacianFilter` function of OpenCV. The output of the Gaussian blurring and Laplacian filter is downloaded back to the host memory for display on the console. The performance of the filtering operations is also measured in the code. The output of the program is shown in the following screenshot:

As can be seen from the output, the Laplacian filter on a blurred image will remove false edges from an image. It will also remove Gaussian noise present in an input image. If an input image is distorted by salt and pepper noise then the median filter should be used as a preprocessing step to a Laplacian filter for edge detection.

To summarize, we have seen different image-processing functions such as image addition, image thresholding and image filtering on Jetson TX1. We have also seen that the performance of these operations on Jetson TX1 is much better than the performance of the same code on a CPU. The next section will describe the interfacing of the camera with a Jetson TX1 so that it can be used in real-life situations.

Interfacing cameras with Jetson TX1

Jetson TX1 can be interfaced with USB cameras or CSI cameras. The development board comes with one camera of 5 MP already interfaced with Jetson TX1. This camera can be used to capture video just like a webcam on a laptop. Camera interfacing is an important feature that makes the Jetson TX1 development board useful in real-time situations. It supports up to six-lane cameras. The detailed list of cameras supported by Jetson TX1 can be found at the following link: `https://elinux.org/Jetson_TX1` .

This section will demonstrate the procedure to capture videos using a camera interfaced with Jetson TX1 and how these videos can be used to develop computer vision applications, like face detection and background subtraction.

Reading and displaying video from onboard camera

This section will describe the method used to capture video from a USB camera or onboard camera interfaced with Jetson TX1. For this, OpenCV should be compiled with GStreamer support; otherwise, the format of the captured video will not be supported by OpenCV.

The following code can be used to capture video from a camera and display it on the screen:

```
#include <opencv2/opencv.hpp>
#include <iostream>
#include <stdio.h>
using namespace cv;
using namespace std;
```

```
int main(int, char**)
{
 Mat frame;
 // open the default camera using default API
 VideoCapture cap("nvcamerasrc ! video/x-raw(memory:NVMM), width=(int)1280,
height=(int)720, format=(string)I420, framerate=(fraction)24/1 ! nvvidconv
flip-method=0 ! video/x-raw, format=(string)I420 ! videoconvert ! video/x-
raw, format=(string)BGR ! appsink");
 if (!cap.isOpened()) {
 cout << "Unable to open camera\n";
 return -1;
 }
 while (1)
 {
 int64 start = cv::getTickCount();
 cap.read(frame);
 // check if we succeeded
 if (frame.empty()) {
  cout << "Can not read frame\n";
  break;
 }
 double fps = cv::getTickFrequency() / (cv::getTickCount() - start);
 std::cout << "FPS : " << fps << std::endl;

 imshow("Live", frame);
 if (waitKey(30) == 'q')
  break;
 }

 return 0;
}
```

The code is more or less similar to a code used for capturing video from a webcam on a desktop. Instead of using a device ID as an argument to capture an object, the string that specifies GStreamer pipeline is used. This is shown as follows:

```
VideoCapture cap("nvcamerasrc ! video/x-raw(memory:NVMM), width=(int)1280,
height=(int)720, format=(string)I420, framerate=(fraction)24/1 ! nvvidconv
flip-method=0 ! video/x-raw, format=(string)I420 ! videoconvert ! video/x-
raw, format=(string)BGR ! appsink");
```

The width and height of the captured video are specified as 1,280 and 720 pixels. The frame rate is also specified. These values will change according to formats supported by interfaced cameras. Use `nvvidconv` to convert video to BGR format that is supported by OpenCV. It is also used for image scaling and flipping. To flip the captured video, the flip method can be specified as an integer value other than zero.

The `cap.isOpened` property is used to check whether capturing from the camera has started or not. Then the frames are read one by one using the read method and displayed on the screen until q is pressed by the user. The rate of frame capturing is also measured in the code.

The output of the live video is captured by the camera for two different frames, and the frame rate is shown in the following screenshot:

To summarize, in this section we have seen the procedure to capture video from a camera interfaced with a Jetson TX1 development board. This captured video can be used to develop useful real-time computer vision applications as described in the next section.

Advanced applications on Jetson TX1

This section will describe the use of a Jetson TX1 embedded platform in the deployment of advanced computer vision applications, like face detection, eye detection, and background subtraction.

Face detection using Haar cascades

A Haar cascade uses rectangular features to detect an object. It uses rectangles of different sizes to calculate different line and edge features. The idea behind the Haar-like feature detection algorithm is to compute the difference between the sum of white pixels and the sum of black pixels inside the rectangle.

The main advantage of this method is the fast sum computation using the integral image approach. This makes the Haar cascade ideal for real-time object detection. It requires less time for processing an image than other algorithms used for object detection. The Haar cascade is ideal for deployment on embedded systems like Jetson TX1 because of its low computational complexity and low memory footprint. So in this section, this algorithm is used to deploy face detection applications on Jetson TX1.

The code for face detection from a video captured by a camera interfaced with Jetson TX1 is as follows:

```
#include <iostream>
#include <opencv2/opencv.hpp>
using namespace cv;
using namespace std;

int main()
{
 VideoCapture cap("images/output.avi");
//cv::VideoCapture cap("nvcamerasrc ! video/x-raw(memory:NVMM),
width=(int)1280, height=(int)720, format=(string)I420,
framerate=(fraction)24/1 ! nvvidconv flip-method=0 ! video/x-raw,
format=(string)I420 ! videoconvert ! video/x-raw, format=(string)BGR !
appsink");
 if (!cap.isOpened()) {
   cout << "Can not open video source";
   return -1;
 }
 std::vector<cv::Rect> h_found;
 cv::Ptr<cv::cuda::CascadeClassifier> cascade =
cv::cuda::CascadeClassifier::create("haarcascade_frontalface_alt2.xml");
 cv::cuda::GpuMat d_frame, d_gray, d_found;
 while(1)
 {
 Mat frame;
 if ( !cap.read(frame) ) {
   cout << "Can not read frame from webcam";
   return -1;
 }
 int64 start = cv::getTickCount();
 d_frame.upload(frame);
 cv::cuda::cvtColor(d_frame, d_gray, cv::COLOR_BGR2GRAY);

 cascade->detectMultiScale(d_gray, d_found);
 cascade->convert(d_found, h_found);

 for(int i = 0; i < h_found.size(); ++i)
 {
```

```
    rectangle(frame, h_found[i], Scalar(0,255,255), 5);
  }
  double fps = cv::getTickFrequency() / (cv::getTickCount() - start);
  std::cout << "FPS : " << fps << std::endl;
  imshow("Result", frame);
  if (waitKey(1) == 'q') {
    break;
  }
  }

  return 0;
}
```

The Haar cascade is an algorithm which needs to be trained to do a particular task. It is difficult to train a Haar cascade from scratch for a particular application, so OpenCV provides some trained XML files which can be used to detect objects. These XML files are provided in the `\usr\local\opencv\data\haarcascades_cuda` directory of the OpenCV and CUDA installations.

The webcam is initialized, and frames from the webcam are captured one by one. The frame is uploaded to the device memory for processing on the GPU. OpenCV and CUDA provide the `CascadeClassifier` class that can be used for implementing the Haar cascade. The create method is used to create an object of that class. It requires the filename of the trained XML file to be loaded.

Inside the `while` loop, the `detectMultiscale` method is applied to every frame so that faces of different sizes can be detected in each frame. The detected location is converted to a rectangle vector, using the convert method. Then, this vector is iterated using the `for` loop so that a bounding box can be drawn using a rectangle function on all the detected faces. This procedure is repeated for every frame captured from the webcam. The performance of the algorithm is also measured in terms of frames per second.

The output of the program is as follows:

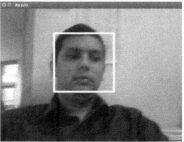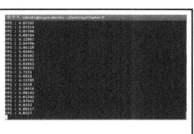

As can be seen from the output, the face is correctly localized in two different frames of the webcam at different positions. The second frame is a little bit blurred, but it is not affecting the algorithm. The performance of the algorithm on Jetson TX1 is also shown in the right image. The algorithm works at around five frames per second.

To summarize, this section demonstrates the use of Jetson TX1 in detecting faces from a live video captured from a webcam. This application can be used for person identification, face locking, attendance monitoring, and so on.

Eye detection using Haar cascades

This section will describe the use of Haar cascades in detecting the eyes of humans. The XML file for a trained Haar cascade for eye detection is provided in the OpenCV installation directory. This file is used to detect eyes. The code for it is as follows:

```
#include "opencv2/objdetect/objdetect.hpp"
#include "opencv2/highgui/highgui.hpp"
#include "opencv2/imgproc/imgproc.hpp"
#include "opencv2/cudaobjdetect.hpp"
#include <iostream>
#include <stdio.h>

using namespace std;
using namespace cv;

int main( )
{
  Mat h_image;
  h_image = imread("images/lena_color_512.tif", 0);
  Ptr<cuda::CascadeClassifier> cascade =
cuda::CascadeClassifier::create("haarcascade_eye.xml");
  cuda::GpuMat d_image;
  cuda::GpuMat d_buf;
  int64 start = cv::getTickCount();
  d_image.upload(h_image);
  cascadeGPU->setMinNeighbors(0);
  cascadeGPU->setScaleFactor(1.02);
  cascade->detectMultiScale(d_image, d_buf);
  std::vector<Rect> detections;
  cascade->convert(d_buf, detections);
  if (detections.empty())
    std::cout << "No detection." << std::endl;
    cvtColor(h_image,h_image,COLOR_GRAY2BGR);
  for(int i = 0; i < detections.size(); ++i)
  {
```

```
    rectangle(h_image, detections[i], Scalar(0,255,255), 5);
  }
  double fps = cv::getTickFrequency() / (cv::getTickCount() - start);
  std::cout << "FPS : " << fps << std::endl;
  imshow("Result image on Jetson TX1", h_image);
  waitKey(0);
  return 0;
}
```

The code is similar to the code for face detection. This is the advantage of using Haar cascades. If an XML file for a trained Haar cascade on a given object is available then the same code will work in all applications. Just the name of the XML file needs to change while creating an object of the `CascadeClassifier` class. In the preceding code, `haarcascade_eye.xml`, which is the trained XML file for eye detection, is used. The other code is self-explanatory. The scale factor is set at `1.02` so that image size will be reduced by `1.02` at every scale. The output of the eye detection program is as follows:

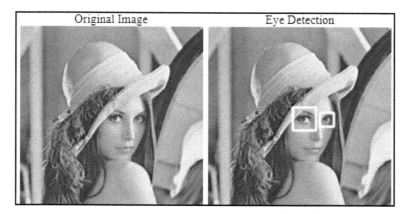

Now that we have detected objects from video and images using a Haar cascade, the captured video can also be used to detect and track objects using the background subtraction method as described in the next section.

Background subtraction using Mixture of Gaussian (MoG)

Background subtraction is an important preprocessing step for object detection and tracking applications. It can also be used for unusual activity detection from CCTV footage. This section demonstrates the use of Jetson TX1 in a background subtraction application. The camera interfaced with Jetson TX1 is mounted in a room for activity detection inside the room. The background of the room is initialized in the first frame.

The MoG, which is a widely used background subtraction method used for separating the foreground from the background based on Gaussian mixtures, is used for activity detection. The background is continuously updated from the sequence of frames. A mixture of K Gaussian distribution is used to categorize pixels as foreground or background. The time sequence of the frame is also weighted to improve background modeling. The intensities that are continuously changing are categorized as foreground, and intensities that are static are categorized as background.

The code for activity monitoring using MoG is as follows:

```
#include <iostream>
#include <string>
#include "opencv2/opencv.hpp"

using namespace std;
using namespace cv;
using namespace cv::cuda;
int main()
{
 VideoCapture cap("nvcamerasrc ! video/x-raw(memory:NVMM), width=(int)1280,
height=(int)720, format=(string)I420, framerate=(fraction)24/1 ! nvvidconv
flip-method=0 ! video/x-raw, format=(string)I420 ! videoconvert ! video/x-
raw, format=(string)BGR ! appsink");
 if (!cap.isOpened())
 {
 cout << "Can not open camera or video file" << endl;
 return -1;
 }
 Mat frame;
 cap.read(frame);
 GpuMat d_frame;
 d_frame.upload(frame);
 Ptr<BackgroundSubtractor> mog = cuda::createBackgroundSubtractorMOG();
 GpuMat d_fgmask,d_fgimage,d_bgimage;
 Mat h_fgmask,h_fgimage,h_bgimage;
 mog->apply(d_frame, d_fgmask, 0.01);
```

```
namedWindow("image", WINDOW_NORMAL);
namedWindow("foreground mask", WINDOW_NORMAL);
namedWindow("foreground image", WINDOW_NORMAL);
namedWindow("mean background image", WINDOW_NORMAL);

while(1)
{
cap.read(frame);
if (frame.empty())
 break;
d_frame.upload(frame);
int64 start = cv::getTickCount();
mog->apply(d_frame, d_fgmask, 0.01);
mog->getBackgroundImage(d_bgimage);
double fps = cv::getTickFrequency() / (cv::getTickCount() - start);
std::cout << "FPS : " << fps << std::endl;
d_fgimage.create(d_frame.size(), d_frame.type());
d_fgimage.setTo(Scalar::all(0));
d_frame.copyTo(d_fgimage, d_fgmask);
d_fgmask.download(h_fgmask);
d_fgimage.download(h_fgimage);
d_bgimage.download(h_bgimage);
imshow("image", frame);
imshow("foreground mask", h_fgmask);
imshow("foreground image", h_fgimage);
imshow("mean background image", h_bgimage);
if (waitKey(1) == 'q')
 break;
}

 return 0;
}
```

The camera interfaced with Jetson TX1 is initialized with the GStreamer pipeline. The createBackgroundSubtractorMOG class is used to create an object for MoG implementation. The apply method of the created object is used to create a foreground mask from the first frame. It requires an input image, an image array to store foreground mask, and learning rate as the input. The image of the room without any activity is initialized as a background for the MoG. So, any activity that will happen will be categorized as foreground by the algorithm.

This foreground mask and the background image are continuously updated after every frame inside the while loop. The getBackgroundImage function is used to fetch the current background model.

The foreground mask is used to create a foreground image, which indicates which objects are currently moving. It is basically logical and operates between the original frame and foreground mask. The foreground mask, foreground image, and the modeled background are downloaded to the host memory after every frame, for displaying on the screen.

The output of two different frames from the video is shown in the following screenshot:

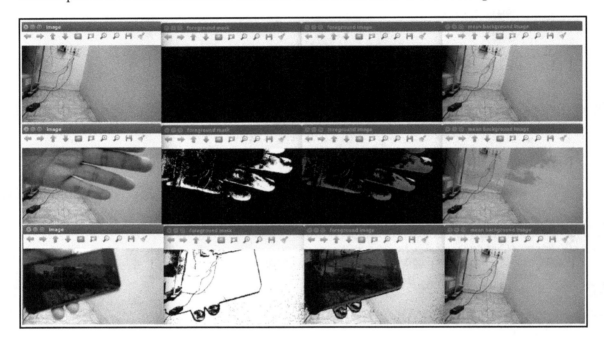

The first row indicates the background of the room without any activity. When someone moves a hand in front of the camera, it will be detected as foreground, as shown in the second frame result. In the same way, if someone puts a cell phone in front of the camera, that will also be categorized as foreground, as shown in the third frame. The performance of the code in terms of frames per second is shown in the following screenshot:

```
ubuntu@tegra-ubuntu: ~/Desktop/Chapter 9
FPS :  45.9451
FPS :  38.3942
FPS :  39.1694
FPS :  39.365
FPS :  38.7298
FPS :  34.2839
FPS :  75.2029
FPS :  59.0898
FPS :  47.6766
FPS :  49.3542
FPS :  34.7506
FPS :  38.3625
FPS :  38.4274
FPS :  44.3814
FPS :  77.2785
FPS :  65.9443
FPS :  58.8832
FPS :  54.1984
FPS :  49.1819
FPS :  78.8699
FPS :  71.9925
FPS :  65.1592
FPS :  60.9173
```

The technique works at around 60-70 frames per second, which can easily be used to take a real-time decision. Though the demonstration in this section is very trivial, this application can be used in many real-life situations. The activity inside a room can be used to control the appliances present in the room. This will help in saving electricity when no person is present. This application can also be used at an ATM for monitoring activity inside it. It can also be used for other video surveillance applications in public places. Python can also be used as the programming language on Jetson TX1, which will be explained in the next section.

Computer vision using Python and OpenCV on Jetson TX1

Up till now, we have developed all computer vision applications using C/C++, OpenCV, and CUDA. Jetson TX1 also supports the Python programming language for computer vision applications. When OpenCV is compiled on Jetson TX1, it also installs Python binaries for OpenCV. So programmers who are comfortable in Python programming language can use a Python interface for OpenCV in developing computer vision applications and deploying them on Jetson TX1. Python also comes preinstalled with Jetson TX1 as is the case for all Linux operating systems. Windows users can install Python separately. The installation procedure and advantages of Python are explained in the next chapter.

One disadvantage of using Python is that OpenCV Python interface is still not greatly benefited by CUDA acceleration. Still, the ease of learning Python and the wide range of applications in which it can be used have encouraged many software developers to use Python for computer vision applications. The sample code for reading and displaying images using Python and OpenCV is as follows:

```
import numpy as np
import cv2
img = cv2.imread('images/cameraman.tif',0)
cv2.imshow("Image read in Python", img)
k = cv2.waitKey(0) & 0xFF
if k == 27: # wait for ESC key to exit
 cv2.destroyAllWindows()
```

In Python,the `import` command is used to include a library in a file. So the `cv2` library is included by using the `import cv2` command. Images are stored as `numpy` arrays so `numpy` is also imported in a file. The `imread` function is used to read an image in the same way as C++. All OpenCV functions have to be prefixed with `cv2.` in Python. The `imshow` function is used to display an image. All OpenCV functions have a similar signature and functionality in Python as C++.

The following command can be used to execute the code from the Terminal:

```
# For Python2.7
$ python image_read.py
# For Python 3
$ python image_read.py
```

The output of the program is shown in the following screenshot:

This section is just included to make you aware that Python can also be used as a programming language for developing computer vision applications using OpenCV and deploying it on Jetson TX1.

Summary

This chapter described the use of Jetson TX1 in the deployment of CUDA and OpenCV code. The properties of the GPU device present on a TX1 board that make it ideal for deploying computationally complex applications are explained in detail. The performance of Jetson TX1 for CUDA applications such as adding two large arrays is measured and compared with GPUs present on laptops. The procedure to work with images on Jetson TX1 is explained in detail in this chapter. The image-processing applications like image addition, image thresholding, and image filtering are deployed on Jetson TX1 and performance is measured for them.

The best part of Jetson TX1 is that multiple cameras can be interfaced with it in an embedded environment, and videos from that camera can be processed to design complex computer vision applications. The procedure to capture video from an onboard or USB camera interfaced with Jetson TX1 is explained in detail.

The chapter also described the deployment of advanced computer vision applications like face detection, eye detection, and background subtraction on Jetson TX1. The Python language can also be used to deploy computer vision applications on Jetson TX1. This concept is explained in the last part of the chapter. So far, we have seen how the C/C++ language can leverage the advantages of CUDA and GPU acceleration.

The next couple of chapters will demonstrate the use of CUDA and GPU acceleration for the Python language using the PyCUDA module.

Questions

1. Compare the performance of a GPU device on Jetson TX1 with a GeForce 940 GPU seen earlier in the book.
2. State True or False: All CUDA programs seen earlier in the book can be executed on Jetson TX1 without modification.
3. What is the need for recompiling OpenCV on Jetson TX1?
4. State True or False: OpenCV can't capture video from a camera connected to the USB port.
5. State True or False: It is better to use a CSI camera for computationally intensive applications than a USB camera.
6. If you are developing computationally intensive computer vision applications using OpenCV, which language would you prefer for faster performance?
7. Is there a need to install separate OpenCV Python binding or Python interpreter on Jetson TX1?

10
Getting Started with PyCUDA

We have seen how we can accelerate various applications using OpenCV and CUDA. We have used C or C++ as a programming language. Nowadays, Python is very popular in many domains, so it will be very useful if we can accelerate Python applications using CUDA. Python provides a PyCUDA module that does exactly that.

It uses the Nvidia CUDA toolkit which, in turn, requires an Nvidia graphics card installed on the computer. This chapter will give an introduction to the Python language and the PyCUDA module, in particular. It will discuss the installation procedure for the PyCUDA module on the Windows and Linux operating systems. Though the chapter requires some familiarity with the Python language, newcomers will also be able to follow most of the procedures.

The following topics will be covered in this chapter:

- Introduction to the Python Programming Language
- Introduction to the PyCUDA module
- Installation of PyCUDA on Windows
- Installation of PyCUDA on Ubuntu

Technical requirements

This chapter requires a good understanding of the Python programming language. It also requires any computer or laptop with an Nvidia GPU on board. The PyCUDA installation file for Windows used in this chapter can be downloaded from the following GitHub link: `https://github.com/PacktPublishing/Hands-On-GPU-Accelerated-Computer-Vision-with-OpenCV-and-CUDA`.

Introduction to Python programming language

Python is continuously gaining popularity as it can be used in many fields with a wide range of applications. It is a high-level programming language that helps in expressing complex systems with a few lines of code. The Python syntax is easy to learn and more readable than other languages such as C++ and Java, which makes it easy to learn for novice programmers.

Python is a lightweight scripting language that can be easily used in embedded applications. Moreover, it is an interpreted language that requires an interpreter rather than a compiler, as is case for other programming languages. This allows the programmer to execute code line by line. It requires a Python interpreter that can be easily installed on all operating systems. Since Python is open source, a large community chooses to work with it. They have developed a wide range of libraries and made it open source, and hence it can be easily used in applications without any cost.

Python can be used in various domains such as data science, machine learning, deep learning, data analytics, image processing, computer vision, data mining, and web development. It has ready-to-use modules for almost all of the OS mentioned domains, which help in the rapid development of applications. OpenCV library, which was explained earlier in this book, also has a Python interface. Thus, it can be easily integrated with Python code for computer vision applications. Python has libraries for machine learning and deep learning that can be used for computer vision applications along with OpenCV.

One disadvantage of an interpreted language like Python is that it is much slower than compiled languages like C or C++. Python has a feature whereby it can integrate C or C++ code within a Python script. This allows you to write computationally intensive code in C or C++ with a Python wrapper.

Introduction to the PyCUDA module

In the last section, we saw many advantages of using the Python programming language. It is also mentioned that Python is much slower than C or C++. So, it will be beneficial if it can leverage the parallel processing capability of a GPU. Python provides a PyCUDA wrapper that can utilize the parallel computing capability of a GPU by using the Nvidia CUDA API. Python also has a `PyOpenCL` module that can be used for parallel computation on any GPU.

Then, one question you might ask is why you have to use PyCUDA, which is specific to Nvidia GPUs. There are many advantages of using PyCUDA over other similar modules; the following are the reasons:

- It provides an easy interface with CUDA API for Python developers and has good documentation, which make it easy to learn.
- The full power of CUDA API provided by Nvidia can be used within Python code using the PyCUDA module.
- The base layer of PyCUDA is written in C++, which makes it faster.
- It has a higher level of abstraction, which makes it easy to use compared to the Nvidia C-based runtime API.
- It has a very efficient memory management mechanism with object cleanup tied to the lifetime of the objects. This feature helps it to write correct code, without memory leak or crashing.
- The errors within the CUDA code can also be handled by Python exceptions, which helps with the error-handling mechanism in the code.

This section described the advantage of using PyCUDA for the acceleration of Python applications. In the next section, we will see the procedure to install PyCUDA on Windows and Ubuntu operating systems.

Installing PyCUDA on Windows

This section will describe the steps to install PyCUDA on a Windows operating system. Windows 10 is used for the demonstration, but the procedure will work on any recent Windows versions. The steps are described below:

1. If you have not installed CUDA toolkit, as described in the first chapter, then download the latest CUDA toolkit from `https://developer.nvidia.com/cuda-downloads`. It will ask for your operating system, CPU architecture, and whether to install using the internet or to download the entire installer first. As can be seen from the following screenshot, we have chosen **Windows 10** with the **local** installer. You can choose values according to your settings:

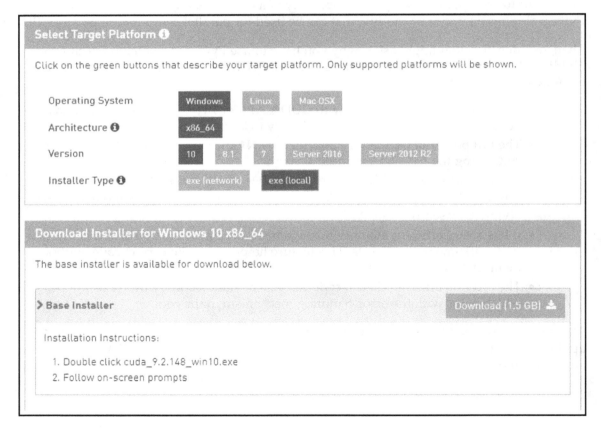

2. Install the CUDA toolkit by double-clicking on the downloaded installer and follow the on-screen prompts.

3. Install the latest Visual Studio edition, which has a visual C++ version. We are using Visual Studio 2017 community edition, which is free to use. The path for visual C++ should be added to the path environment variable. The environment variable can be accessed by right-clicking on **My Computer (This PC)** | **Properties** | **Advanced System Settings** | **Environment Variables** | **System variables**. Add the path for the bin folder of the visual C++ installation and CUDA toolkit installation in the path environment variable, as shown in the following screenshot:

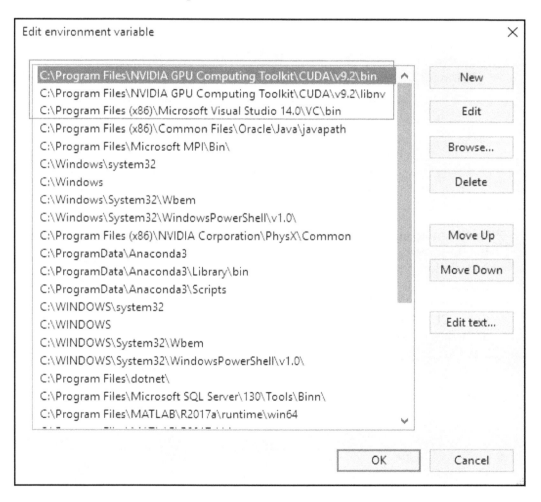

4. Anaconda distribution will be used as a Python interpreter so it can be downloaded from the site: `https://www.anaconda.com/download/`. We are using **Anaconda 5.2** with the **Python 3.6** version, as shown in the following screenshot:

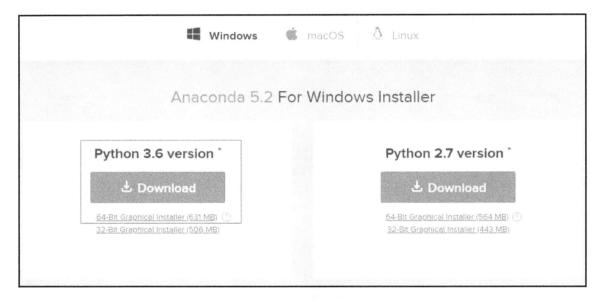

5. Install Anaconda by double-clicking on the downloaded installer and following the on-screen prompts. Make sure you check the checkbox for adding the installation path to the path environment variable.

6. Download the latest PyCUDA binary according to your system settings from the following link: `https://www.lfd.uci.edu/~gohlke/Pythonlibs/#pycuda`. We are using CUDA 9.2148 and Python 3.6, so the PyCUDA version is chosen accordingly, as the following shows:

pycuda-2017.1.1-cuda9185-cp34-cp34m-win32.whl

pycuda-2017.1.1-cuda9185-cp34-cp34m-win_amd64.whl

pycuda-2017.1.1-cuda9185-cp35-cp35m-win32.whl

pycuda-2017.1.1-cuda9185-cp35-cp35m-win_amd64.whl

pycuda-2017.1.1-cuda9185-cp36-cp36m-win32.whl

pycuda-2017.1.1-cuda9185-cp36-cp36m-win_amd64.whl

pycuda-2018.1-cuda92148-cp27-cp27m-win32.whl

pycuda-2018.1-cuda92148-cp27-cp27m-win_amd64.whl

pycuda-2018.1-cuda92148-cp34-cp34m-win32.whl

pycuda-2018.1-cuda92148-cp34-cp34m-win_amd64.whl

pycuda-2018.1-cuda92148-cp35-cp35m-win32.whl

pycuda-2018.1-cuda92148-cp35-cp35m-win_amd64.whl

pycuda-2018.1-cuda92148-cp36-cp36m-win32.whl

pycuda-2018.1-cuda92148-cp36-cp36m-win_amd64.whl

pycuda-2018.1-cuda92148-cp37-cp37m-win32.whl

pycuda-2018.1-cuda92148-cp37-cp37m-win_amd64.whl

7. Open Command Prompt, go to the folder where the PyCUDA binary is downloaded and execute the command as shown in the following screenshot:

```
PS C:\Users\bhaum\Downloads> pip install .\pycuda-2017.1.1+cuda92148-cp36-cp36m-win_amd64.whl
Processing c:\users\bhaum\downloads\pycuda-2017.1.1+cuda92148-cp36-cp36m-win_amd64.whl
Requirement already satisfied: pytest>=2 in c:\programdata\anaconda3\lib\site-packages (from pycuda==2017.1.1+cuda92148)
Requirement already satisfied: pytools>=2011.2 in c:\programdata\anaconda3\lib\site-packages (from pycuda==2017.1.1+cuda
92148)
Requirement already satisfied: decorator>=3.2.0 in c:\programdata\anaconda3\lib\site-packages (from pycuda==2017.1.1+cud
a92148)
Requirement already satisfied: appdirs>=1.4.0 in c:\programdata\anaconda3\lib\site-packages (from pycuda==2017.1.1+cuda9
2148)
Requirement already satisfied: py>=1.5.0 in c:\programdata\anaconda3\lib\site-packages (from pytest>=2->pycuda==2017.1.1
+cuda92148)
Requirement already satisfied: six>=1.10.0 in c:\programdata\anaconda3\lib\site-packages (from pytest>=2->pycuda==2017.1
.1+cuda92148)
Requirement already satisfied: setuptools in c:\programdata\anaconda3\lib\site-packages (from pytest>=2->pycuda==2017.1.
1+cuda92148)
Requirement already satisfied: attrs>=17.2.0 in c:\programdata\anaconda3\lib\site-packages (from pytest>=2->pycuda==2017
.1.1+cuda92148)
Requirement already satisfied: pluggy<0.7,>=0.5 in c:\programdata\anaconda3\lib\site-packages (from pytest>=2->pycuda==2
017.1.1+cuda92148)
Requirement already satisfied: colorama in c:\programdata\anaconda3\lib\site-packages (from pytest>=2->pycuda==2017.1.1+
cuda92148)
Requirement already satisfied: numpy>=1.6.0 in c:\programdata\anaconda3\lib\site-packages (from pytools>=2011.2->pycuda=
=2017.1.1+cuda92148)
Installing collected packages: pycuda
  Found existing installation: pycuda 2017.1.1+cuda9185
    Uninstalling pycuda-2017.1.1+cuda9185:
      Successfully uninstalled pycuda-2017.1.1+cuda9185
Successfully installed pycuda-2017.1.1+cuda92148
You are using pip version 9.0.1, however version 18.0 is available.
You should consider upgrading via the 'python -m pip install --upgrade pip' command.
```

The command will complete the installation of PyCUDA in the Python distribution.

Steps to check PyCUDA installation

The following steps are to be followed to check whether PyCUDA has been installed correctly or not:

1. Open Spyder, which is a Python IDE, that comes with Anaconda installations. You can open it by writing `Spyder` in the start menu.
2. In Spyder IDE, type `import pycuda` on the **IPython console** as shown in the following screenshot. If no error is reported, then PyCUDA is installed correctly.

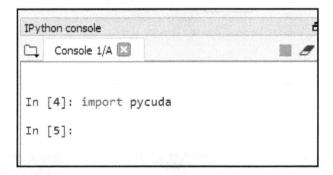

Installing PyCUDA on Ubuntu

This section will describe the steps to install PyCUDA on Linux operating systems. Ubuntu is used for demonstration but the procedure will work on any recent Linux distribution. The steps are described below:

1. If you have not installed the CUDA toolkit, as described in the first chapter, then download the latest CUDA toolkit from `https://developer.nvidia.com/cuda-downloads`. It will ask for your operating system, CPU architecture, and whether to install using the internet or to download the entire installer first. As can be seen from the following screenshot, we have chosen **Ubuntu** with the **runfile (local)** installer. You can choose values according to your settings:

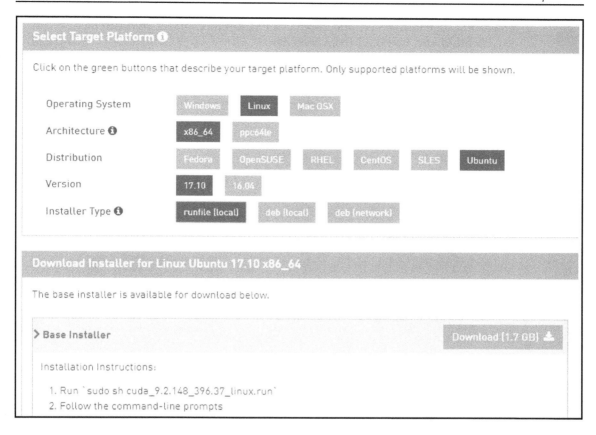

2. Run the **sudo sh cuda_9.2.148_396.37_linux.run** command on Command Prompt to install the CUDA toolkit.

3. Anaconda distribution will be used as a Python interpreter so it can be downloaded and installed from the site: `https://www.anaconda.com/download/`. We are using **Anaconda 5.2** with the **Python 3.6** version, as shown in the following screenshot:

4. After installing Anaconda, execute the following command on the Terminal, as shown in the following screenshot to install PyCUDA:

```
bhaumik@bhaumik-Lenovo-ideapad-520-15IKB:~$ conda install -c lukepfister pycuda
Solving environment: done


==> WARNING: A newer version of conda exists. <==
  current version: 4.4.10
  latest version: 4.5.8

Please update conda by running

    $ conda update -n base conda



## Package Plan ##

  environment location: /home/bhaumik/anaconda3

  added / updated specs:
    - pycuda


The following packages will be downloaded:

    package                    |            build
    ---------------------------|-----------------
    ca-certificates-2018.03.07 |                0      124 KB
    pycuda-2017.1              |          py36_0      627 KB  lukepfister
    appdirs-1.4.3              |   py36h28b3542_0       16 KB
    pytools-2018.4             |          py36_0      110 KB  lukepfister
    mako-1.0.4                 |          py36_0      116 KB  lukepfister
    openssl-1.0.2o             |       h20670df_0      3.4 MB
    certifi-2018.4.16          |          py36_0      142 KB
    ---------------------------------------------------------
                                          Total:      4.6 MB
```

The command will complete the installation of PyCUDA in the Python
distribution.

Steps to check the PyCUDA installation

The following steps are to be followed to check whether PyCUDA has been installed correctly or not:

- Open Spyder, which is the Python IDE that comes with the Anaconda installation. You can open it by writing `Spyder` in the Terminal.
- In Spyder IDE, type `import pycuda` on the **IPython console** as shown in the following screenshot. If no error is reported then PyCUDA is installed correctly.

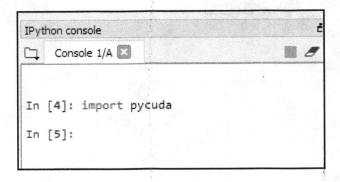

Summary

To summarize, this chapter gave an introduction to the Python programming language and how it is used in various domains for a vast range of applications. It is lightweight but slow compared to the C or C++ languages. So, if it can leverage the advantages of the parallel computing capability of the GPU then it will be very useful. PyCUDA is a Python wrapper that allows the Python code to take advantage of Nvidia CUDA APIs. The advantage of PyCUDA over other parallel processing modules available in Python is explained in detail. PyCUDA uses an Nvidia CUDA runtime API and Python interpreter. Anaconda, which is a famous Python distribution, comes with many useful Python libraries and IDEs installed, along with the CUDA toolkit. The detailed steps to install PyCUDA on Windows and Ubuntu operating systems are discussed in this chapter.

We will see how to use PyCUDA to accelerate Python applications in detail in the next two chapters.

Questions

1. What are the advantages of Python over programming languages like C or C++?
2. What is the difference between compiled type languages and interpreted languages?
3. State true or false: Python is faster than C or C++.
4. What is the advantage of PyOpenCL over PyCUDA?
5. State true or false: Python allows the use of C or C++ code within Python script.

11
Working with PyCUDA

In the last chapter, we saw the procedure to install PyCUDA for Windows and Linux operating systems. In this chapter, we will start by developing the first PyCUDA program that displays a string on the console. It is very important to know and access the device properties of the GPU on which PyCUDA is running; the method for doing this will be discussed in detail in this chapter. We will also look at the execution of threads and blocks for a kernel in PyCUDA. The important programming concepts for any CUDA programming, such as allocating and deallocating the memory on the device, transferring data from host to device and vice versa, and the kernel call will be discussed in detail, using an example of the vector addition program. The method to measure the performance of PyCUDA programs using CUDA events and to compare it with the CPU program will also be discussed. These programming concepts will be used to develop some complex PyCUDA programs, such as the squaring of elements in an array and matrix multiplication. The last part of the chapter describes some advanced methods to define kernel functions in PyCUDA.

The following topics will be covered in this chapter:

- Writing the first "Hello, PyCUDA!" program in PyCUDA
- Accessing device properties from a PyCUDA program
- Thread and block execution in PyCUDA
- Basic PyCUDA programming concepts using a vector addition program
- Measuring the performance of PyCUDA programs using CUDA events
- Some complex programs in PyCUDA
- Advanced kernel functions in PyCUDA

Technical requirements

This chapter requires a good understanding of the Python programming language. It also requires any computer or laptop with the Nvidia GPU onboard. All the code used in this chapter can be downloaded from the following GitHub link: `https://github.com/PacktPublishing/Hands-On-GPU-Accelerated-Computer-Vision-with-OpenCV-and-CUDA`.

Check out the following video to see the code in action:
`http://bit.ly/2QPWojV`

Writing the first program in PyCUDA

This section describes the procedure for writing a simple "Hello, PyCUDA!" program using PyCUDA. It will demonstrate the workflow for writing any PyCUDA programs. As Python is an interpreted language, the code can also be run line by line from the Python terminal, or it can be saved with the `.py` extension and executed as a file.

The program for displaying a simple string from the kernel using PyCUDA is shown as follows:

```
import pycuda.driver as drv
import pycuda.autoinit
from pycuda.compiler import SourceModule

mod = SourceModule("""
  #include <stdio.h>

  __global__ void myfirst_kernel()
  {
    printf("Hello,PyCUDA!!!");
  }
""")

function = mod.get_function("myfirst_kernel")
function(block=(1,1,1))
```

The first step while developing PyCUDA code is to include all libraries needed for the code. The import directive is used to include a library, module, class, or function in a file. This is similar to including a directive in C or C++, and it can be done in three different ways, as shown in the following steps. The use of three imported modules is also shown as follows:

1. Import `pycuda.driver as drv`
   This indicates that the driver submodule of the pymodule is imported and it is given a short notation `drv`, so wherever functions from the `pycuda.driver` module are to be used then they can be used as `drv.functionname`. This module contains memory management functions, device properties, data direction functions, and so on.
2. Import `pycuda.autoinit`
   This command indicates the `autoint` module from `pycuda` is imported. It is not given any shorthand notation. The `autoint` module is used for device initialization, context creation, and memory cleanup. This module is not mandatory, and all the above functions can also be done manually.
3. From `pycuda.compiler` import `SourceModule`
   This command indicates that only the `SourceModule` class from the `pycuda.compiler` module is imported. This is important when you only want to use one class of a large module. The `SourceModule` class is used to define C-like kernel functions in PyCUDA.

The C or C++ kernel code is fed as a constructor to the `Sourcemodule` class and the mod object is created. The kernel code is very simple as it is just printing a `Hello, PyCUDA!` string on the console. As the `printf` function is used inside kernel code, it is very important to include the `stdio.h` header file. The `myfirst_kernel` function is defined inside the kernel code using the `__global__` directive to indicate that the function will be executed on the GPU. The function does not take any arguments. It just prints a string on the console. This kernel function will be compiled by the `nvcc` compiler.

This function can be used inside Python code by creating a pointer to the function using the `get_function` method of the `mod` object. The name of the kernel function is given as arguments in quotes. The pointer variable can be given any name. This pointer variable is used to call the kernel in the last line of the code. The arguments to the kernel function can be specified here, but the `myfirst_kernel` function does not have any arguments, so no arguments are specified. The number of threads per block and blocks per grid to be launched for a kernel can also be provided as an argument by using optional block and grid arguments. The block argument is given a value of (1,1,1) which is a 1 x 3 Python tuple, which indicates a block size of 1 x 1 x 1. So one thread will be launched that will print the string on the console.

The output of the program is shown as follows:

```
PS G:\cude opencv book material\CUDA book code\Chapter11> python .\hello_pycuda.py
Hello,PyCUDA!!!
PS G:\cude opencv book material\CUDA book code\Chapter11> _
```

To summarize, this section demonstrated the procedure to develop a simple PyCUDA program step by step.

A kernel call

The device code that is written using ANSI C keywords along with CUDA extension keywords is called a **kernel**. It is launched from a Python code by a method called **Kernel Call**. Basically, the meaning of a kernel call is that we are launching a device code from the host code. A kernel call typically generates a large number of blocks and threads to exploit data parallelism on a GPU. Kernel code is very similar to that of normal C functions; it is just that this code is executed by several threads in parallel. It has a very simple syntax in Python, which can be shown as follows:

```
kernel (parameters for kernel,block=(tx,ty,tz) , grid=(bx,by,bz))
```

It starts with the pointer of the kernel function that we want to launch. You should make sure that this kernel pointer is created using the get_function method. Then, it can include parameters of the kernel function separated by a comma. The block parameter indicates the number of threads to be launched, and the grid parameter indicates the number of blocks in the grid. The block and grid parameters are specified using a 1 x 3 Python tuple, which indicates blocks and threads in three dimensions. The total number of threads started by a kernel launch will be the multiplication of these numbers.

Accessing GPU device properties from PyCUDA program

PyCUDA provides a simple API to find information such as, which CUDA-enabled GPU devices (if any) are present and which capabilities each device supports. It is important to find out the properties of a GPU device that is being used before writing PyCUDA programs so that the optimal resources of the device can be used.

The program for displaying all properties of CUDA-enabled devices on a system by using PyCUDA is shown as follows:

```
import pycuda.driver as drv
import pycuda.autoinit
drv.init()
print("%d device(s) found." % drv.Device.count())
for i in range(drv.Device.count()):
  dev = drv.Device(i)
  print("Device #%d: %s" % (i, dev.name()))
  print(" Compute Capability: %d.%d" % dev.compute_capability())
  print(" Total Memory: %s GB" % (dev.total_memory()//(1024*1024*1024)))
  attributes = [(str(prop), value)
    for prop, value in list(dev.get_attributes().items())]
    attributes.sort()
    n=0
    for prop, value in attributes:
      print(" %s: %s " % (prop, value),end=" ")
      n = n+1
      if(n%2 == 0):
        print(" ")
```

First, it is important to get a count of how many CUDA-enabled devices are present on the system, as a system may contain more than one GPU-enabled device. This count can be determined by the `drv.Device.count()` function of a driver class in PyCUDA. All the devices present on a system are iterated to determine the properties of each device. A pointer object to each device is created using the `drv.Device` function. This pointer is used to determine all properties of a particular device.

The `name` function will give the name of a particular device and `total_memory` will give the size of the GPU global memory available on the device. The other properties are stored as a Python dictionary that can be fetched by the `get_attributes().items()` function. This is converted to a list of tuples by using list comprehension in Python. All the rows of this list contain the 2 x 1 tuple, which has the name of the property and its value.

This list is iterated using the `for` loop to display all the properties on the console. This program is executed on the laptop with a GeForce 940 GPU and CUDA 9. The output of the program is as shown:

The properties were discussed in detail in earlier chapters of the book, so we won't discuss them again; however, to summarize, this section demonstrated the method to access GPU device properties from a PyCUDA program.

Thread and block execution in PyCUDA

We saw in the *A kernel call* section that we can start multiple blocks and multiple threads in parallel. So, in which order do these blocks and threads start and finish their execution? It is important to know this if we want to use the output of one thread in other threads. To understand this, we have modified the kernel in the `hello, PyCUDA!` program, seen in the earlier section, by including a print statement in a kernel call, which prints the block number. The modified code is shown as follows:

```
import pycuda.driver as drv
import pycuda.autoinit
from pycuda.compiler import SourceModule
```

```
mod = SourceModule("""
  #include <stdio.h>
  __global__ void myfirst_kernel()
  {
    printf("I am in block no: %d \\n", blockIdx.x);
  }
""")

function = mod.get_function("myfirst_kernel")
function(grid=(4,1),block=(1,1,1))
```

As can be seen from the code, we are launching a kernel with 10 blocks in parallel, with each block having a single thread. In the kernel code, we are printing the block ID of the kernel execution. We can think of that as 10 copies of the same `myfirstkernel` start execution in parallel. Each of these copies will have a unique block ID, which can be accessed by the `blockIdx.x` directive, and unique thread ID, which can be accessed by `threadIdx.x`. These IDs will tell us which block and thread are executing the kernel. When you run the program many times, you will find that each time, blocks execute in different orders. One sample output can be shown as follows:

```
Windows PowerShell
PS G:\cude opencv book material\CUDA book code\Chapter11> python .\thread_execution.py
I am in block no: 2
I am in block no: 7
I am in block no: 0
I am in block no: 8
I am in block no: 1
I am in block no: 3
I am in block no: 5
I am in block no: 4
I am in block no: 6
I am in block no: 9
PS G:\cude opencv book material\CUDA book code\Chapter11>
```

It can produce *n* factorial number of different outputs, where *n* indicates the number of blocks started in parallel. So, whenever you are writing the program in PyCUDA, you should be careful that blocks execute in random order.

Basic programming concepts in PyCUDA

We will start developing some useful stuff using PyCUDA in this section. The section will also demonstrate some useful functions and directives of PyCUDA, using a simple example of adding two numbers.

Adding two numbers in PyCUDA

Python provides a very fast library for numerical operations which is called **numpy (Numeric Python)**. It is developed in C or C++ and is very useful for array manipulations in Python. It is used frequently in PyCUDA programs as arguments to PyCUDA kernel functions are passed as numpy arrays. This section explains how to add two numbers using PyCUDA. The basic kernel code for adding two numbers is shown as follows:

```
import pycuda.autoinit
import pycuda.driver as drv
import numpy
from pycuda.compiler import SourceModule
mod = SourceModule("""
    __global__ void add_num(float *d_result, float *d_a, float *d_b)
  {
      const int i = threadIdx.x;
      d_result[i] = d_a[i] + d_b[i];
  }
""")
```

The `SourceModule` class and driver class are imported as explained earlier. The `numpy` library is also imported as it will be required for passing arguments to the kernel code. The `add_num` kernel function is defined as a constructor to the `SourceModule` class. The function takes two device pointers as input and one device pointer that points to the answer of the addition as output. It is important to note that, though we are adding two numbers, the kernel function is defined so that it can work on two array additions as well. Two single numbers are nothing but two arrays with one element each. If there aren't any errors, this code will be compiled and loaded onto the device. The code to call this kernel code from Python is shown as follows:

```
add_num = mod.get_function("add_num")

h_a = numpy.random.randn(1).astype(numpy.float32)
h_b = numpy.random.randn(1).astype(numpy.float32)

h_result = numpy.zeros_like(h_a)
d_a = drv.mem_alloc(h_a.nbytes)
d_b = drv.mem_alloc(h_b.nbytes)
d_result = drv.mem_alloc(h_result.nbytes)
drv.memcpy_htod(d_a, h_a)
drv.memcpy_htod(d_b, h_b)

add_num(
  d_result, d_a, d_b,
  block=(1,1,1), grid=(1,1))
```

```
drv.memcpy_dtoh(h_result,d_result)
print("Addition on GPU:")
print(h_a[0],"+", h_b[0] , "=" , h_result[0])
```

The pointer reference to the kernel function is created using `get_function`. Two random numbers are created using the `numpy.random.randn(1)` function, which is used to create a random number in the normal distribution. These numbers are converted to single precision floating point numbers, using the `astype(numpy.float32)` method. The numpy array to store the result on the host is initialized to zero.

The memory on the device can be allocated using the `mem_alloc` function of a driver class in PyCUDA. The size of memory is passed as an argument to the function. The size for input is found using the `h_a.nbytes` function. PyCUDA provides a `memcpy` function in the driver class to copy data from host memory to the device memory and vice versa.

The `drv.memcpy_htod` function copies data from the host memory to the device memory. The pointer to the device memory is passed as the first argument and the host memory pointer is passed as the second argument. The `add_num` kernel is called by passing device pointers as arguments along with numbers that specify the number of blocks and threads to be launched. In the code given before, one block is launched with one thread. The result computed by the kernel is copied back to the host by using the `drv.memcpy_dtoh` function. The result is displayed on the console, which is shown as follows:

```
In [11]: runfile('G:/cude opencv book material/CUDA book code/Chapter11/add_n.py',
wdir='G:/cude opencv book material/CUDA book code/Chapter11')
Addition on GPU:
1.2273334 + 1.3404454 = 2.5677788
```

To summarize, this section demonstrated the structure of a PyCUDA program. It started with a kernel definition code. Then inputs are defined in Python. The memory is allocated on the device and inputs are transferred to the device memory. This is followed by a kernel call, which will compute the result. This result is transferred to the host for further processing. PyCUDA provides even simpler APIs to do this operation, which is explained in the next section.

Simplifying the addition program using driver class

PyCUDA provides an even simpler API for kernel calling that does not require memory allocation and memory copying. It is done implicitly by the API. This can be accomplished by using the In and Out functions of the driver class in PyCUDA. The modified array addition code is shown as follows:

```
import pycuda.autoinit
import pycuda.driver as drv
import numpy
N = 10
from pycuda.compiler import SourceModule
mod = SourceModule("""
    __global__ void add_num(float *d_result, float *d_a, float *d_b)
    {
        const int i = threadIdx.x;
        d_result[i] = d_a[i] + d_b[i];
    }
""")
add_num = mod.get_function("add_num")
h_a = numpy.random.randn(N).astype(numpy.float32)
h_b = numpy.random.randn(N).astype(numpy.float32)
h_result = numpy.zeros_like(h_a)
add_num(
    drv.Out(h_result), drv.In(h_a), drv.In(h_b),
    block=(N,1,1), grid=(1,1))
print("Addition on GPU:")
for i in range(0,N):
    print(h_a[i],"+", h_b[i] , "=" , h_result[i])
```

Ten elements of an array are added instead of single elements in the preceding code. The kernel function is exactly the same as the code seen previously. Two arrays of ten random numbers are created on the host. Now instead of creating the memory of them and transferring that to the device, the kernel is called directly. The kernel call is modified by specifying the direction of data using drv.Out or drv.In. It simplifies the PyCUDA code and reduces the size of the code.

The kernel is called with one block and *N* threads per block. These *N* threads add *N* elements of the array in parallel, which accelerates the addition operation. The result of the kernel is automatically downloaded to the host memory by using the drv.out directive so this result is directly printed on the console using the for loop. The result for an addition of ten elements using PyCUDA is shown as follows:

```
Addition on GPU:
0.7673203 + 0.5080069 = 1.2753272
0.28488383 + 0.15324554 = 0.43812937
-0.3220178 + -0.10700232 = -0.4290201
-0.501334 + -1.7047318 = -2.206066
0.023053076 + 0.34796545 = 0.37101853
-0.44806996 + -2.071736 = -2.5198061
2.9193559 + 0.7721601 = 3.691516
-0.8016763 + -0.31726292 = -1.1189392
0.607628 + -1.2539302 = -0.6463022
-0.80436313 + 1.2789425 = 0.47457933
```

To summarize, this section described the important concepts and functions of PyCUDA by taking a simple array addition program. The performance improvement of using PyCUDA can be quantified using CUDA events, which are explained in the next section.

Measuring performance of PyCUDA programs using CUDA events

So far, we have not determined the performance of the PyCUDA programs explicitly. In this section, we will see how to measure the performance of the programs using CUDA events. This is a very important concept in PyCUDA because it will allow you to choose the best performing algorithms for a particular application from many options.

CUDA events

We can use Python time measuring options for measuring the performance of CUDA programs, but it will not give accurate results. It will include the time overhead of thread latency in the OS and scheduling in the OS among many other factors. The time measured using the CPU will also depend on the availability of a high-precision CPU timer. Many times, the host is performing asynchronous computations while the GPU kernel is running, and hence CPU timers of Python may not give correct times for kernel executions. So, to measure the time for GPU kernel computations, PyCUDA provides an event API.

A CUDA event is a GPU timestamp recorded at a specified point in a PyCUDA program. In this API, the GPU records the timestamp, which eliminates the issues that were present when using CPU timers for measuring performance. There are two steps to measure time using CUDA events: creating an event and recording an event. We can record two events, one at the start of our code and one at the end. Then we will try to calculate the difference in time between the two events that will give an overall performance for our code.

In PyCUDA code, the following lines can be included to measure performance using a CUDA event API:

```
import pycuda.driver as drv
start = drv.Event()
end=drv.Event()
#Start Time
start.record()
#The kernel code for which time is to be measured
#End Time
end.record()
end.synchronize()
#Measure time difference
secs = start.time_till(end)*1e-3
```

The `record` method is used to measure a current timestamp. The timestamp is measured before and after the kernel code to measure time for the kernel execution. The difference between timestamps can be measured using the `time_till` method, as shown in the preceding code. It will give time in milliseconds, which is converted to seconds. In the next section, we will try to measure the performance of code using a CUDA event.

Measuring performance of PyCUDA using large array addition

This section will demonstrate the method to use CUDA events to measure the performance of PyCUDA programs. The comparison of the performance of PyCUDA code with simple Python code is also described. The arrays with a million elements are taken so that performance can be accurately compared. The kernel code for large array addition is shown as follows:

```
import pycuda.autoinit
import pycuda.driver as drv
import numpy
import time
import math
```

```
from pycuda.compiler import SourceModule
N = 1000000
mod = SourceModule("""
__global__ void add_num(float *d_result, float *d_a, float *d_b,int N)
{
  int tid = threadIdx.x + blockIdx.x * blockDim.x;
   while (tid < N)
    {
      d_result[tid] = d_a[tid] + d_b[tid];
      tid = tid + blockDim.x * gridDim.x;
    }
}
""")
```

As the number of elements is high, multiple blocks and threads are launched. So, both the thread ID and block ID are used to calculate the thread index. If the total number of threads launched is not equal to the number of elements, then multiple elements are added by the same thread. This is done by the `while` loop inside the kernel function. It will also ensure that the thread index does not go beyond the array elements. Apart from the input array and the output array, the size of an array is also taken as a parameter for the kernel function, as Python global variables are not accessible to kernel code in `SourceModule`. The Python code for adding large arrays is shown as follows:

```
start = drv.Event()end=drv.Event()
add_num = mod.get_function("add_num")

h_a = numpy.random.randn(N).astype(numpy.float32)
h_b = numpy.random.randn(N).astype(numpy.float32)

h_result = numpy.zeros_like(h_a)
h_result1 = numpy.zeros_like(h_a)
n_blocks = math.ceil((N/1024))
start.record()
add_num(
   drv.Out(h_result), drv.In(h_a), drv.In(h_b),numpy.uint32(N),
   block=(1024,1,1), grid=(n_blocks,1))
end.record()
end.synchronize()
secs = start.time_till(end)*1e-3
print("Addition of %d element of GPU"%N)
print("%fs" % (secs))
```

Two events, `start` and `stop` are created to measure timings for the GPU code.The `Event()` function from the driver class is used to define event objects. Then, the pointer reference to the kernel function is created using the `get_function`. Two arrays with a million elements each are initialized with random numbers using the `randn` function of the `numpy` library. It will generate floating point numbers so they are converted to the single precision number to speed up computation on the device.

Each block supports 1,024 threads as we saw in the device property section. So based on that, the total number of blocks is calculated by dividing N by 1,024. It can be a float value so it is converted to next highest integer value using the `ceil` function of the `numpy` library. Then the kernel is launched with the calculated value number of blocks and 1,024 threads per block. The size of the array is passed with the `numpy.uint32` datatype.

The time is recorded before and after calling the kernel function using the record function, and the time difference is calculated to measure the timing of the kernel function. The calculated time is printed on the console. To compare this performance with CPU timings, the following code is added to the program:

```
start = time.time()
for i in range(0,N):
    h_result1[i] = h_a[i] +h_b[i]
end = time.time()
print("Addition of %d element of CPU"%N)
print(end-start,"s")
```

The time library from Python is used to measure CPU timings. The `for` loop is used to iterate through every element in an array. (Note: you can also use `h_result1 = h_a + h_b` as both arrays are numpy arrays.) Time is measured before and after the `for` loop using the `time.time()` function and the difference between this time is printed on the console. The output from the program is shown as follows:

```
In [9]: runfile('G:/cude opencv book material/CUDA book code/Chapter11/add_number.py',
wdir='G:/cude opencv book material/CUDA book code/Chapter11')
Addition of 1000000 element of GPU
0.009422s
Addition of 1000000 element of CPU
0.41515421867370605 s
```

As can be seen from the output, GPU takes 9.4 ms to add a million elements, while the CPU takes 415.15 ms, so around a 50-times improvement can be accomplished by using a GPU.

To summarize, this section demonstrated the use of events to measure timings for GPU code. The performance of the GPU is compared with CPU performance to quantify the performance improvement while using the GPU.

Complex programs in PyCUDA

The PyCUDA syntax and terminology will be familiar by now. We will use this knowledge to develop advanced programs and learn some advanced concepts in PyCUDA. In this section, we will develop a program to square elements of an array using three different methods in PyCUDA. We will also learn the code for doing matrix multiplication in PyCUDA.

Element-wise squaring of a matrix in PyCUDA

In this section, the program to perform element-wise squaring of numbers in a matrix is performed using three different methods. While doing this, the concepts of using multidimensional threads and blocks, the `inout` directive of the driver class, and the `gpuarray` class is explained in detail.

Simple kernel invocation with multidimensional threads

A simple kernel function using PyCUDA to square every element of a matrix is implemented in this section. The kernel function of squaring every element of a 5 x 5 matrix is shown as follows:

```
import pycuda.driver as drv
import pycuda.autoinit
from pycuda.compiler import SourceModule
import numpy
mod = SourceModule("""
  __global__ void square(float *d_a)
  {
    int idx = threadIdx.x + threadIdx.y*5;
    d_a[idx] = d_a[idx]*d_a[idx];
  }
""")
```

The kernel function square takes only one device pointer that points to the matrix as input and replaces every element with the square of it. As multidimensional threads are launched, the thread index in both x and y directions are used to index the value from a matrix. You can assume that a 5 x 5 matrix is flattened to a 1 x 25 vector to understand the indexing mechanism. Please, note that the size of a matrix is hardcoded to 5 in this code, but it can also be user-defined like the size of an array in the last section. The Python code to use this kernel function is shown as follows:

```
start = drv.Event()
end=drv.Event()
h_a = numpy.random.randint(1,5,(5, 5))
h_a = h_a.astype(numpy.float32)
h_b=h_a.copy()

start.record()

d_a = drv.mem_alloc(h_a.size * h_a.dtype.itemsize)
drv.memcpy_htod(d_a, h_a)

square = mod.get_function("square")
square(d_a, block=(5, 5, 1), grid=(1, 1), shared=0)

h_result = numpy.empty_like(h_a)
drv.memcpy_dtoh(h_result, d_a)
end.record()
end.synchronize()
secs = start.time_till(end)*1e-3
print("Time of Squaring on GPU without inout")
print("%fs" % (secs))
print("original array:")
print(h_a)
print("Square with kernel:")
print(h_result)
```

Two events are created to measure timings of a kernel function. The matrix of 5 x 5 is initialized with random numbers on the host. It is done by using a randint function of the numpy.random module. It requires three arguments. The first two arguments define the range of numbers used to generate random numbers. The first argument is the minimum value and the second argument is the maximum value used for generating numbers. The third argument is the size, which is specified as a tuple (5,5). This generated matrix is again converted to a single precision number for faster processing. The memory for the matrix is allocated on the device and the generated matrix of random numbers is copied to it.

The pointer reference to the kernel function is created and the kernel is called by passing a device memory pointer as an argument. The kernel is called with multidimensional threads with the value of 5 in the x and y directions. So the total number of threads launched is 25, with each thread calculating a square of a single element of the matrix. The result calculated by the kernel is copied back to the host and displayed on the console. The time needed for the kernel is displayed on the console along with the input and output matrix. The output is displayed on the console.

```
Time of Squaring on GPU without inout
0.149003s
original array:
[[3. 2. 1. 4. 3.]
 [1. 1. 1. 2. 2.]
 [2. 1. 1. 3. 2.]
 [3. 4. 2. 3. 1.]
 [4. 1. 4. 3. 1.]]
Square with kernel:
[[ 9.  4.  1. 16.  9.]
 [ 1.  1.  1.  4.  4.]
 [ 4.  1.  1.  9.  4.]
 [ 9. 16.  4.  9.  1.]
 [16.  1. 16.  9.  1.]]
```

It takes 149 ms to calculate the square of each element of a 5 x 5 matrix. The same calculation can be simplified by using the `inout` directive of the driver class. This is explained in the next section.

Using inout with the kernel invocation

As can be seen from the kernel function of the program in the last section, the same array is used as both input and output. The driver module in PyCUDA provides an `inout` directive for this kind of cases. It removes the need for the separate allocation of memory for the array, uploading it to the device and downloading the result back to the host. All operations are performed simultaneously during a kernel call. This makes the code simpler and easier to read. The Python code for using the `inout` directive of driver class is shown as follows:

```
start.record()
start.synchronize()

square(drv.InOut(h_a), block=(5, 5, 1))

end.record()
```

```
end.synchronize()

print("Square with InOut:")
print(h_a)
secs = start.time_till(end)*1e-3
print("Time of Squaring on GPU with inout")
print("%fs" % (secs))
```

The CUDA events are initialized to measure the performance of the code using the `inout` directive. The kernel call is the same as in the last section so it is not repeated here. As can be seen, while calling the square kernel, a single variable is passed as an argument with the `drv.inout` directive. So, all device-related operations are performed in this single step. The kernel is called with multidimensional threads as is the case in the last section. The computed result and the time taken is printed on the console as the following shows:

```
Square with InOut:
[[ 9.  4.  1. 16.  9.]
 [ 1.  1.  1.  4.  4.]
 [ 4.  1.  1.  9.  4.]
 [ 9. 16.  4.  9.  1.]
 [16.  1. 16.  9.  1.]]
Time of Squaring on GPU with inout
0.004260s
```

The time taken is comparatively less than the original kernel. So, by using the `inout` directive the of driver class, the PyCUDA code can be made efficient and easy to read. PyCUDA also provides a `gpuarray` class for array-related operations. It can be also used for squaring operations, which is explained in the next section.

Using gpuarray class

Python provides a `numpy` library for numeric computations in Python. PyCUDA provides a `gpuarray` class, similar to `numpy`, that stores its data and performs its computations on the GPU device. The shape and datatype of the arrays work exactly as in `numpy`. The `gpuarray` class provides many arithmetic methods for computations. It removes the need to specify the kernel code in C or C++ using `SourceModule`. So, the PyCUDA code will contain only a Python code. The code of squaring every element of the matrix using the `gpuarray` class is shown as follows:

```
import pycuda.gpuarray as gpuarray
import numpy
import pycuda.driver as drv
```

```
start = drv.Event()
end=drv.Event()
start.record()
start.synchronize()

h_b = numpy.random.randint(1,5,(5, 5))
d_b = gpuarray.to_gpu(h_b.astype(numpy.float32))
h_result = (d_b**2).get()
end.record()
end.synchronize()

print("original array:")
print(h_b)
print("doubled with gpuarray:")
print(h_result)
secs = start.time_till(end)*1e-3
print("Time of Squaring on GPU with gpuarray")
print("%fs" % (secs))
```

The gpuarray class needs to be imported for using in the code. It is available in the pycuda.gpuarray module. The matrix is initialized with random integers from 1 to 5 for computation. This matrix is uploaded to the device memory by using the to_gpu() method of the gpuarray class. The matrix to be uploaded is provided as an argument to this method. The matrix is converted to a single precision number. All the operations on this uploaded matrix will be performed on the device. The square operation is performed in a similar way as we do in Python code but, as the variable is stored on the device using gpuarray, this operation will also be performed on the device. The result is downloaded back to the host by using the get method. This result along with the time needed to perform element-wise squaring using gpuarray is displayed on the console as follows:

```
original array:
[[1 1 3 1 4]
 [4 3 4 2 1]
 [4 1 1 4 4]
 [2 3 2 4 1]
 [2 1 2 4 3]]
Squared with gpuarray:
[[ 1.  1.  9.  1. 16.]
 [16.  9. 16.  4.  1.]
 [16.  1.  1. 16. 16.]
 [ 4.  9.  4. 16.  1.]
 [ 4.  1.  4. 16.  9.]]
Time of Squaring on GPU with gpuarray
0.058682s
```

It takes around 58 ms to compute the square. It completely removes the need to define kernel functions in C language, and its functionality is similar to the numpy library so Python programmers can easily work with it.

To summarize, in this section we have developed an element-wise squaring program using PyCUDA in three different fashions. We have also seen the concepts of multidimensional threads, the inout directive and the gpuarray class in PyCUDA.

Dot product using GPU array

The dot between two vectors is an important mathematical operation used in various applications. The gpuarray class used in the last section can be used to calculate the dot product between two vectors. The performance of the gpuarray method to calculate the dot product is compared with the numpy operation. The code used to calculate the dot product using numpy is shown as follows:

```
import pycuda.gpuarray as gpuarray
import pycuda.driver as drv
import numpy
import time
import pycuda.autoinit
n=100
h_a=numpy.float32(numpy.random.randint(1,5,(1,n)))
h_b=numpy.float32(numpy.random.randint(1,5,(1,n)))

start=time.time()
h_result=numpy.sum(h_a*h_b)

#print(numpy.dot(a,b))
end=time.time()-start
print("Answer of Dot Product using numpy")
print(h_result)
print("Time taken for Dot Product using numpy")
print(end,"s")
```

Two vectors with 100 elements each are initialized with random integers for calculating the dot product. The time module of Python is used to calculate the time needed for the computation of the dot product. The * operator is used to calculate the element-wise multiplication of two vectors and the result of this is summed up to calculate the overall dot product. Please, note that the numpy.dot method calculated is used in matrix multiplication, which can't be used for the dot product. The calculated dot product and time are displayed on the console. The code to perform the same operation on a GPU using gpuarray is shown as follows:

```
d_a = gpuarray.to_gpu(h_a)
d_b = gpuarray.to_gpu(h_b)

start1 = drv.Event()
end1=drv.Event()
start1.record()

d_result = gpuarray.dot(d_a,d_b)
end1.record()
end1.synchronize()
secs = start1.time_till(end1)*1e-3
print("Answer of Dot Product on GPU")
print(d_result.get())
print("Time taken for Dot Product on GPU")
print("%fs" % (secs))
if(h_result==d_result.get()):
    print("The computed dor product is correct")
```

The `to_gpu` method is used to upload two vectors on a GPU for calculating the dot product. The `gpuarray` class provides a dot method, which can be used to calculate the dot product directly. It needs two GPU arrays as an argument. The calculated result is downloaded back to the host by using the `get()` method. The calculated result and time measured using CUDA events are displayed on the console. The result of the program is shown as follows:

```
In [3]: runfile('G:/cude opencv book material/CUDA book code/Chapter11/gpu_dot.py',
wdir='G:/cude opencv book material/CUDA book code/Chapter11')
Answer of Dot Product using numpy
633.0
Time taken for Dot Product using numpy
0.03769350051879883 s
Answer of Dot Product on GPU
633.0
Time taken for Dot Product on GPU
0.000108s
The computed dor product is correct
```

As can be seen from the output, that same result is obtained by calculating the dot product using `numpy` and `gpuarray`. The `numpy` library takes 37 ms to compute the dot product, while the GPU takes only 0.1 ms to do the same operation. This further exemplifies the benifit of using GPU and PyCUDA to do complex mathematical operations.

Matrix multiplication

An important mathematical operation used frequently is matrix multiplication. This section will demonstrate how it can be performed on a GPU using PyCUDA. It is a very complicated mathematical operation when the sizes of the matrix are very large. It should be kept in mind that for matrix multiplication, the number of columns in the first matrix should be equal to the number of rows in the second matrix. Matrix multiplication is not a cumulative operation. To avoid complexity, in this example, we are taking a square matrix of the same size. If you are familiar with the mathematics of matrix multiplication, then you may recall that a row in the first matrix will be multiplied with all the columns in the second matrix. This is repeated for all rows in the first matrix. The example of a 3 x 3 matrix multiplication is shown as follows:

$$\begin{bmatrix} 4 & 1 & 1 \\ 1 & 2 & 3 \\ 1 & 1 & 3 \end{bmatrix} + \begin{bmatrix} 3 & 3 & 4 \\ 2 & 3 & 3 \\ 4 & 1 & 1 \end{bmatrix} = \begin{bmatrix} 4*3+1*2+1*4 & 16 & 20 \\ 1*3+2*2+3*4 & 12 & 13 \\ 1*3+1*2+3*4 & 9 & 10 \end{bmatrix}$$

Every element in the resultant matrix will be calculated by multiplying the corresponding row in the first matrix and column in the second matrix. This concept is used to develop a kernel function shown as follows:

```
import numpy as np
from pycuda import driver
from pycuda.compiler import SourceModule
import pycuda.autoinit
MATRIX_SIZE = 3

matrix_mul_kernel = """
__global__ void Matrix_Mul_Kernel(float *d_a, float *d_b, float *d_c)
{
  int tx = threadIdx.x;
  int ty = threadIdx.y;
  float value = 0;
  for (int i = 0; i < %(MATRIX_SIZE)s; ++i) {
    float d_a_element = d_a[ty * %(MATRIX_SIZE)s + i];
    float d_b_element = d_b[i * %(MATRIX_SIZE)s + tx];
    value += d_a_element * d_b_element;
  }

  d_c[ty * %(MATRIX_SIZE)s + tx] = value;
} """
matrix_mul = matrix_mul_kernel % {'MATRIX_SIZE': MATRIX_SIZE}
mod = SourceModule(matrix_mul)
```

The kernel function takes two input arrays and one output array as arguments. The size of a matrix is passed as a constant to the kernel function. This removes the need to pass the size of a vector as one of the parameters of the kernel function, as was explained earlier in the chapter. Both methods are equally correct, and it is up to the programmer which they find more convenient. Each thread computes one element of a resultant matrix. All elements of the row from the first matrix and columns from the second matrix are multiplied and summed up inside the `for` loop. The answer is copied to the location in the resultant matrix. The details of calculating the index inside the kernel function can be found in earlier chapters of the book. The Python code to use this kernel function is shown as follows:

```
h_a = np.random.randint(1,5,(MATRIX_SIZE, MATRIX_SIZE)).astype(np.float32)
h_b = np.random.randint(1,5,(MATRIX_SIZE, MATRIX_SIZE)).astype(np.float32)

d_a = gpuarray.to_gpu(h_a)
d_b = gpuarray.to_gpu(h_b)
d_c_gpu = gpuarray.empty((MATRIX_SIZE, MATRIX_SIZE), np.float32)

matrixmul = mod.get_function("Matrix_Mul_Kernel")
matrixmul(d_a, d_b,d_c_gpu,
   block = (MATRIX_SIZE, MATRIX_SIZE, 1),
)
print("*" * 100)
print("Matrix A:")
print(d_a.get())

print("*" * 100)
print("Matrix B:")
print(d_b.get())

print("*" * 100)
print("Matrix C:")
print(d_c_gpu.get())

   # compute on the CPU to verify GPU computation
h_c_cpu = np.dot(h_a, h_b)
if h_c_cpu == d_c_gpu.get() :
    print("The computed matrix multiplication is correct")
```

Two matrices with the size of 3 x 3 are initialized with random integers from 1 to 5. These matrices are uploaded to the device memory using the `to_gpu` method of the `gpuarray` class. The empty GPU array is created to store the result on the device. These three variables are passed as arguments to the kernel function. The kernel function is called with the matrix size as dimensions in x and y directions. The result is downloaded back to the host using the `get()` method. The two input matrices and the result calculated by the GPU are printed on the console. The matrix multiplication is also calculated on a CPU using the dot method of the `numpy` library. The result is compared with the GPU result for verifying the result of the kernel computation. The result of the program is displayed as follows:

```
In [7]: runfile('G:/cude opencv book material/CUDA book code/Chapter11/matrix_mmulfinal.py', wdir='G:/cude opencv book material/CUDA book code/Chapter11')
***********************************************************************************
Matrix A:
[[4. 1. 1.]
 [1. 2. 3.]
 [1. 1. 3.]]
***********************************************************************************
Matrix B:
[[3. 3. 4.]
 [2. 3. 3.]
 [4. 1. 1.]]
***********************************************************************************
Matrix Multiplication result:
[[18. 16. 20.]
 [19. 12. 13.]
 [17.  9. 10.]]

The computed matrix multiplication is correct
```

To summarize, We have developed a simple kernel function to perform matrix multiplication using PyCUDA. This kernel function can be further optimized by using shared memory, as explained earlier in the book.

Advanced kernel functions in PyCUDA

So far, we have seen the use of the `SourceModule` class for defining kernel functions in C or C++. We have also used the `gpuarray` class for doing device computations without defining kernel functions explicitly. This section describes the advanced kernel definition features available in PyCUDA. These features are used to develop kernel functions for various parallel communication patterns like the map, reduce, and scan operations.

Element-wise kernel in PyCUDA

This feature allows the programmer to define a kernel function that works on every element of an array. It allows the programmer to execute the kernel on complex expressions that are made of one or more operands into a single computational step. The kernel function for the element-wise addition of a large array can be defined in the following way:

```
import pycuda.gpuarray as gpuarray
import pycuda.driver as drv
from pycuda.elementwise import ElementwiseKernel
from pycuda.curandom import rand as curand
add = ElementwiseKernel(
  "float *d_a, float *d_b, float *d_c",
  "d_c[i] = d_a[i] + d_b[i]",
  "add")
```

The `PyCuda.elementwise.ElementwiseKernel` function is used to define the element-wise kernel function. It requires three arguments. The first argument is the list of parameters for the kernel function. The second argument defines the operation to be performed on each element, and the third argument specifies the name of the kernel function. The Python code to use this kernel function is shown as follows:

```
n = 1000000
d_a = curand(n)
d_b = curand(n)
d_c = gpuarray.empty_like(d_a)
start = drv.Event()
end=drv.Event()
start.record()
add(d_a, d_b, d_c)
end.record()
end.synchronize()
secs = start.time_till(end)*1e-3
print("Addition of %d element of GPU"%shape)
print("%fs" % (secs))
# check the result
if d_c == (d_a + d_b):
  print("The sum computed on GPU is correct")
```

The two arrays are initialized with random numbers using the `curand` function of the `pycuda.curandom` class. It is again a useful functionality, as it removes the need to initialize on the host and then upload to the device memory. An empty GPU array is created to store the result. The `add` kernel is called by passing these three variables as an argument. The time needed for the addition of a million elements is calculated using CUDA events and is displayed on the console.

The output of the program is shown as follows:

```
In [4]: runfile('G:/cude opencv book material/CUDA book code/Chapter12/
element_wise_addition.py', wdir='G:/cude opencv book material/CUDA book code/Chapter12')
Addition of 1000000 element of GPU
0.000629s
The sum computed on GPU is correct
```

The element-wise kernel only needs 0.6 ms for the addition of a million elements in an array. This performance is better than the program seen earlier in this chapter. So element-wise, kernel definition is a very important concept to remember when element-wise operations are to be performed on a vector.

Reduction kernel

The reduction operation can be defined as reducing a collection of elements to a single value by using some expressions. It can be very useful in various parallel computation applications. The example of calculating the dot product between vectors is taken to demonstrate the concept of reduction in PyCUDA. The program for calculating the dot product using the feature of a reduction kernel in PyCUDA is shown as follows:

```
import pycuda.gpuarray as gpuarray
import pycuda.driver as drv
import numpy
from pycuda.reduction import ReductionKernel
import pycuda.autoinit
n=5
start = drv.Event()
end=drv.Event()
start.record()
d_a = gpuarray.arange(n,dtype= numpy.uint32)
d_b = gpuarray.arange(n,dtype= numpy.uint32)
kernel =
ReductionKernel(numpy.uint32,neutral="0",reduce_expr="a+b",map_expr="d_a[i]
*d_b[i]",arguments="int *d_a, int *d_b")
d_result = kernel(d_a,d_b).get()
end.record()
end.synchronize()
secs = start.time_till(end)*1e-3
print("Vector A")
print(d_a)
print("Vector B")
print(d_b)
print("The computed dot product using reduction:")
```

```
print(d_result)
print("Dot Product on GPU")
print("%fs" % (secs))
```

PyCUDA provides the `pycuda.reduction.ReductionKernel` class to define reduction kernels. It requires many arguments. The first argument is the data type for the output. The second argument is neutral, which is mostly defined as 0. The third argument is the expression used to reduce the collection of elements. The addition operation is defined in the preceding code. The fourth argument is defined as the expression used for mapping operations between operands before reduction. The element-wise multiplication is defined in the code. The final argument defines the argument for the kernel function.

The reduction kernel for computing the dot product requires element-wise multiplication between two vectors and then the addition of all elements. Two vectors are defined using the `arange` function. It works in a similar way as the `range` function in Python but `arange` saves the array on the device. The kernel function is called by passing these two vectors as an argument, and the result is fetched to the host. The time needed for computing is calculated using CUDA events and displayed on the console along with the result of the dot product, shown as follows:

```
In [6]: runfile('G:/cude opencv book material/CUDA book code/Chapter12/gpu_dot.py',
wdir='G:/cude opencv book material/CUDA book code/Chapter12')
Vector A
[0 1 2 3 4]
Vector B
[0 1 2 3 4]
The computed dot product using reduction:
30
Dot Product on GPU
2.546338s
```

The reduction kernel takes around 2.5 s to compute the dot product, which is a relatively long time compared to the explicit kernel seen in the last section. Still, it is quite useful in parallel computing applications where reduction operation is required.

Scan kernel

The scan operation is again a very important parallel computing paradigm. The scan operator applies a specified function to the first item in the input. The result of that function is provided as the input along with the second item from the original input. All the intermediate results form the output sequence. This concept can be used for various applications. The example of a cumulative addition is taken as an example to demonstrate the concept of the scan kernel in PyCUDA. The cumulative addition is nothing but applying addition to every element of a vector sequentially. The example is shown as follows:

```
Input Vector
[7 5 9 2 9]
Scan Operation for cumulative sum
[7,7+5,7+5+9,7+5+9+2,7+2+9+2+7]
```

As can be seen, the output of the previous addition is added to the current element to calculate the output at the current position. This is called an **inclusive scan** operation. If the current element of the input is not involved, then it is known as an **exclusive scan**. The program to perform cumulative summation using an inclusive scan is shown as follows:

```
import pycuda.gpuarray as gpuarray
import pycuda.driver as drv
import numpy
from pycuda.scan import InclusiveScanKernel
import pycuda.autoinit
n=10
start = drv.Event()
end=drv.Event()
start.record()
kernel = InclusiveScanKernel(numpy.uint32,"a+b")
h_a = numpy.random.randint(1,10,n).astype(numpy.int32)
d_a = gpuarray.to_gpu(h_a)
kernel(d_a)
end.record()
end.synchronize()
secs = start.time_till(end)*1e-3
assert(d_a.get() == numpy.cumsum(h_a,axis=0)).all()
print("The input data:")
print(h_a)
print("The computed cumulative sum using Scan:")
print(d_a.get())
print("Cumulative Sum on GPU")
print("%fs" % (secs))
```

PyCUDA provides the `pycuda.scan.InclusiveScanKernel` class to define an inclusive scan kernel. It requires the data type of the output and the operation to be used for scanning as arguments. The addition operation is specified for a cumulative summation. The array with random integers is applied as an input to this kernel function. The kernel output will have the same size as the input. The input and output vector along with the time needed for calculating the cumulative sum is displayed on the console, as shown in the following:

```
In [3]: runfile('G:/cude opencv book material/CUDA book code/Chapter12/gpu_scan.py',
wdir='G:/cude opencv book material/CUDA book code/Chapter12')
The input data:
[7 5 9 2 9 7 7 7 2 6]
The computed cumulative sum using Scan:
[ 7 12 21 23 32 39 46 53 55 61]
Cumulative Sum on GPU
0.002032s
```

It takes around 2 ms to run a scan operation on 10 elements of an array. To summarize, in this section we saw various special methods for defining kernels for mapping, reduction, and scanning operations.

Summary

This chapter demonstrated the concepts of programming in PyCUDA. It started with the development of a simple `Hello, PyCUDA` program using PyCUDA. The concepts of kernel definition in C or C++ and calling it from Python code and the API for accessing GPU device properties from a PyCUDA program were discussed in detail. The execution mechanism for multiple threads and blocks in a PyCUDA program was explained with a simple program. The basic structure of a PyCUDA program was described with a simple example of an array addition. The simplification of PyCUDA code was described by using directives from a driver class. The use of CUDA events to measure the performance of the PyCUDA programs was explained in detail. The functionality of the `inout` directive of the driver class and the `gpuarray` class was explained using an element-wise squaring example. The `gpuarray` class was used to develop code for calculating the dot product using PyCUDA. The PyCUDA code for a complex mathematical operation of matrix multiplication was explained in detail. The last part of the chapter described various kernel-defining methods used for mapping, reduction, and scanning operations.

The next chapter will build on this knowledge and describe some advanced kernels available in PyCUDA along with the development of computer vision applications using PyCUDA.

Questions

1. Which programming language is used to define the kernel function using the `SourceModule` class in PyCUDA? Which compiler will be used to compile this kernel function?
2. Write a kernel call function for the `myfirst_kernel` function used in this chapter, with the number of blocks equal to 1024 x 1024 and threads per block equal to 512 x 512.
3. State true or false: The block execution inside PyCUDA program is in sequential order.
4. What is the advantage of using the `In`, `Out`, and `inout` driver class primitives in PyCUDA programs?
5. Write a PyCUDA program to add two to every element of a vector with an arbitrary size using the `gpuarray` class.
6. What is the advantage of using CUDA events to measure the time for a kernel execution?
7. State true or false: The `gpuarray` class is the GPU device version of the `numpy` library in Python.

12
Basic Computer Vision Applications Using PyCUDA

In the previous chapter, we saw important programming concepts related to PyCUDA. We also learned how to develop some programs in PyCUDA using these programming concepts. This chapter will build on this knowledge and we will use PyCUDA for developing basic image processing and computer vision applications. The parallel programming concepts of atomic operations and shared memory will also be explained in detail. The histogram of an image conveys important information related to the contrast of an image and it can also be used as an image feature for computer vision tasks. The program to calculate the histogram using PyCUDA will be explained in detail in this chapter. Other basic computer vision applications, such as the conversion of color spaces, image addition, and image inversion using PyCUDA, will also be described.

The following topics will be covered in this chapter:

- Histogram calculation using atomic operations and shared memory
- Basic computer vision applications using PyCUDA
- Color space conversion for an image and video from a webcam
- Image addition
- Image inversion

Technical requirements

This chapter requires a good understanding of the Python programming languages. It also requires any computer or laptop with an Nvidia GPU on board. All the code used in this chapter can be downloaded from the following GitHub link: `https://github.com/PacktPublishing/Hands-On-GPU-Accelerated-Computer-Vision-with-OpenCV-and-CUDA`. Check out the following video to see the code in action: `http://bit.ly/2prC1wI`

Histogram calculation in PyCUDA

The histogram of an image conveys important information related to the contrast of an image, and it can also be used as an image feature for computer vision tasks. A histogram indicates the frequency of the occurrence of a particular pixel value. While calculating the histogram of an 8-bit image that is 256 x 256 in size, the 65,535-pixel values will work on arrays of intensity values from 0-255. If one thread is launched per pixel, then 65,535 threads will work on 256 memory locations of intensity values.

Consider a situation in which a large number of threads try to modify a small portion of memory. While calculating the histogram of an image, read-modify-write operations have to be performed for all memory locations. This operation is d_out[i] ++, where first d_out[i] is read from memory, then incremented, and then written back to the memory. However, when multiple threads are doing this operation on the same memory location, it can give an incorrect output.

Suppose one memory location has an initial value of 0 and the a and b threads try to increment this memory location, then the final answer should be 2. However, at the time of execution, it may happen that both the a and b threads read this value simultaneously, then both threads will get the value 0. They increment it to 1 and both will store this 1 on the memory. So instead of 2, the calculated answer is 1, which is incorrect.

To understand how this can be dangerous, consider the example of an ATM cash withdrawal. Suppose you have a balance of $50,000 in your account. You have two ATM cards for the same account. You and your friend go to two different ATMs simultaneously to withdraw $40,000. Both of you swipe cards simultaneously; so, when the ATMs check the balance, both will get $50,000. If you both withdraw $40,000, then both machines will look at the initial balance, which is $50,000. The amount to withdraw is less than the balance, hence both machines will give $40,000. Even though your balance was $50,000, you got $80,000, which is dangerous. To avoid these scenarios, atomic operations are used when parallel programming, which is explained in the next section.

Using atomic operations

CUDA provides an API called `atomicAdd` operations to avoid problems with parallel access of memory locations. It is a blocking operation, which means that when multiple threads try to access the same memory location, only one thread can access the memory location at a time. Other threads have to wait for this thread to finish and write its answer to memory. The kernel function to calculate a histogram using an `atomicAdd` operation is shown as follows:

```
import pycuda.autoinit
import pycuda.driver as drv
import numpy
import matplotlib.pyplot as plt
from pycuda.compiler import SourceModule
mod = SourceModule("""
__global__ void atomic_hist(int *d_b, int *d_a, int SIZE)
{
 int tid = threadIdx.x + blockDim.x * blockIdx.x;
 int item = d_a[tid];
 if (tid < SIZE)
 {
  atomicAdd(&(d_b[item]), 1);
 }
}
""")
```

The kernel function has three arguments. The first argument is the output array in which the histogram will be stored after calculation. The size of this array will be 256 for an 8-bit image. The second argument is the flattened array of image intensities. The third argument is the size of a flattened array. The memory location of the histogram array indexed by pixel intensity at the thread index will be incremented for every thread. The number of threads is equal to the size of a flattened image array.

The `atomicAdd` function is used to increment memory location. It takes two arguments. The first is the memory location we want to increment, and the second is the value by which this location has to be incremented. The `atomicadd` function will increase the cost in terms of execution time for histogram calculation. The Python code for histogram calculation using atomic operations is as follows:

```
atomic_hist = mod.get_function("atomic_hist")
import cv2
h_img = cv2.imread("cameraman.tif",0)

h_a=h_img.flatten()
h_a=h_a.astype(numpy.int)
```

```
h_result = numpy.zeros(256).astype(numpy.int)
SIZE = h_img.size
NUM_BIN=256
n_threads= int(numpy.ceil((SIZE+NUM_BIN-1) / NUM_BIN))
start = drv.Event()
end=drv.Event()
start.record()
atomic_hist(
    drv.Out(h_result), drv.In(h_a), numpy.uint32(SIZE),
    block=(n_threads,1,1), grid=(NUM_BIN,1))

end.record()
end.synchronize()
secs = start.time_till(end)*1e-3
print("Time for Calculating Histogram on GPU with shared memory")
print("%fs" % (secs))
plt.stem(h_result)
plt.xlim([0,256])
plt.title("Histogram on GPU")
```

The pointer reference to the kernel function is created using the `get_function()` method. The image is read using the OpenCV library. If it is not installed for Python, you can execute the following command from the Command Prompt:

$pip install opencv-python

Then, `OpenCV` library can be imported from any Python program using the `import cv2` command. The image read function is similar to what has been explained earlier in this book. The image is read as a grayscale image. The image is stored as a `numpy` array in Python. This array is flattened to a vector so that it can be operated upon by one-dimensional threads and blocks. It is also possible to work on an image with two-dimensional threads without flattening it. The `numpy` library provides a `flatten()` method to perform this operation.

The total number of blocks and threads are calculated from the size of an image and the number of bins for the histogram. The flattened image array, blank histogram array, and size of the flattened array are passed as arguments while calling the kernel function along with the number of blocks and threads to be launched. The kernel function returns the calculated histogram, which can be displayed or plotted.

Python provides a `matplotlib` library that contains a rich set of plotting functions. The `stem` function from this library is used to plot a discrete `histogram` function. The `xlim` function is used to set limits of the X axis. The `title` function is used to give a title to the plot. The output of the program is shown in the following diagram:

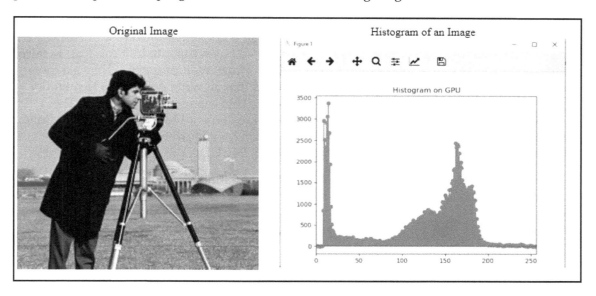

If a histogram does not have a uniform distribution of all intensities, then it can result in poor contrast images. The contrast can be enhanced by performing histogram equalization, which converts this distribution to a uniform one. A histogram also conveys information about the brightness of an image. If the histogram is concentrated on the left-hand side of the plot, then the image will be too dark and if it is concentrated on the right-hand side, then the image will be too bright. Again, histogram equalization can be used to correct this issue.

The kernel function for calculating a histogram can also be developed using the concept of shared memory in parallel programming. This is illustrated in the following section.

Using shared memory

Shared memory is available on-chip on a GPU device, hence it is much faster than global memory. Shared memory latency is roughly 100 times lower than uncached global memory latency. All the threads from the same block can access shared memory. This is very useful in many applications where threads need to share their results with other threads. However, it can also create chaos or false results if this is not synchronized. If one thread reads data from memory before the other thread has written to it, it can lead to false results. So, this memory access should be controlled or managed properly. This is done with the __syncthreads() directive, which ensures that all write operations to memory are completed before moving ahead in the programs. This is also called a **barrier**. The meaning of barrier is that all threads will reach this line and wait for other threads to finish. After all the threads have reached this barrier, they can move further. This section will demonstrate how shared memory can be used from a PyCUDA program.

This concept of shared memory can be utilized for calculating the histogram of an image. The kernel function is shown as follows:

```
import pycuda.autoinit
import pycuda.driver as drv
import numpy
import matplotlib.pyplot as plt
from pycuda.compiler import SourceModule

mod1 = SourceModule("""
__global__ void atomic_hist(int *d_b, int *d_a, int SIZE)
{
 int tid = threadIdx.x + blockDim.x * blockIdx.x;
 int offset = blockDim.x * gridDim.x;
 __shared__ int cache[256];
 cache[threadIdx.x] = 0;
 __syncthreads();

 while (tid < SIZE)
 {
  atomicAdd(&(cache[d_a[tid]]), 1);
  tid += offset;
 }
 __syncthreads();
 atomicAdd(&(d_b[threadIdx.x]), cache[threadIdx.x]);
}
""")
```

The number of bins is 256 for an 8-bit image, so we are defining shared memory of size equal to the number of threads in a block, which is equal to a number of bins. We will calculate a histogram for the current block, so shared memory is initialized to zero and the histogram is computed for this block in the same way as discussed earlier. But this time, the result is stored in shared memory and not in global memory. In this case, only 256 threads are trying to access 256 memory elements in shared memory instead of all 65,535 elements from the previous code. This will help in reducing the overhead time in the atomic operation. The final atomic add in the last line will add a histogram of one block to overall histogram values. As addition is a cumulative operation, we do not have to worry about the order in which each block is executed. The Python code to use this kernel function to calculate a histogram is shown as follows:

```
atomic_hist = mod.get_function("atomic_hist")

import cv2
h_img = cv2.imread("cameraman.tif",0)

h_a=h_img.flatten()
h_a=h_a.astype(numpy.int)
h_result = numpy.zeros(256).astype(numpy.int)
SIZE = h_img.size
NUM_BIN=256
n_threads= int(numpy.ceil((SIZE+NUM_BIN-1) / NUM_BIN))
start = drv.Event()
end=drv.Event()
start.record()
atomic_hist(
  drv.Out(h_result), drv.In(h_a), numpy.uint32(SIZE),
  block=(n_threads,1,1), grid=(NUM_BIN,1),shared= 256*4)

end.record()
end.synchronize()
secs = start.time_till(end)*1e-3
print("Time for Calculating Histogram on GPU with shared memory")
print("%fs" % (secs))
plt.stem(h_result)
plt.xlim([0,256])
plt.title("Histogram on GPU")
```

The code is almost similar to that in the last section. The only difference is in the kernel call. The size of the shared memory should be defined while calling the kernel. This can be specified using the shared argument in the kernel call function. It is specified as 256*4 because the shared memory has a size of 256 integer elements, which require 4 bytes of storage each. The same histogram will be displayed as shown in the previous section.

To check the authenticity of the calculated histogram and compare the performance, the histogram is also calculated using the OpenCV inbuilt function, `calcHist`, as shown in the following code:

```
start = cv2.getTickCount()
hist = cv2.calcHist([h_img],[0],None,[256],[0,256])
end = cv2.getTickCount()
time = (end - start)/ cv2.getTickFrequency()
print("Time for Calculating Histogram on CPU")
print("%fs" % (secs))
```

The `calcHist` function requires five arguments. The first argument is the name of the image variable. The second argument specifies the channels in the case of a color image. It is zero for a grayscale image. The third argument specifies the mask if you want to calculate the histogram for a particular portion of an image. The fourth argument specifies the number of bins, and the fifth argument specifies the range of intensity values. OpenCV also provides `getTickCount` and `getTickFrequency` functions in Python for calculating the performance of the OpenCV code. The performance of the code without shared memory, with shared memory, and using the OpenCV function, is shown as follows:

```
In [4]: runfile('G:/cude opencv book material/CUDA book code/Chapter12/
histogram_without_shared.py', wdir='G:/cude opencv book material/CUDA book code/
Chapter12')
Time for Calculating Histogram on GPU without shared memory
0.001040s
Time for Calculating Histogram using OpenCV
0.001040s

In [5]: runfile('G:/cude opencv book material/CUDA book code/Chapter12/histogram.py',
wdir='G:/cude opencv book material/CUDA book code/Chapter12')
Time for Calculating Histogram on GPU with shared memory
0.000839s
```

The time taken by the kernel function without shared memory is 1 ms while, using shared memory, it is 0.8 ms, which further proves the point that the use of shared memory improves the performance of kernel functions. To summarize, in this section, we have seen two different methods of calculating histograms on the GPU. We have also seen the concept of atomic operations and shared memory, along with how they can be used in PyCUDA.

Basic computer vision operations using PyCUDA

This section will demonstrate the use of PyCUDA in developing simple computer vision applications. Images in Python are nothing but two- or three-dimensional numpy arrays, hence working and manipulating images in PyCUDA is similar to working with multidimensional arrays. This section will give you a basic idea of developing a simple application that you can utilize in developing complex computer vision applications using PyCUDA.

Color space conversion in PyCUDA

Most computer vision algorithms work on grayscale images, so there is a need for converting a color image captured from a camera to a grayscale image. Though OpenCV provides an inbuilt function to do this operation, it can be done by developing your own function. This section will demonstrate the method to develop a PyCUDA function for converting a color image to a grayscale image. If formulas for converting an image from one color space into another are known, then the function shown in this section can be written for any color space conversion by just replacing formulas.

OpenCV captures and stores image in BGR format, where blue is the first channel followed by green and red. The formula to convert from BGR format to grayscale is given as follows:

```
gray = 0.299*r+0.587*g+0.114*b Where r,g,b are color intensities of red,
green and blue channel at a particular location
```

The implementation of this function for an image and video is shown in the following two subsections.

BGR to gray conversion on an image

In this section, we will try to develop the kernel function for converting a BGR image into a grayscale image. The kernel function for converting a color image into grayscale is shown as follows:

```
import pycuda.driver as drv
from pycuda.compiler import SourceModule
import numpy as np
import cv2
mod = SourceModule \
  (
```

```
"""
#include<stdio.h>
#define INDEX(a, b) a*256+b

__global__ void bgr2gray(float *d_result,float *b_img, float *g_img, float
*r_img)
{
 unsigned int idx = threadIdx.x+(blockIdx.x*(blockDim.x*blockDim.y));
 unsigned int a = idx/256;
 unsigned int b = idx%256;
 d_result[INDEX(a, b)] = (0.299*r_img[INDEX(a, b)]+0.587*g_img[INDEX(a,
b)]+0.114*b_img[INDEX(a, b)]);

}
 """
)
```

A small `INDEX` function is defined to calculate a particular index value for a two-dimensional image of 256 x 256 in size. The flattened image arrays of three channels of a color image are taken as the input of the kernel function and its output is the grayscale image of the same size. The `INDEX` function is used to convert the thread index into a particular pixel location in an image. The grayscale value at that location is calculated using the function shown. The Python code for converting a color image to a grayscale image is shown as follows:

```
h_img = cv2.imread('lena_color.tif',1)
h_gray=cv2.cvtColor(h_img,cv2.COLOR_BGR2GRAY)
#print a
b_img = h_img[:, :, 0].reshape(65536).astype(np.float32)
g_img = h_img[:, :, 1].reshape(65536).astype(np.float32)
r_img = h_img[:, :, 2].reshape(65536).astype(np.float32)
h_result=r_img
bgr2gray = mod.get_function("bgr2gray")
bgr2gray(drv.Out(h_result), drv.In(b_img),
drv.In(g_img),drv.In(r_img),block=(1024, 1, 1), grid=(64, 1, 1))

h_result=np.reshape(h_result, (256,256)).astype(np.uint8)
cv2.imshow("Grayscale Image",h_result)
cv2.waitKey(0)
cv2.destroyAllWindows()
```

The color image is read using the OpenCV `imread` function. The size of an image should be 256 x 256, so if it isn't, then it should be converted into that size using the `cv2.resize` function. The color image is stored in BGR format so blue, green, and red channels are separated from it using array slicing in Python. These arrays are flattened so that they can be passed to a kernel function.

The kernel function is called with three color channels as input and an array to store the output grayscale image. The kernel function will calculate a grayscale value at every pixel location and return a flattened array of a grayscale image. This resultant array is converted back to the original image size using the reshape function from the numpy library. The OpenCV imshow function needs an unsigned integer data type for displaying the image so that an array is also converted to the uint8 data type. The grayscale image is displayed on the screen, as shown in the following screenshot:

BGR to gray conversion on a webcam video

The same kernel function developed in the last section to convert an image into grayscale can be utilized to convert a video captured from a webcam into grayscale. The Python code for this is shown as follows:

```
cap = cv2.VideoCapture(0)
bgr2gray = mod.get_function("bgr2gray")
while(True):
  # Capture frame-by-frame
  ret, h_img = cap.read()
  h_img = cv2.resize(h_img,(256,256),interpolation = cv2.INTER_CUBIC)

  b_img = h_img[:, :, 0].reshape(65536).astype(np.float32)
  g_img = h_img[:, :, 1].reshape(65536).astype(np.float32)
  r_img = h_img[:, :, 2].reshape(65536).astype(np.float32)
  h_result=r_img
  bgr2gray(drv.Out(h_result), drv.In(b_img),
drv.In(g_img),drv.In(r_img),block=(1024, 1, 1), grid=(64, 1, 1))
```

```
    h_result=np.reshape(h_result,(256,256)).astype(np.uint8)
    cv2.imshow("Grayscale Image",h_result)

    # Display the resulting frame
    cv2.imshow('Original frame',h_img)
    if cv2.waitKey(50) & 0xFF == ord('q'):
      break

# When everything done, release the capture
cap.release()
cv2.destroyAllWindows()
```

OpenCV in Python provides a `VideoCapture` class to capture video from a webcam. It requires a camera device index as an argument. It is specified as zero for a webcam. Then, a continuous `while` loop is started to capture frames from the webcam. The frames are read using the `read` method of a capture object. These frames are resized to 256 x 256 using the `resize` function of the `cv2` library. These frames are color images, so three channels are separated from them and flattened so that they can be passed to a kernel function. The kernel function is called in the same way as in the last section, and the result from it is reshaped for displaying on the screen. The output of the code for one frame of webcam stream is shown as follows:

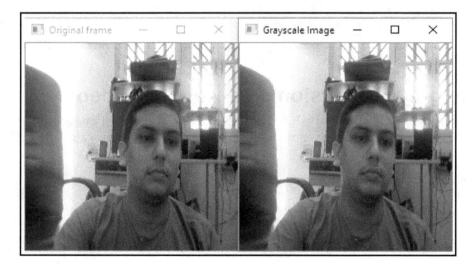

The webcam streaming will continue until the *q* key is pressed on the keyboard. To summarize, we have developed a kernel function in PyCUDA to convert a color image in BGR format into a grayscale image, which can work on an image as well as video. These kernel functions can be modified for other color space conversions by replacing equations for the same.

Image addition in PyCUDA

The addition of two images can be performed when two images are of the same size. It performs a pixel-wise addition of two images. Suppose that, in two images, the pixel at (0,0) has intensity values of 100 and 150 respectively, then the intensity value in the resultant image will be 250, which is the addition of two intensity values, as shown in the following equation:

```
result = img1 + img2
```

OpenCV addition is a saturated operation, which means that if an answer of addition goes above 255, then it will be saturated at 255. So, the same functionality is implemented as a PyCUDA kernel function. The code to perform image addition is shown as follows:

```
import pycuda.driver as drv
from pycuda.compiler import SourceModule
import numpy as np
import cv2
mod = SourceModule \
  (
"""
  __global__ void add_num(float *d_result, float *d_a, float *d_b,int N)
{
 int tid = threadIdx.x + blockIdx.x * blockDim.x;
 while (tid < N)
   {
 d_result[tid] = d_a[tid] + d_b[tid];
 if(d_result[tid]>255)
 {
 d_result[tid]=255;
 }
 tid = tid + blockDim.x * gridDim.x;
 }
}
"""
 )
img1 = cv2.imread('cameraman.tif',0)
img2 = cv2.imread('circles.png',0)
h_img1 = img1.reshape(65536).astype(np.float32)
h_img2 = img2.reshape(65536).astype(np.float32)
N = h_img1.size
h_result=h_img1
add_img = mod.get_function("add_num")
add_img(drv.Out(h_result), drv.In(h_img1),
drv.In(h_img2),np.uint32(N),block=(1024, 1, 1), grid=(64, 1, 1))
h_result=np.reshape(h_result, (256,256)).astype(np.uint8)
cv2.imshow("Image after addition",h_result)
```

```
cv2.waitKey(0)
cv2.destroyAllWindows()
```

The kernel function is similar to the array addition kernel function seen in the last chapter. The saturation condition is added to the kernel function, which indicates that if pixel intensity goes beyond 255 after addition, then it will be saturated at 255. Two images of the same size are read, flattened, and converted into a single precision floating point data type. These flattened images, along with their size, are passed as arguments to the kernel function. The result calculated by the kernel function is reshaped to the original image size and converted into an unsigned integer type for displaying, using the imshow function. The result is shown in the following screenshot, along with the original images:

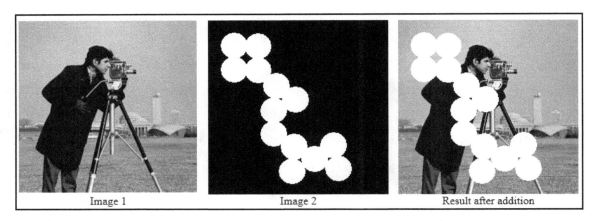

| Image 1 | Image 2 | Result after addition |

The same kernel functions can be used for other arithmetic and logical operations with minor modifications.

Image inversion in PyCUDA using gpuarray

Apart from arithmetic operations, the NOT operation is also widely used for inverting an image where black is converted into white and white is converted into black. It can be represented by the following equation:

```
result_image = 255 - input_image
```

In the preceding equation, 255 indicates the maximum intensity value for an 8-bit image. The gpuarray class provided by PyCUDA is used to develop a program for image inversion, as follows:

```
import pycuda.driver as drv
import numpy as np
```

```
import cv2
import pycuda.gpuarray as gpuarray
import pycuda.autoinit

img = cv2.imread('circles.png',0)
h_img = img.reshape(65536).astype(np.float32)
d_img = gpuarray.to_gpu(h_img)
d_result = 255- d_img
h_result = d_result.get()
h_result=np.reshape(h_result, (256,256)).astype(np.uint8)
cv2.imshow("Image after addition",h_result)
cv2.waitKey(0)
cv2.destroyAllWindows()
```

The image is read as a grayscale image, flattened and converted into a single precision floating point data type for further processing. It is uploaded to the GPU using the `to_gpu` method of a `gpuarray` class. The inversion is performed on the GPU using the preceding equation and the result is downloaded back to the host using the `get()` method. The result is displayed on the screen by reshaping it to the original image size, as shown in the following screenshot:

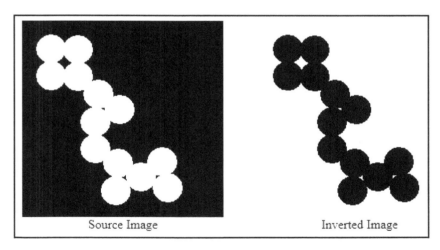

Source Image   Inverted Image

To summarize, this section demonstrated the use of PyCUDA in developing basic computer vision operations, such as color space conversions, image addition, and image inversion. This concept can be used to develop complex computer vision applications using PyCUDA.

Summary

This chapter described the use of PyCUDA in the development of simple computer vision applications. It described the use of PyCUDA in calculating the histogram of an array. The histogram is a very important statistical global feature of an image that can be used to find out important information about it. The concept of atomic operations and shared memory was explained in detail, using histogram calculation as an example. Images in Python are stored as `numpy` arrays, so manipulating images in PyCUDA is similar to modifying multidimensional `numpy` arrays. This chapter described the use of PyCUDA in various basic computer vision applications, such as image addition, image inversion, and color space conversion. The concepts described in this chapter can be utilized for developing complex computer vision applications using PyCUDA.

This chapter also marks an end to this book, which described the use of CUDA programming and GPU hardware in accelerating computer vision applications.

Questions

1. State true or false: The use of the `d_out[i]++` line instead of the `atomicadd` operation will yield an accurate result in histogram calculation.
2. What is the advantage of using shared memory with atomic operations?
3. What is the modification in the kernel call function when shared memory is used in the kernel?
4. Which information can be obtained by calculating the histogram of an image?
5. State true or false: The kernel function developed in this chapter for BGR into grayscale conversion will also work for RGB into grayscale conversion.
6. Why is the image flattened in all of the examples shown in this chapter? Is it a compulsory step?
7. Why is the image converted into the `uint8` data type from the `numpy` library before being displayed?

Assessments

Chapter 1

1. The three options to increase the performance are as follows:
   - Having faster clock speed
   - More work per clock cycle by a single processor
   - Many small processors that can work in parallel. This option is used by GPU to improve performance.
2. True
3. CPUs are designed to improve latency and GPUs are designed to improve Throughput.
4. The car will take 4 hours to reach the destination but it can only accommodate 5 persons, while the bus that can accommodate 40 persons takes 6 hours to reach the destination. The bus can transport 6.66 persons per hour, while the car can transport 1.2 persons per hour. Thus, car has better latency, and bus has better throughput.
5. Image is nothing but a two dimensional array. Most of the computer vision applications involve processing of these two-dimensional arrays. It involves similar operations on a large amount of data, which can be efficiently performed by GPUs. So GPUs and CUDA are very useful in computer vision applications.
6. False
7. `printf` statement is executed on the host

Chapter 2

1. CUDA program to subtract two numbers by passing parameters as value is as follows:

```
include <iostream>
#include <cuda.h>
#include <cuda_runtime.h>
__global__ void gpuSub(int d_a, int d_b, int *d_c)
{
 *d_c = d_a - d_b;
```

```
}
int main(void)
{
  int h_c;
  int *d_c;
  cudaMalloc((void**)&d_c, sizeof(int));
  gpuSub << <1, 1 >> > (4, 1, d_c);
  cudaMemcpy(&h_c, d_c, sizeof(int), cudaMemcpyDeviceToHost);
  printf("4-1 = %d\n", h_c);
  cudaFree(d_c);
  return 0;
}
```

2. CUDA program to multiply two numbers by passing parameters as reference is as follows:

```
#include <iostream>
#include <cuda.h>
#include <cuda_runtime.h>
__global__ void gpuMul(int *d_a, int *d_b, int *d_c)
{
 *d_c = *d_a * *d_b;
}
int main(void)
{
 int h_a,h_b, h_c;
 int *d_a,*d_b,*d_c;
 h_a = 1;
 h_b = 4;
 cudaMalloc((void**)&d_a, sizeof(int));
 cudaMalloc((void**)&d_b, sizeof(int));
 cudaMalloc((void**)&d_c, sizeof(int));
 cudaMemcpy(d_a, &h_a, sizeof(int), cudaMemcpyHostToDevice);
 cudaMemcpy(d_b, &h_b, sizeof(int), cudaMemcpyHostToDevice);
 gpuMul << <1, 1 >> > (d_a, d_b, d_c);
 cudaMemcpy(&h_c, d_c, sizeof(int), cudaMemcpyDeviceToHost);
 printf("Passing Parameter by Reference Output: %d + %d = %d\n",
h_a, h_b, h_c);
 cudaFree(d_a);
 cudaFree(d_b);
 cudaFree(d_c);
 return 0;
 }
```

3. Three ways to launch 5000 threads for `gpuMul` kernel as are follows:

```
1. gpuMul << <25, 200 >> > (d_a, d_b, d_c);
2. gpuMul << <50, 100 >> > (d_a, d_b, d_c);
3. gpuMul << <10, 500 >> > (d_a, d_b, d_c);
```

4. False

5. The program to find GPU Devices with version 5.0 or greater is as follows

```
int main(void)
{
  int device;
  cudaDeviceProp device_property;
  cudaGetDevice(&device);
  printf("ID of device: %d\n", device);
  memset(&device_property, 0, sizeof(cudaDeviceProp));
  device_property.major = 5;
  device_property.minor = 0;
  cudaChooseDevice(&device, &device_property);
  printf("ID of device which supports double precision is: %d\n",
device);
  cudaSetDevice(device);
}
```

6. CUDA program to find Cube of Number is as follows:

```
#include "stdio.h"
#include<iostream>
#include <cuda.h>
#include <cuda_runtime.h>
#define N 50
__global__ void gpuCube(float *d_in, float *d_out)
{
    //Getting thread index for current kernel
    int tid = threadIdx.x; // handle the data at this index
    float temp = d_in[tid];
    d_out[tid] = temp*temp*temp;
 }
int main(void)
{
    float h_in[N], h_out[N];
    float *d_in, *d_out;
    cudaMalloc((void**)&d_in, N * sizeof(float));
    cudaMalloc((void**)&d_out, N * sizeof(float));
     for (int i = 0; i < N; i++)
    {
        h_in[i] = i;
```

```
        }
    cudaMemcpy(d_in, h_in, N * sizeof(float),
cudaMemcpyHostToDevice);
    gpuSquare << <1, N >> >(d_in, d_out);
   cudaMemcpy(h_out, d_out, N * sizeof(float),
cudaMemcpyDeviceToHost);
    printf("Cube of Number on GPU \n");
    for (int i = 0; i < N; i++)
    {
        printf("The cube of %f is %f\n", h_in[i], h_out[i]);
    }
    cudaFree(d_in);
    cudaFree(d_out);
    return 0;
}
```

7. Communication pattern for a particular application is given as shown here:
    1. Image Processing - stencil
    2. Moving Average - gather
    3. Sorting Array in ascending order - Scatter
    4. Finding cube of numbers in Array - Map

Chapter 3

1. The best method to choose the number of threads and number of blocks is as follows:

```
gpuAdd << <512, 512 >> >(d_a, d_b, d_c);
```

There is a limit to the number of threads that can be launched per block which is 512 or 1024 for the latest processors. The same way there is a limit to the number of blocks per grid. So if there are a large number of threads then it is better to launch kernel by a small number of blocks and threads as described.

2. Following is the CUDA program to find the cube of 50000 number:

```
#include "stdio.h"
#include<iostream>
#include <cuda.h>
#include <cuda_runtime.h>
#define N 50000
__global__ void gpuCube(float *d_in, float *d_out)
{
        int tid = threadIdx.x + blockIdx.x * blockDim.x;
```

```
while (tid < N)
{
    float temp = d_in[tid];
    d_out[tid] = temp*temp*temp;
    tid += blockDim.x * gridDim.x;
  }
}
int main(void)
{
    float h_in[N], h_out[N];
    float *d_in, *d_out;
    cudaMalloc((void**)&d_in, N * sizeof(float));
    cudaMalloc((void**)&d_out, N * sizeof(float));
    for (int i = 0; i < N; i++)
    {
        h_in[i] = i;
    }
    cudaMemcpy(d_in, h_in, N * sizeof(float),
cudaMemcpyHostToDevice);
    gpuSquare << <512, 512 >> >(d_in, d_out);
    cudaMemcpy(h_out, d_out, N * sizeof(float),
cudaMemcpyDeviceToHost);
    printf("Cube of Number on GPU \n");
    for (int i = 0; i < N; i++)
    {
        printf("The cube of %f is %f\n", h_in[i], h_out[i]);
    }
    cudaFree(d_in);
    cudaFree(d_out);
    return 0;
}
```

3. True, because it only needs to access local memory, which is a faster memory.

4. When variables of the kernel do not fit in register files, they uses local memory. This is called as register spilling. Because some of the data is not in the registers, it will need more time to fetch it from memory. This will take more time, and hence the performance of the program will be affected.

5. No, because all the threads are running in parallel. So data might be read before it has been written, and thus it might not give the desired output.

6. True. In atomic operations, all the other threads have to wait when one thread is accessing a particular memory location. This will incur time overhead when many threads are accessing the same memory locations. So, atomic operations will increase the execution time of the CUDA program.

7. Stencil communication pattern is ideal for texture memory.

8. When __syncthreads directive is used inside an if statement, then for threads that have this condition, false will never reach this point and __syncthreads will continuously wait for all the threads to reach this point. Thus, the program will never be terminated.

Chapter 4

1. CPU timers will include time overhead of thread latency in OS and scheduling in OS, among many other factors. The time measured using CPU will also depend on the availability of high precision CPU timer. The host is frequently performing asynchronous computation while GPU kernel is running, and hence CPU timers may not give correct time for kernel executions.

2. Open **Nvidia Visual profiler** from C:\Program Files\NVIDIA GPU Computing Toolkit\CUDA\v9.0\libnvvp. Then, go to **-> New Session** and Select .exe file for matrix multiplication example. You can visualize the performance of your code.

3. Divide by zero, incorrect variable types or sizes, nonexistent variables, subscripts out of range etc are examples of semantic errors.

4. An example of thread divergence can be given as follows:

```
__global__ void gpuCube(float *d_in, float *d_out)
{
    int tid = threadIdx.x;
if(tid%2 == 0)
{
    float temp = d_in[tid];
    d_out[tid] = temp*temp*temp;
 }
else
{
    float temp = d_in[tid];
    d_out[tid] = temp*temp*temp;
}
}
```

In the code, odd and even number of threads are performing different operations, and hence they will take different amount of time for completion. After if statement, these threads will again merge. This will incur time overhead because fast threads have to wait for slow threads. This will slow down the performance of the code.

5. `cudaHostAlloc` function should be used with proper care because this memory is not swapped out of disk; your system may run out of memory. It may affect the performance of other applications running on the system.

6. The order of operation is important in CUDA stream operations as we want to overlap memory copy operations with kernel execution operations. So, operation queues should be made in such a way that these operations can overlap with each other, or else using CUDA stream won't help the performance of the program.

7. For 1024 x 1024 image, number of threads should be 32x32 (if your system supports 1024 threads per block), and the number of blocks should be 32 x 32, which can be determined by image size divided by number of threads per block.

Chapter 5

1. There is a difference between image processing and computer vision fields. Image processing is concerned with improving the visual quality of images by modifying pixel values, whereas computer vision is concerned with extracting important information from the images. So, in image processing, both input and output are images, while in computer vision, input is an image but the output is the information extracted from that image.

2. The OpenCV library has an interface in C, C++, Java, and Python languages and it can be used in all operating systems like Windows, Linux, Mac, and Android without modifying the single line of code. This library can also take advantage of multi-core processing. It can take advantage of OpenGL and CUDA for parallel processing. As OpenCV is lightweight, it can be used on embedded platforms like Raspberry Pi as well. This makes it ideal for deploying computer vision applications on embedded systems in real life scenarios.

3. The command to initialize image with red color is as follows:

```
Mat img3(1960,1960, CV_64FC3, Scalar(0,0,255) )
```

4. The program to capture video from webcam and store it on disk is as follows:

```
#include <opencv2/opencv.hpp>
#include <iostream>

using namespace cv;
using namespace std;

int main(int argc, char* argv[])
{
```

```
        VideoCapture cap(0);
        if (cap.isOpened() == false)
        {
          cout << "Cannot open Webcam" << endl;
          return -1;
    }
      Size frame_size(640, 640);
      int frames_per_second = 30;

      VideoWriter v_writer("images/video.avi", VideoWriter::fourcc('M',
    'J', 'P', 'G'), frames_per_second, frame_size, true);
      cout<<"Press Q to Quit" <<endl;
      String win_name = "Webcam Video";
      namedWindow(win_name); //create a window
        while (true)
        {
          Mat frame;
          bool flag = cap.read(frame); // read a new frame from video
          imshow(win_name, frame);
          v_writer.write(frame);
      if (waitKey(1) == 'q')
      {
          v_writer.release();
          break;
      }
      }
    return 0;
    }
```

5. BGR color format is used by OpenCV to read and display an Image.

6. Program to capture video from a webcam and convert it to gray scale is as follows:

```
#include <opencv2/opencv.hpp>
#include <iostream>

using namespace cv;
using namespace std;

int main(int argc, char* argv[])
{
    VideoCapture cap(0);
  if (cap.isOpened() == false)
  {
      cout << "Cannot open Webcam" << endl;
      return -1;
  }
  cout<<"Press Q to Quit" <<endl;
```

```
    String win_name = "Webcam Video";
    namedWindow(win_name); //create a window
    while (true)
    {
        Mat frame;
        bool flag = cap.read(frame); // read a new frame from video
        cvtColor(frame, frame,cv::COLOR_BGR2GRAY);
        imshow(win_name, frame);
      if (waitKey(1) == 'q')
      {
          break;
      }
    }
    return 0;
}
```

7. OpenCV program to measure the performance of add and subtract operation is as follows:

```
#include <iostream>
#include "opencv2/opencv.hpp"

int main (int argc, char* argv[])
{
    //Read Two Images
    cv::Mat h_img1 = cv::imread("images/cameraman.tif");
    cv::Mat h_img2 = cv::imread("images/circles.png");
    //Create Memory for storing Images on device
    cv::cuda::GpuMat d_result1,d_result2,d_img1, d_img2;
    cv::Mat h_result1,h_result2;
int64 work_begin = getTickCount();
    //Upload Images to device
    d_img1.upload(h_img1);
    d_img2.upload(h_img2);

    cv::cuda::add(d_img1,d_img2, d_result1);
    cv::cuda::subtract(d_img1, d_img2,d_result2);
    //Download Result back to host
    d_result1.download(h_result1);
     d_result2.download(h_result2);
    int64 delta = getTickCount() - work_begin;
//Frequency of timer
    double freq = getTickFrequency();
    double work_fps = freq / delta;
    std::cout<<"Performance of Thresholding on CPU: " <<std::endl;
    std::cout <<"Time: " << (1/work_fps) <<std::endl;
    cv::waitKey();
    return 0;
```

```
    }
```

8. OpenCV program for bitwise AND and OR operations is as follows:

```
include <iostream>
#include "opencv2/opencv.hpp"

int main (int argc, char* argv[])
{
    cv::Mat h_img1 = cv::imread("images/cameraman.tif");
    cv::Mat h_img2 = cv::imread("images/circles.png");
    cv::cuda::GpuMat d_result1,d_result2,d_img1, d_img2;
    cv::Mat h_result1,h_result2;
    d_img1.upload(h_img1);
    d_img2.upload(h_img2);

    cv::cuda::bitwise_and(d_img1,d_img2, d_result1);
    cv::cuda::biwise_or(d_img1, d_img2,d_result2);

    d_result1.download(h_result1);
     d_result2.download(h_result2);
cv::imshow("Image1 ", h_img1);
    cv::imshow("Image2 ", h_img2);
    cv::imshow("Result AND operation ", h_result1);
cv::imshow("Result OR operation ", h_result2);
    cv::waitKey();
    return 0;
}
```

Chapter 6

1. OpenCV function to print pixel intensity at location (200, 200) of any color image on the console is as follows:

```
cv::Mat h_img2 = cv::imread("images/autumn.tif",1);
cv::Vec3b intensity1 = h_img1.at<cv::Vec3b>(cv::Point(200, 200));
std::cout<<"Pixel Intensity of color Image at (200,200) is:" <<
intensity1 << std::endl;
```

2. OpenCV function to resize an image to (300, 200) pixels using bilinear Interpolation method is as follows:

```
cv::cuda::resize(d_img1,d_result1,cv::Size(300, 200),
cv::INTER_LINEAR);
```

3. OpenCV function to upsample an image by 2 using AREA interpolation is as follows:

```
int width= d_img1.cols;
int height = d_img1.size().height;
cv::cuda::resize(d_img1,d_result2,cv::Size(2*width, 2*height),
cv::INTER_AREA);
```

4. False. Blurring increases as we increase the size of a filter.
5. False. The median filter can't remove Gaussian noise. It can remove salt and pepper noise.
6. The image has to be blurred using an Averaging or Gaussian filter before applying lapacian operator to remove noise sensitivity.
7. OpenCV function to implement top hat and black hat morphological operation is as follows:

```
cv::Mat element =
cv::getStructuringElement(cv::MORPH_RECT,cv::Size(5,5));
  d_img1.upload(h_img1);
  cv::Ptr<cv::cuda::Filter> filtert,filterb;
  filtert =
cv::cuda::createMorphologyFilter(cv::MORPH_TOPHAT,CV_8UC1,element);
  filtert->apply(d_img1, d_resulte);
  filterb =
cv::cuda::createMorphologyFilter(cv::MORPH_BLACKHAT,CV_8UC1,element
);
  filterb->apply(d_img1, d_resultd);
```

Chapter 7

1. OpenCV code to detect objects with yellow color from a video is as follows: Note that the boilerplate code is not repeated here.

```
cuda::cvtColor(d_frame, d_frame_hsv, COLOR_BGR2HSV);

//Split HSV 3 channels
cuda::split(d_frame_hsv, d_frame_shsv);

//Threshold HSV channels for Yellow color
cuda::threshold(d_frame_shsv[0], d_thresc[0], 20, 30,
THRESH_BINARY);
cuda::threshold(d_frame_shsv[1], d_thresc[1], 100, 255,
THRESH_BINARY);
cuda::threshold(d_frame_shsv[2], d_thresc[2], 100, 255,
```

```
THRESH_BINARY);

//Bitwise AND the channels
cv::cuda::bitwise_and(d_thresc[0], d_thresc[1],d_intermediate);
cv::cuda::bitwise_and(d_intermediate, d_thresc[2], d_result);
d_result.download(h_result);
imshow("Thresholded Image", h_result);
imshow("Original", frame);
```

2. When the color of an object is the same as the color of background, then color based object detection will fail. If there is a change in illumination, even then it can fail.

3. The first step of canny edge detection algorithm is Gaussian blurring, which removes the noise present in the image. After that, the gradient is computed. Thus, the edges detected will be less affected by noise here, than other edge detection algorithms seen earlier.

4. When the image is affected by Gaussian or salt-pepper noise, then the result of the Hough transform is very poor. To improve the result image must be filtered by Gaussian and Median filter, as a preprocessing step.

5. When the intensity threshold for computing FAST keypoints is low, then more keypoints will pass the segment test and will be categorized as key-points. As this threshold is increased, the number of key-points detected will gradually decrease.

6. The larger value of hessian threshold in SURF will result in fewer but more salient interest points and a smaller value will result in more numerous but less salient points.

7. When the scale factor of Haar cascade is increased from 1.01 to 1.05, then image size will be reduced by a larger factor at every scale. Thus, fewer images need to be processed per frame, which reduces computation time; however, this may fail to detect some of the objects.

8. MoG is faster and less noisy compared to GMG algorithm for background subtraction. The morphological operation like opening and closing can be applied to the output of GMG to reduce the noise present.

Chapter 8

1. Jetson TX1 offers performance in terms of Tera floating point operations per second, which is far better than Raspberry Pi. So Jetson TX1 can be used in computationally intensive applications like computer vision and deep learning for deployment in real time.

2. Jetson TX1 development board supports up to six 2-lane or three 4-lane cameras. It has one 5 megapixel camera attached to it.

3. The USB hub has to be used to connect more than two USB peripherals with Jetson TX1.

4. True

5. False. Jetson TX1 contains one ARM Cortex A57 quad-core CPU operating at 1.73 GHz.

6. Though Jetson TX1 comes with pre-flashed Ubuntu, it does not contain any software packages needed for Computer Vision applications. The Jetpack contains Linux of Tegra (L4T) board support packages, TensorRT, which is used for deep learning inference in computer vision applications, latest CUDA toolkit, cuDNN, which is CUDA deep neural network library, Visionworks, which is also used for computer vision and deep learning applications, and OpenCV. So, by installing Jetpack, we can install all software packages needed to build computer vision applications rapidly.

Chapter 9

1. The global memory for the GPU device on Jetson TX1 is around 4 GB with a GPU clock speed of around 1 GHz. This clock speed is slower than Geforce 940 GPU used earlier in this book. The memory clock speed is only 13 MHz compared to 2.505 GHz on Geforce 940, which makes Jetson TX1 slower. The L2 cache is 256 KB compared to 1 MB on Geforce 940. Most of the other properties are similar to GeForce 940.

2. True

3. In the latest Jetpack, OpenCV is not compiled with CUDA support nor does it have GStreamer support, which is needed for accessing the camera from the code. So, it is a good idea to remove OpenCV installation that comes with Jetpack and compile the new version of OpenCV with CUGA and GStreamer support.

4. False. OpenCV can capture video from both USB and CSI camera connected to Jetson TX1 board.

5. True. CSI camera is more close to hardware so frames are read quickly than USB camera so it is better to use CSI camera for computationally intensive applications.

6. Python OpenCV binding is not supported by CUDA acceleration so it is better to use C++ OpenCV binding for a computationally intensive task.

7. No. Jetson TX1 comes preinstalled with python2 and python3 interpreter, while OpenCV is compiled for Jetson TX1; it also installs python binaries so there is no need to install separate python OpenCV bindings.

Chapter 10

1. Python is Open Source and has a large user community contributing to the language in terms of modules. These modules can be used easily to develop applications in a small time with few lines of code. The syntax of Python language is easy to read and interpret, which makes it easier to learn for a new programmer. It is an interpreted language that allows line by line execution of the code. These are the few advantages of python over C/C++.

2. The whole code is checked and converted to machine code in compiled type languages, while one statement at a time is translated in an interpreted language. An interpreted language requires less amount of time to analyze the source code, but the overall execution time is slower compared to compile type languages. Interpreted languages do not generate intermediate code as in the case of compiled type languages.

3. False. Python is an interpreted language, which makes it slower than C/C++.

4. PyOpenCL can take advantage of any Graphics processing Unit, while PyCUDA requires Nvidia GPU and CUDA toolkit.

5. True. Python allows C/C++ code in a python script, and hence the computationally complex task can be written in C/C++ for faster processing, and python wrapper can be created for it. PyCUDA can leverage this capability for kernel code.

Chapter 11

1. C/C++ programming language is used to write kernel function inside `SourceModule` class, and this kernel function is compiled by `nvcc` (Nvidia C) Compiler.

2. The kernel call function is as follows:

```
myfirst_kernel(block=(512,512,1),grid=(1024,1014,1))
```

3. False. The order of block execution is random in PyCUDA program, and it can't be determined by PyCUDA programmer.

4. The directives from driver class remove the need of separate allocation of memory for the Array, uploading it to the device and downloading the result back to host. All operations are performed simultaneously during a kernel call. This makes the code simpler and easy to read.

5. The PyCUDA code for adding two to every element in an array is shown below:

```
import pycuda.gpuarray as gpuarray
import numpy
import pycuda.driver as drv

start = drv.Event()
end=drv.Event()
start.record()
start.synchronize()
n=10
h_b = numpy.random.randint(1,5,(1,n))
d_b = gpuarray.to_gpu(h_b.astype(numpy.float32))
h_result = (d_b + 2).get()
end.record()
end.synchronize()

print("original array:")
print(h_b)
print("doubled with gpuarray:")
print(h_result)
secs = start.time_till(end)*1e-3
print("Time of adding 2 on GPU with gpuarray")
print("%fs" % (secs))
```

6. The use of Python time measuring options for measuring the performance of PyCUDA programs will not give accurate results. It will include time overhead of thread latency in OS and scheduling in OS, among many other factors. The time measured using time class will also depend on the availability of high precision CPU timer. Many a times, host is performing asynchronous computation while GPU kernel is running, and hence CPU timers of Python may not give correct time for kernel executions. We can overcome these drawbacks by using CUDA events.

7. True

Chapter 12

1. False. This line represents a read-modify-write operation that can yield wrong results when multiple threads are trying to increment the same memory location, as in the case of histogram calculation.

2. In the case of using shared memory, fewer threads are trying to access 256 memory elements in shared memory, instead of all threads as in the case without shared memory. This will help in reducing time overhead in the atomic operation.

3. The kernel call function in case of using share memory is as follows:

```
atomic_hist(
        drv.Out(h_result), drv.In(h_a), numpy.uint32(SIZE),
        block=(n_threads,1,1), grid=(NUM_BIN,1),shared= 256*4)
```

The size of the shared memory should be defined, while calling the kernel. This is specified by using the shared argument in the kernel call function.

4. The histogram is a statistical feature that gives important information regarding the contrast and brightness of an image. If it has a uniform distribution, then the image will have a good contrast. The histogram also conveys the information about the brightness of an image. If the histogram is concentrated on the left-hand side of the plot, then the image will be too dark, and if it is concentrated on the right-hand side, then the image will be too bright.

5. True. As RGB and BGR color format is same just the order of channels is different. The equation of conversion will still remain the same.

6. It is simpler to work with single dimensional threads and blocks than multidimensional. It simplifies the indexing mechanism inside the kernel function, and hence it is performed in every example that appears in the chapter. It is not mandatory if we are working with multidimensional threads and blocks.

7. The imshow function, used to display an image on the screen, requires an image in unsigned integer format. So all the results computed by kernel function are converted uint8 datatype of numpy library before displaying on the screen.

Other Books You May Enjoy

If you enjoyed this book, you may be interested in these other books by Packt:

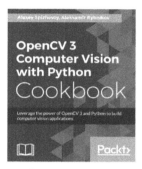

OpenCV 3 Computer Vision with Python Cookbook
Alexey Spizhevoy

ISBN: 978-1-78847-444-3

- Get familiar with low-level image processing methods
- See the common linear algebra tools needed in computer vision
- Work with different camera models and epipolar geometry
- Find out how to detect interesting points in images and compare them
- Binarize images and mask out regions of interest
- Detect objects and track them in videos

Computer Vision with OpenCV 3 and Qt5
Amin Ahmadi Tazehkandi

ISBN: 978-1-78847-239-5

- Get an introduction to Qt IDE and SDK
- Be introduced to OpenCV and see how to communicate between OpenCV and Qt
- Understand how to create UI using Qt Widgets
- Know to develop cross-platform applications using OpenCV 3 and Qt 5
- Explore the multithreaded application development features of Qt5
- Improve OpenCV 3 application development using Qt5
- Build, test, and deploy Qt and OpenCV apps, either dynamically or statically
- See Computer Vision technologies such as filtering and transformation of images, detecting and matching objects, template matching, object tracking, video and motion analysis, and much more
- Be introduced to QML and Qt Quick for iOS and Android application development

Leave a review - let other readers know what you think

Please share your thoughts on this book with others by leaving a review on the site that you bought it from. If you purchased the book from Amazon, please leave us an honest review on this book's Amazon page. This is vital so that other potential readers can see and use your unbiased opinion to make purchasing decisions, we can understand what our customers think about our products, and our authors can see your feedback on the title that they have worked with Packt to create. It will only take a few minutes of your time, but is valuable to other potential customers, our authors, and Packt. Thank you!

Index

error handling
    about 95
    debugging tools, using 97, 98
    within code 96, 97
errors
    semantic errors 97
    syntax errors 97
exclusive scan 320
eye detection
    with Haar cascades 222, 224, 270

F

face detection
    with Haar cascades 219, 220, 267, 268, 270
Fast Library for Approximate Nearest Neighbors
    (FLANN) matcher 216
Features from Accelerated Segment Test (FAST)
    feature detector 209, 211
file
    images, saving 144
filtering operations
    convolution operations, on image 177, 178
    high-pass filtering, on image 184
    low pass filtering, on image 178, 179
    on images 177
frames per second (FPS) 162

G

gather pattern 50
Gaussian filter 181
General-Purpose GPUs (GPGPUs) 9
geometric transformation
    image, resizing 174, 175
    image, rotation 175, 177
    image, translation 175, 177
    on images 174
global memory 61
GMG
    using 228, 230, 231
GNU C Complier (GCC) 15
GPU device properties
    accessing, from CUDA programs 37
    general device properties 38
    memory-related properties 39
    thread-related properties 40, 41

gpuarray
    used, for image inversion in PyCUDA 336
graphics processing unit (GPU)
    about 8
    architecture 9, 10
grayscale images
    histogram equalization 171, 172

H

Haar cascades
    face, detecting from videos 221, 222
    used, for eye detection 222, 224, 270
    used, for face detection 219, 220, 267, 268,
    270
    used, for object detection 218, 219
high-pass filtering
    Laplacian filters 188
    on images 184
    Scharr filters 186, 187, 188
    Sobel filters 184, 185, 186
histogram calculation
    in OpenCV 169, 170, 171
    in PyCUDA 324
    in PyCUDA, with atomic operations 325, 327
    in PyCUDA, with shared memory 328, 329, 330
    on GPU, with CUDA 110, 111, 112, 114, 115
histogram equalization
    for color images 172
    for grayscale images 171, 172
    in OpenCV 171
histogram of oriented (HoG) 164
Hough transform
    used, for circle detection 207, 208
    used, for straight line detection 203, 205, 206
Hue Saturation Value (HSV) 198

I

image addition
    in PyCUDA 335
image inversion
    in PyCUDA, with gpuarray 336
image processing
    about 120, 121
    image thresholding 260, 261, 263
    image, adding 258, 260

S

scan kernel 320, 321
scatter pattern 51
Scharr filters 186, 187, 188
semantic errors 97
shapes
  circle, drawing 142
  drawing, on blank image 141
  ellipse, drawing 143
  line, drawing 141, 142
  rectangle, drawing 142
shared memory
  about 64, 66
  used, for histogram calculation in PyCUDA 328,
    329, 330
Sobel filters 184, 185, 186
software development kit (SDK) 238
sorting algorithms
  acceleration, with CUDA 106
  rank sort algorithms, implementing 107, 108,
    109
Standard C compiler
  about 15
  for Linux 15
  for Mac 15
  for Windows 15
stencil pattern 51
straight line detection
  with Hough transform 203, 205, 206
streaming multiprocessors (SMs) 11
strided memory access
  using 99
Support Vector Machine (SVM) 164
SURF 213, 214, 216, 218
syntax errors 97

T

text
  writing, on image 143
texture memory 74, 75, 77
thread divergence

avoiding 99, 100
thread synchronization
  about 64
  atomic operations 67, 68, 69, 70
  shared memory 64, 66
threads
  about 56, 57, 58
  executing, on device 35, 37
transpose pattern 51

U

Ubuntu
  CUDA C program, creating 22, 23
  PyCUDA, installing 286, 288, 289

V

vector operations
  about 42
  latency, comparing between CPU and GPU code
    47, 48
  two-vector addition program 43, 45, 46, 47
  vectors, elementwise squaring 48, 50
video
  displaying, from onboard camera 265, 267
  processing, from webcam 148, 149
  processing, on computer 145, 147
  reading, from onboard camera 265, 267
  saving, to disk 149
  working with, in OpenCV 145

W

webcam
  videos, processing 148, 149
Windows
  CUDA C program, creating 22
  CUDA toolkit, installing 16, 17
  OpenCV, installing 122
  PyCUDA, installing 282, 283, 284, 285, 286

Y

YCrCb 198